BirthBond

BirthBond

Reunions Between Birthparents and
Adoptees - What Happens After . . .

Judith S. Gediman
Linda P. Brown

NEW HORIZON PRESS
Far Hills, New Jersey

Library of Congress Catalog Card Number: 89-43405

Judith S. Gediman
Linda P. Brown
  BirthBond

ISBN: 0-88282-052-4
New Horizon Press

Acknowledgment

A book of this kind could not be written without the contributions of numerous people. We have woven their voices together, but without these individuals there would be no book.

For contributing their time and their expertise, we wish to thank Annette Baran, Lee Campbell, Susan Darke, Gail Davenport, Florence Fisher, Carol Gustavson, Donald Humphrey, Reuben Pannor, Penny Partridge, and Joyce Pavao. Most especially, we thank the birthmothers, birthfathers, adoptive parents and adoptees who, with generous spirits, shared with us their stories of reunion and post-reunion.

Lewis M. Gediman and the Gediman Research Group also deserve a resounding thank you for nourishing the enterprise in countless ways. The book could not have been written without their support.

"Only connect"
E. M. Forster

Contents

Introduction

by

Judith S. Gediman

I knew Linda Brown's husband before I knew Linda. He and my husband had been college roommates, and the four of us became friends in the mid 1960s, after they married. We lived in the same city until career moves took us in separate directions, but we maintained our friendship over the next twenty years. Linda and her husband had two children, both boys, and I went on to divorce and remarry—ordinary enough life events in the 1960s and 1970s.

In the spring of 1985, my (second) husband and I were visiting Providence, Rhode Island, where his son attended college and where the Browns had settled. We arranged to meet at a restaurant for our more or less annual visit, but we realized that this was not going to be an ordinary evening as soon as the waiter had taken our order. "We'd like to take the floor; we have something to tell you," they announced and proceeded to tell us a story we could never have imagined.

A few years before I met her, when she and her husband were dating, Linda, who was in college, had become pregnant. She was expelled from school, sent away to stay with relatives and gave birth to her baby far from home. The child, a girl, had been given up for adoption. Our friends' parents knew all this—both mothers and fathers had been instrumental, in fact, in deciding how the situation was to be handled—and the two students didn't see one another again until a few years after the adoption. Linda had found it impossible to return to school and, by then, was working; her future husband was in his last year of medical school. They resumed dating and a short time later decided to marry. The rest we knew. Recently, years after the pregnancy, the child Linda had relinquished for adoption had searched for and found her mother; and, in finding Linda, the young woman had recovered not just her birthmother but her birthfather and two full brothers as well! They had been seeing each other for a year.

I was stupefied to discover that the people I thought I

knew so well and for so long had been living with a secret of this magnitude for so many years. How could I anticipate their reactions to being found by their daughter? Should I be concerned about them or not? Were they happy or distressed about Karen's sudden appearance?

They assured me it was all right. In 1975, after seeing a television talk show about reunions between birthmothers and the children they had surrendered for adoption, Linda had written to the agency that had arranged her baby's adoption back in 1962. Her letter gave her current address along with permission to inform her daughter of her whereabouts if she should ever request it.

The experience of reunion was proving to be tumultuous. Everyone was coming to grips with the events of the past and trying to forge a relationship in the present. There was no renowned or recognized authority like Dr. Spock to consult about how to handle any of the unknowns, they pointed out, so everyone was feeling his or her own way, one day at a time. The Browns were getting to know Karen and her history. She was getting to know the Browns and their family. There were highs. There were lows. Much of what was happening felt bittersweet. But one thing was certain: the secret was out of the closet, and Karen was in their lives to stay.

After the startling revelations of that evening, I couldn't stop thinking about Linda and her family. I kept wondering what I would have done had I been in her position all those years ago; I thanked my lucky stars that I hadn't been. We began to call each other more frequently than before, and, each time we spoke, Linda had a new piece of information, a new problem to contend with, a new insight into the past or the fast-developing present, a new slant on what she'd previously told me. I thought how ironic it was, and poignant too, that a couple whose other children were almost ready to leave the nest should suddenly have this new child fall into their lives. I was struck by the ways in which Linda and her family would never be the same and listened in wonder as she shared the extraordinary complex of feelings and events associated with Karen's

Introduction

return. Linda's feelings sometimes seemed contradictory. The situation always seemed intense.

Our mutual friends were equally fascinated, and I tried to give the best answers I could when they asked me how things were going with the Browns. What did I think Karen "wanted," they asked, and did I know how Karen's adoptive parents were feeling? We were all curious to meet Karen, and Linda assured us that we would.

Our meeting finally occurred about a year later, on a weekend when everyone had occasion to be in New York. The plan was for Karen, and the boyfriend with whom she was now involved, to join us for dessert at the restaurant where we would be dining with the Browns.

She walked in smiling, a beauty of twenty-two so lovely that neither my husband nor I could take our eyes off her for the entire hour we were together. (He thought she looked like Ava Gardner, but I learned in the course of writing this book that staring is very common in reunion meetings no matter *what* the new person looks like.) After the introductions ("this is our daughter" were the exact words), the six of us entered into small talk about the desserts on the menu. No one mentioned the word adoption, and nothing was said about Karen's history until the time had come to say good-bye. Then it was she who refused to let the meeting end without acknowledging her identity. "Well, who do you think I look like?" she asked out of the blue. I was flustered, stunned by the implicit demand that I directly confront her origins.

When I discussed it later with Linda, I discovered that Karen's desire for us to acknowledge her adoption openly was not an unusual occurrence. Two years after having met Karen, Linda was beginning to become aware, having met other adult adoptees, that not everything Karen said or did could be attributed to her daughter's unique personality. Rather, the fact of being adopted seemed to generate a variety of *common* feelings among adult adoptees—and a hunger to know who they look like is one of the most immediate. Linda was also beginning to realize that there were commonalities between her own situation and that of the other birthmothers she was meeting, women whose histories were similar to hers in many important ways. Hearing about the circumstances of their various pregnancies and adoptions—and talking about the reunions they were undergoing with their adult sons and daughters—was proving to be a revealing experience.

Several weeks later, amazed at some of the things Linda was learning and encouraged by the curiosity of our own friends and acquaintances, I asked Linda if she would be interested in working on a book: "After the Reunion." The idea would be to explore the subject more systematically than had yet been done, using the double edge of my research and writing background coupled with her first-hand experience and growing circle of adoption contacts. First, we would familiarize ourselves with whatever reading material we could find about adoption, reunion and post-reunion; then, we would conduct original research: personal interviews with birthmothers, all of whom were currently experiencing reunions with the children (now grown) whom they surrendered to adoption years ago.

In proposing the project, I was looking for a way to use my professional skills outside the business domain in an area that would make a social and humanist contribution. Linda was looking for a vehicle that would help her understand her adoption/reunion experience more completely and also help remove some of the guilt and secrecy that surround such reunions taking place all over the country. She agreed to the idea without hesitation, and our project was born.

We began to make decisions. First, we realized that there was a distinction to be made between search, reunion, and post-reunion. We intended to concentrate on *post*-reunion, but realized that we would need to attend to the predecessors, search and reunion, as well.

Although we would talk to many members of birthfamilies, we decided to conduct intensive interviews with thirty birthmothers who were engaged in post-reunion situations. The reunion must be of at least six months' duration, a restriction we imposed so that interviewing would take place after the massive confusion of the initial meeting had settled down.[1] Given our focus on post-reunion, we also wanted to be reasonably

Introduction

sure we had eliminated rejection situations and were dealing with enduring relationships.[2] Among the interviews on which we ultimately focused, about half the reunions were three years or less in duration, the other half between three to ten years.

We knew it would be nearly impossible to identify birth-mothers-in-reunion unless they were willing to come forth. For this reason, we concentrated our efforts within what is generally referred to as the search and support movement or the adoption reform movement—a loose affiliation of groups around the country that assist adoptees, birthmothers, adoptive parents, and other individuals who wish to locate and re-connect with missing birth relatives. We advertised in support group newsletters; we got suggestions from search experts who had assisted in large numbers of reunions and could identify birthmothers who might be willing to be interviewed; we found people by word-of-mouth.

Our focus was post-reunion, but we decided that we ought to ask the women, first, about the circumstances years ago that had led to giving up their babies. We also wanted to know how they felt over the years about the adoptions, and what the search and initial contact was like. As it turned out, this decision to start with the past was the right one; the birthmothers insisted that it would simply not have been possible to discuss post-reunion at all without first referring to the long-ago days and events when their stories actually began. For them, all of the events are intimately and intrinsically connected. Generally speaking, post-reunion represents a completion and affords the birthmothers a feeling of having come full-circle. (It also represents a new beginning, but that's jumping ahead.)

In a sample comprised simply of volunteers, it was no surprise to find that almost everyone we interviewed had spoken before of these matters, usually to close family and friends, often to other birthmothers, adoptees or various "interested others." Several of the women had become accustomed to telling "my story," by which they meant a detailed historical account of how it happened that they became pregnant and relinquished a baby, how they felt about it as the years passed, and how they were found by, or searched for, their child. This account would then be followed by a less detailed, less analytic, and only partially digested account of what had happened since, because post-reunion, unlike its historical underpinnings, is very much an ongoing event. It exists in the here and now, a story in the making, and the story is constantly evolving and changing. Often, the birthmothers had considerably more difficulty narrating and understanding the intricacies of their post-reunion drama than they did with "Act One" (pregnancy and relinquishment) or "Act Two" (search and reunion).

One consequence of our decision to interview birth-mothers first was that, for the purposes of this study, their perspective would be our initial focus. It would not yield objective answers to all the dilemmas of closed adoption, but, hopefully, would reveal new information and critical insights into the short and long term consequences of relinquishment for adoptees and birthmothers. We asked these birthmothers to speak about their own feelings and to discuss the feelings of everyone in their post-reunion circle.[3]

Willingness to answer our questions was rarely a problem. Once birthmothers are out of the closet, many welcome the opportunity to discuss their experiences. After years of silence and secrecy (half a century, in one case), being able to speak out freely is generally therapeutic. Many told us that the opportunity to be interviewed was welcome and useful for this reason. Similarly, several gave us permission, even encouraged us, to use their names, explaining that guarantees of anonymity only perpetuate shame and stigma for birthmothers as a group.[4]

Beyond the in-depth interviews, our understanding has been augmented and enriched by other sources. We interviewed people with professional expertise in adoption and reunion and asked them to share their perceptions of post-reunion events, dynamics, patterns and meanings. We spoke to adoptees and adoptive parents. We read books, periodicals and unpublished materials. We listened to audio tapes and watched video tapes about reunion and post-reunion.[5] We spoke to birthfathers and birthsiblings. We heard birthmothers speak at national conferences, as well as at local search and support group meetings; we read their stories in newsletters around the country. Others, hearing about our study, called us. All told, we have looked in on hundreds of reunions, though thirty cases are highlighted in this book.

We do not claim to be able to generalize what we have learned for every birthmother out there somewhere, silent and unseen; however, we feel confident that the voices we are hearing speak for a sizable segment of that population.

Post-reunion between birthmothers and the children they relinquished constitutes a phenomenon which is virtually unprecedented in the adoption history of this country. As the people in this book tell their stories, they are changing our understanding of what adoption is all about. Most of them would also like to change the future of adoption practices in the United States.

English is impoverished and clumsy in its ability to provide simple and accurate nomenclature for many of the people, events and processes about which we are talking in this book. For example, there is no word in the English language for the child who grows up. As a parent, both the newborn, the eighteen-year-old and the fifty-year-old is your "child." So, while we speak about reunions between birthmothers and their children, we have to remember these "children" are actually grown-ups themselves. In adoption circles, they are referred to as "adult adoptees," a term more accurate than graceful and one which tells us that adoption is a lifelong reality.

Limited language also makes it difficult for the birthmother to express her relationship to this (grown-up) child. If we were to hear someone talk about "my adopted child" out of context, we would assume that an adoptive parent was speaking. Some birthmothers try to solve the problem by referring to the child as "my adopted-away" child. Some leave the adoption confusion out of the picture and simply say "my son" or "my daughter."

What to call the woman who surrenders a child for adoption presents another semantic problem. She has been referred to as the real mother, the natural mother, the birth mother, the birthing mother, the first mother, the original mother, and more—all to differentiate her from the woman who will come to be known as the adoptive (not adopted) mother. For the purposes of this book, we have reluctantly opted to follow the current fashion—birth mother—but presented as one word—birthmother—despite considerable reservations about the term. We prefer the term natural mother, but defer to the sensibilities of those who take the position that if one mother is "natural" the suggestion is that the other is "unnatural." We need better words.

The language problem is not just a problem for writers. It is part and parcel of the discomfort that accompanies adoption on every front. Adoptive parents first confront the issue when the time comes to reveal the existence of the other mother to their youngster, a revelation that adoption advisors recommend making at a very young age, before the child can hear it from someone else, but also before the child can really comprehend the meaning of the concept of adoption. One adoptive mother tells the story of how her son cut through the linguistic fog:

> *"He came to me once and he said, 'I grew in your tummy, didn't I Mommy?' and I said, 'No, you didn't grow in my tummy, but'—and I was searching for the words—'you grew in another lady's tummy.' I couldn't even say mother because I really wasn't comfortable sharing that. I remember saying, 'But she couldn't be your mother.' We always referred to her as that lady or the other lady. Roger was about seven or eight and he looked at me and he said, 'Stop calling her that. She was my mother, wasn't she?' At that point, my husband and I decided that we had to become more comfortable with talking about his mother. Roger is a very sensitive young man."*

Language problems also exist when siblings enter the conversational scene. The phrase "his adopted sister," for example, is unclear. Does the phrase mean the sister he grew up with in his adoptive home? Does it mean the girl was also adopted? What if, unlike him, she is the *biological* child of his adoptive parents?

Other cultures respect family lineage more than ours and have languages more finely tuned for family relationships. In Danish, for example, there are different words to denote the aunt who is your mother's sister and the aunt who is your father's sister. English ignores most such subtleties. It wouldn't matter if language were not so important in helping us perceive and comprehend our experience. Linguists and philosophers tell us that without words to name things, their reality is compromised, and they can even fail to exist. Naming, it's been said, is a way of possessing.[6]

The inadequacies of adoption language, in other words, are more than just a nuisance. Finding the words to describe how they feel and what they are experiencing is a problem faced by nearly everyone in their reunion and post-reunion situations. Ironically, the need to communicate can be especially urgent because the experience is so unique and powerful. It is not unusual for birthmothers and adoptees to write poems about relinquishment, adoption and reunion, turning to the rhythms and symbols of a less literal expression to unburden themselves of the strong, but ill-defined, forces that swell below the surface of ordinary discourse.

The difficulty of converting reunion experiences into everyday language, and sharing these thoughts and feelings with the uninitiated outsider, is a mutuality that draws adoption-insiders together. You have to experience it, the participants insist, to comprehend it. Many experts tend to agree. According to one woman who is an adoptee, a birthmother and a support person herself, "In nearly fifteen years of working with individuals (in search and reunion), I have yet to find anyone who can well define the emotions or the experience. Even after long reconnection, it is difficult to explain."[7]

Despite the inadequacies of language, defining the emotions and the experience is precisely what this book will attempt to do. Although it is about a very particular relationship, at a point in social history when the words and concepts

Introduction

by which to communicate it still lag behind people's apprehensions, in the final analysis, it is also about the most fundamental issues and concerns we share as human beings, adopted or not.

This book is about all the close relationships in our lives and what makes them endure—the ties of obligation and affection that bind us to one another, so tightly woven sometimes that we are unable to say where one begins and the other ends. It is about attachment and separation, family and kinship, inclusion and exclusion. It is about trust and doubt, loyalty and betrayal, generosity of spirit and meanness of spirit. It is about loss and grief, wounding and healing, anger and shame, joy and sorrow. It is about the development of personal identity and how our identity is shaped by the groups from which we come and the groups to which we belong. It is also about love.

Reunion and post-reunion are processes we can all appreciate or imagine. What must it feel like to live with a secret year after year? How does it feel to look back and conclude that you were trapped by the existing culture in which you grew? What must it be like to confront your past, the actions you took, and have the opportunity to rewrite it? Would you do it differently this time? Can we exorcise our ghosts?

Beyond all this, reunion and post-reunion are events which, however imperfectly understood or articulated, are surely primal. For there is little more primal than the attachment between a mother and her baby and little more wrenching than their separation. And there is little more stunning than the sight of their reunion decades later, each reaching out, cautious or jubilant, for a future which includes the other.

Prologue: Two Stories

Marcie and Irene are two birthmothers whose reunions are represented, directly or indirectly, in this book. Collectively, the stories make a powerful statement for the fact that being a mother does not leave with the surrender of the child.

Marcie is a woman in her mid-forties, dark-haired with streaks of grey, attractive and mild-mannered. Nothing remarkable about her appearance or demeanor would single her out. Until she speaks, there is nothing to suggest the extent of the damage that being pregnant and giving up her baby caused her, and nothing to suggest the profound healing that reunion and post-reunion have brought. When she tells you how restorative these processes have been, her conviction is persuasive, her inner feelings certainly hard to dismiss.

Compared with other reunions we heard about, Marcie's story is more than just happy; and, unusual for these post-reunion sagas, it is, also, in some important sense, complete. We interviewed Marcie when she had known her thirty-year-old daughter, Lee, for eight years, an extended stretch by post-reunion standards. Theirs is one of the few reunions which has come "full-term." Whatever "work" post-reunion entails has essentially been done; whatever upheavals it produces have mainly been resolved. All families have met; all relationships have been established and resolved. No unexpected shock waves are lurking in any quarter. Marcie and Lee have advanced through assorted events and issues that post-reunion brings, simultaneously moving through the changing "regular life" circumstances of both women. Over time, they have developed a shared history so that Lee no longer seems to have landed full-blown out of nowhere. What lies ahead now, says Marcie, is "just to continue and to grow."

Marcie's Story

In 1956, as a fifteen-year-old teenager, Marcie did not make a "decision" to surrender her baby for adoption on her own. Her parents decided for her, and they didn't want anyone to know about her pregnancy. She remembers feeling angry and powerless, but, at that age, in her condition, and with no income, there was nothing, she felt, she could do about it. She remained at home during the entire pregnancy and was as isolated as she would have been in any home for unwed mothers. "I can remember not having any clothes," she says, "I had to wear bathrobes. I had one maternity dress that was my mother's. She allowed me to wear that to the doctor's. Other than that, I stayed home. No aunts and uncles knew, so, if anyone came to the house, even the delivery boy, I had to go to my room or to the attic and hide. I didn't go to school. The story was that I was sick."

In the years that followed the adoption, Marcie was convinced that she had done the right thing. "I was so beaten. I bought it hook, line and sinker," she recalls, "the only way you can do it is to be convinced that the child is better off, that you aren't worthy of bringing up the child." But she married at eighteen and had a daughter two years later. She was pleased that the baby was a girl because she had been hoping it would replace the child she gave away—a vain hope, but she had no way of knowing at the time. A son followed the next year and Marcie proceeded to live her life, largely unaware of the indelible impression that the earlier events had left.

In 1979, Lee, now twenty-two, called Marcie on the phone. She had been living within thirty miles all her life. Marcie was simultaneously shocked and thrilled, and they arranged to meet that very evening at Marcie's empty workplace. "I knew I would become unglued," remembers Marcie. Their meeting was warm and full of feeling. "I put my arms around her and I said, 'I never thought I would see you alive again,' and I started crying and hugged her."

There was a torrent of questions and answers on both sides. Marcie needed to find out how her daughter had grown up. Lee needed to find out why Marcie had given her up. The most difficult thing Marcie had to answer that first evening was why she hadn't searched for Lee. Her reason was, "I didn't think I had the right; I was told not to." But that answer did not impress Lee because, she, too, had been told the same thing. "I tried to do the best for her by not bugging her," Marcie reflects, *"and she felt betrayed." It is an irony that continually repeats itself in reunion stories, for Marcie was to learn that her daughter, like herself, had become pregnant as a teenager.*

But Lee had married at sixteen, kept the baby, and was now the mother of two small children. So Marcie was a grandmother of two boys, four and seven. Small wonder that it was not possible for her to assimilate so much so fast. Unlike Lee, who had thought about searching for years, Marcie had no time to psychologically prepare herself. She thought she had accepted her past loss, but she was still unaware of the grief that lay buried beneath her elation and still unprepared for the mourning that would follow in the days and months ahead.

To complicate matters further, Marcie was in the middle of a nasty divorce when Lee arrived in her life. Afraid of what would happen if she revealed Lee's existence to her husband, Marcie also delayed telling her other children (now fifteen and sixteen) about Lee, fearing that they would turn against her. Lee took the position, "I don't care if you never tell my brother and sister," an assertion Marcie didn't believe, but which she appreciated nonetheless. At least Lee wasn't pressuring her; she was being considerate, giving her time. Two years passed before Marcie finally informed her other children that they had a sister. If she had it to do again, she says, she would "worry and fret" less, and tell earlier.

The secrecy which Marcie imposed on Lee and herself made the first years of post-reunion "crazier" than they might have been, and Marcie believes that Lee felt somewhat rejected during this period despite her intellectual understanding of Marcie's position. For one thing, the need for secrecy brought a quick (though temporary) end to personal visits. Lee could not call Marcie at home, so mother and daughter began communicating by mail. The writing was not without advantages. "A lot got taken care of in those little notes and cards back and forth," Marcie explains, because it enabled them to say things that would simply have been too charged to say face to face. Marcie analyzes this early period in their history as a time when both women were evaluating their positions. "The initial emo-

tion was over with, and we were trying to figure out where we fit in. Do I dare go into her territory?"

The tension of the situation had relaxed a little, but the stress in Marcie's 'regular' life did not abate. A few weeks after her divorce became final, she went into the hospital for surgery. Lee came to visit and brought a gift, the first book on adoption and reunion that Marcie had seen and the first of many that she would read. Shortly after the surgery, her ex-husband re-married, causing "a real turmoil" with their two children. With so much to deal with, Marcie couldn't dwell on Lee. In retrospect, she thinks, perhaps that was for the best.

Nor did the course of Lee's own life run smooth. Several years after meeting Marcie, she, too, underwent an unpleasant divorce, followed by a series of destructive romantic relation-ships. The two women had known each other for four years before Marcie finally risked expressing her anger: "I was trying not to be controlling, trying to be nice but to say to her 'please shape up,' and when she wouldn't, I was frightened to be angry with her; I was afraid she'd leave. I put up with so much whining and seeing her hurt that I finally said, 'I can't deal with this.' When I found out that I could get angry at her and she wouldn't leave me, it was finally okay. But I had to take that risk."

Another stage of passage in their post-reunion was Marcie's meeting with Lee's adoptive parents, an event that took place during the first year. "I remember feeling so inade-quate, so grateful," says Marcie. (She looked like a "whipped dog" that day, Lee's adoptive mother later recalled.) These were "super human people," Marcie recalls; they had "taken care of my mistake." The couple was kind and welcoming, both on that day and shortly afterward when Marcie called for per-mission to visit Lee, who was in the hospital for exploratory surgery. "Why are you calling me?" the woman asked, "Of course you can go. There's enough love to go around." (A few years later, the adoptive parents retired and moved South. The two mothers remain in touch by phone, sharing news of Lee.)

Eight years later, Marcie has become extremely com-fortable with Lee and knows her well enough to be able to predict what she'll do in most situations. The stance she presents these days is mainly "unqualified acceptance." Still, she wishes Lee were different in some important ways: less submissive, more able to confront other people directly, more independent, free of the feeling that she owes something to her adoptive parents. Marcie would like to help Lee grow, but often feels "powerless" to effect real change. When Lee was still in the hospital, Marcie gave Lee a teddy bear, but she wonders how much impact she can have on a woman who is thirty-years-old. Still, she sees instances where Lee has acted more independently and in more secure a manner than when they first met; Lee has even been known to get angry at her adoptive parents these days, an emotion she used to stifle.

The impact of reunion and post-reunion on Marcie has been enormous. She credits it with producing "a whole new life." Only after her shattered self-esteem had begun to mend, and relieved of the burden of secrecy—a burden whose weight she understood only when it was lifted—was Marcie finally able to move forward. She went back to college, and now laughingly contrasts her active student life with the frightened homebody she used to be. At the time we met, Marcie was a sophomore, planning to pursue a master's degree. She considers herself "transformed back to the person I was before I surrendered—like a whole person now." One of the best results of post-reunion, she says, is "being accepted for who I am." And because she's not living "a phony life" any more, she's calmer, too. When she thinks about what it means to be a birthmother, she often finds the words of an old television commercial swirling around in her head: "You can't fool Mother Nature."

It is interesting to note, however, that, despite the positive accomplishments of this reunion, and, despite feeling that her daughter's adoptive parents were fine, loving people, Marcie still asserts, "Nobody could raise my child the way I would like them to, but they're as close as anybody."

Marcie believes that the system of closed adoption, as she and her daughter experienced it, was a failure. "It hurt too much. It didn't solve the problem; it complicated it." Like many of the other birthmothers we interviewed, she had become committed to bringing about changes in the system—changes *which would purge adoption of its stigma of secrecy and which would allow, and even encourage, some channel of information between birthmothers and the children they give up.*

Her self-esteem is largely restored now, and Marcie will always be grateful to the daughter who found her: "She had the guts to do what I couldn't do."

Because reunion adventures are still so new, long-term relationships like Marcie's (i.e., anything more than a few years) are less common than those of the one, two or three years duration. Searching did not begin in large numbers until the 1970s; few reunions happened before the 1980s. In the case of our interviews, about half are reunions of three years or less, about half between three and ten years. Almost all have the potential to survive, but whether they will flourish or flounder is an open question.

Irene's reunion is the longest we came across (it has persisted for ten years) and it differs from Marcie's in many important ways. Time alone, even ten years, does not necessarily insure that the "work" will be over or that an unruly union will magically bring about a tranquil association. Reunion, like adoption, appears to be a lifelong process.

Unlike Marcie, Irene is a birthmother who set out to find her child. Rita, her daughter, had been looking for her, too. But Irene's post-reunion history is less a chronicle of her own healing than of her grown child's considerable neediness—a characteristic that many adoptees share. The easy reciprocity that Marcie and Lee have achieved continues to elude these two. As in marriage, each reuniting pair has its own special pace and character.

Irene's Story

Irene was thirty-nine and her daughter nineteen when they met. Rita was "all mixed up" when the two found one another. "She had gone to college and quit, was into marijuana, was in a relationship with a young man her adoptive parents disapproved of, had run away to California and come back. She

Prologue: Two Stories

just couldn't find herself." Rita still considers herself "pretty messed up in the head," but maintains that if she hadn't found Irene she "doesn't know what would have happened." Rita's problems have definitely been a factor in the constant seesaw of their relationship. Irene considers it a close one, but she is candid about their conflicts.

A few months after they met, Rita moved in with Irene's family. They got to know one another in a way that only living together makes possible, but emotions ran high: "We argued; we fought; she liked me; she didn't like me; I didn't like things she did; She didn't like things I did." Rita wanted complete attention, to be in the house "every minute of every day," to stay up late each night talking. She stayed for four months.

The unrelenting need for her birthmother "to do" for her and "be there" for her at any time, on call, has persisted. "She's trying to make up for the nurturing that she didn't get in the past," Irene explains, "and it's just not possible." Irene gave Rita a doll for Christmas three years ago; Rita was twenty-seven. It was the first doll she had ever received. She had asked for it when she and Irene were discussing what Irene should buy Rita's child for the holiday. Should she get the girl a doll? "Yes," Rita said, "and you know something else, I'd like one, too. The gifts I got were always 'educational'."

On many occasions, her daughter's needs for mothering "smothered" Irene, who describes Rita as a "difficult personality," a "taker," a "prima donna." Slowly, Irene learned that she would have to set limits, say no, and express her own feelings honestly, behaviors that do not seem to come easily to most of the birthmothers we interviewed. They are often suffused with guilt and fearful of losing their children a second time. One concern Irene expressed was that she would be overstepping her rights with Rita's adoptive parents, whom she knew and respected, if she acquiesced to Rita in everything. So, while Irene foresees that Rita will always be part of her life, "Honestly," she confesses, "it's easier with her living far away."

Irene's reunion with her daughter has touched, with great force, many people besides the principals. These include: Irene's younger sister who has always looked up to her as "a mother figure" and who is jealous of the new person in Irene's life (though she will not admit it); friends' daughters, who have been close to Irene over the years, call her Mom, and are hurt at being displaced by Irene's natural daughter; nieces and nephews who have been an integral part of her life. They also include her husband and her two sons, both of whom find their new sister's interpersonal style quite different from their own.

Irene's boys, in contrast to Rita, who is accustomed to "having everything revolve around her," are the opposite, says Irene, never "spoiled." For a while, they resented anything she did for Rita, finding her self-centered. "It still goes up and down." But Irene, a no-nonsense kind of person, looks back upon the siblings' history with one another as consisting of mostly "stupid things, the usual immature bickering, natural but exaggerated rivalries" which ran their normal course. As for the other people whose feelings were jolted, Irene explains their reactions this way: "Because I missed Rita, I gave everywhere else."

Regardless of the effects around the edges, the main line in Irene's story remains the union between mother and daughter—still less than comfortable, with Rita still pressing and Irene still trying to protect herself from being smothered. Speculating about what the future may hold, she anticipates that the shape of post-reunion may depend on her relationship with Rita's children, her grandchildren, as the years go on. "I really haven't tuned into my grandchildren being my grandchildren yet," she says. She is content to remain in the background, letting Rita's adoptive mother, age seventy-one, enjoy being the grandma for now. The children are my "flesh and blood," she notes, "My time will come."

In addition to Marcie and Irene, six of the other women are also engaged in relatively long reunions (more than five years). The rest have more recent, but not necessarily less mature, relationships. Each story is both unique and similar, and how the reunioning birthmothers all deal with the pleasures and trials of their unprecedented situations is the subject of Chapters 3 through 12.

Prologue: Two Stories

Our purpose, however, is not simply to tell stories—fascinating, moving, and instructive as they may be. Taken together, the individual histories form a body of information, and we have searched the information to see what patterns it presents and what general understandings it suggests. We have attempted to describe the world of post-reunion in a systematic way, and to provide a sense of the possibilities that can occur in these most remarkable, and most profound, human dramas of mother and child.

The birthmothers whose stories are presented in this book come from a broad spectrum of society and from a variety of geographic areas. As mothers-to-be, they came from "snooty small towns" and from Philadelphia's Main Line, as well as from the middle-class and lower-middle-class regions of the fifteen states where they lived. Like Marcie, they have grown into middle-aged women whose lives, from the outside, don't appear to be all that different from anyone else's. When they "got into trouble" years ago, many of them were "the girl-next-door" type.[1]

At the time of our interviews, the "typical" birthmother was a woman in her forties, married, the mother of other children, college-educated, and working outside the home. The first contact in all the reunions represented took place between 1977 and 1987, during which this "typical" woman was reunited with her child, more likely a daughter, born in the 1960s.

More specifically . . .

• At the time of the interviews, the birthmothers ranged in age from a low of thirty-five to a high of seventy-seven, with half in their forties. At the time of first meeting the adoptee, the large majority were in their thirties or forties.

• Twice as many of the adoptees were female.

• When the birthmothers took the active role in searching and making initial contact, they looked for sons and daughters equally. When the adoptee was the activist, the adoptees were more often daughters than sons.

• The adult adoptees were born between 1931 and 1969. Mainly, their birthdays were in the 1950s and '60s, with only a scattering born earlier.

• At the time of meeting, the sons and daughters ranged between seventeen and forty-nine-years-old, with the majority in their late teens or twenties. Almost all of the adoptees who had married had become parents themselves.

• About two-thirds of the birthmothers were married: the rest single, divorced or separated. Three had never married, but each has had a long-term relationship with a man.

• Eight of the women married their child's birthfather a few years after the baby had been adopted.[2] Four of the eight later divorced.

• Eight women had no other children. Collectively, the other mothers had sixty-eight other (biological) children. One woman adopted five children (in addition to her six biological ones). Several of the birthmothers are stepmothers, too.

• The birthmothers' other children cluster in their teens and in their twenties. Several have younger children (under twelve), and several have reached the stage where their children are fully mature (thirties, forties, fifties).

• Collectively, the women are well-educated. About half have either college or graduate school degrees; the remainder have either some college experience or technical/trade school training. Only two stopped their schooling when they completed high school.

• The majority of the birthmothers work, either full-time or part-time. Their occupations include: a factory worker, a bookkeeper, a secretary, an actress, a computer specialist, an editor, an advertising specialist, a yoga instructor, a psychologist, a nurse and a social worker. Several are self-employed.

• At some point, at least half worked in the helping professions (teaching, social work, nursing, mental health)—a route that has always been accessible to women and one that turns out to be particularly magnetic to birthmothers. A few explained that they went into social work, or into jobs where they worked with pregnant girls, as a way of dealing with their own feelings about their personal adoption history. "I went into child welfare," one told us wryly, "so I could place children for adoption. That was the repetition compulsion. I repeated it over and over again to show me it was right!"

• When they relinquished their babies, twenty-eight of the thirty were single; one was married and one separated. With the exception of these two, the baby they gave up was their first child.

• The majority were teenagers, but the group also includes a sizeable minority who were in their twenties, many of whom were working, not in school.

These, then, are the demographic characteristics of the women whose stories we weave in and out of this book. It is their voices we hear directly and, through them, the uncounted multitude for whom they stand.

1

Adoption and Reunion: Coming Into Focus

Tens of thousands of birthmothers are having reunions all over America. In the privacy of their own lives, sometimes furtively, behind closed doors, scenes like the following are actually happening.

- After ten years of searching, a thirty-one-year-old woman reaches her birthmother on the telephone and says, "You may not remember me. The last time we met was December 18, 1950." The birthmother, unable to speak, knows immediately who it is because that is the date her first daughter was born.

- An adopted woman, age twenty-five, spends four years looking for her birthmother, but is repeatedly rebuffed by the woman's sister-in-law, whom she has successfully located and whom she continues to telephone every six months. Ironically, the birthmother, always aware of where her daughter is living, would ride by the house to get a glimpse of her, but had resisted the desire to come forward.

- A woman of forty-nine meets her son, twenty-six, at a restaurant for the first time, while her husband sits unobtrusively at the bar, a few feet away, to be sure she's safe. She signals the husband to leave after an hour or so, and, by the time the evening is over, she thinks she may be falling in love with the son.

• A woman who was raped at seventeen meets the child she bore as a result of that trauma. She is shocked to see that her daughter has "Asian eyes" (the man was Hawaiian) and that both she and her daughter are painfully shy. (Shyness is a trait which scientists have identified as extremely inheritable.)

• A woman of forty-two receives a letter from her nineteen-year-old son informing her of his desire to meet. Several weeks later, the character of her sexual relationship with her husband changes dramatically, and they begin to experience "this incredible sexual life" that they never had before.

• An adoptive mother helps her twenty-year-old son find his birthmother. The birthmother and the son have trouble becoming close, but the two mothers become fast friends.

• A thirty-four-year-old birthmother helps her adopted daughter find the girl's birthfather. The man and the birthmother meet, and the two become involved with one another all over again, putting her marriage in serious jeopardy.

Fifteen or twenty years ago, scenes like these would have been unimaginable. Now, they are becoming commonplace. Why?

To understand reunion and post-reunion, one needs to be educated about adoption and to move beyond the stereotypes and myths that have worked their way into the collective consciousness. Adoption is not the simple and benign procedure we were led to believe: the perfect solution to the problems of unwed mothers and for couples who can't have their own children. Growing up adopted is *not* the same as growing up non-adopted. Adoptive situations and relationships are *different* from non-adopted ones, not necessarily better or worse, adoptees and adoptive parents will sometimes hasten to add, but still different.

To understand reunion and post-reunion, it also helps to understand why adoptions take place, how society has thought about illegitimate babies and unwed mothers,[1] and how society has acted to "protect" the babies, mothers, and the newly formed adoptive families. For any of these understandings to emerge, adoption must not be a forbidden subject. People must be allowed to talk about it. Until recently, that was not the case.

Adoption is different by definition. It is built on different, usually problematic foundations. It occurs when the parents who conceived a child are unable, unwilling, or unfit to care for it. With infant adoptions, one person's misfortune becomes another person's fortune. For every adoptive mother and her joy, there is a birthmother and her sorrow. And for all the joy that adoptive parents experience, many of them turn to adoption only as a last resort after years of frustration and failure in attempts to bear their own children.

Everyone in the adoption triad deals with the issue of loss, because the experience of loss is the fundamental ground upon which the event of adoption is built. For the birthmother, it is the loss of her baby; for the adoptive parents, the loss of the ability to reproduce. For the adoptee, there is a separation from and loss of the first mother, a separation which one author calls the "primal abandonment" that accompanies every adoptee into the adoptive home (and possibly throughout life). Even if an adoptive mother is there waiting immediately after birth, the substitution of one for the other cannot erase the experience of losing the mother to whom the infant was so intimately connected before birth.[2] (In actual practice, the separation of mother and infant may not be followed by immediate placement in an adoptive home anyway. One or more foster homes may come first.)[3]

With loss comes grief. Grief and its companion, mourning, work their way into the adoption culture as well. But often the grief is repressed, as when new birthmothers are assured that any sadness they feel will ultimately disappear—the routine message that was delivered a generation ago. Sometimes, a birthmother's repressed grief becomes twisted, manifesting itself not as grief but as some other feeling or behavior, such as anger or depression. But when the grief remains unresolved, it can be activated by reunion, setting off the mourning that should have taken place years earlier. Similarly, if adoptive parents never come to terms with whatever sense of loss *they* felt at their inability to have (biological) children, reunion can activate the unresolved grief and mourning in them as well.

Turning to the child, the one who is "rejected" by one mother and "chosen" by another, the loss of the birthparents is a psychic trauma, and the fact of adoption becomes an integral part of life, woven into the fabric of one's sense of self. Being adopted becomes an inescapable element of identity.[4]

Some adoptees are able to thrust their adoption into the background of their sense of self. For others, it is absolutely primary, an awareness that begins the moment they learn they are adopted and is never outgrown.[5] But whether the fact of being adopted occupies a greater or lesser place in one's overall identity, the adopted person feels different from the non-adopted, as the words of this adopted person, a woman in her late forties, clearly indicate:

> *"Being aware that I was adopted was a cloak that I wore around me at all times. I was always aware of my adoption; it had become a part of me. Wherever I looked, whatever I did, I took the feeling of adoption with me. It was a continuous part of my life."*

That adoption and identity are fused no doubt helps explain three surprising facts.

Fact 1: It is common to find people with adoption connections who wear more than one hat in the adoption triad—that is, a person who is both an adoptee *and* a birthmother, or both birthmother *and* an adoptive mother, or even all three.

Fact 2: Those who become professional specialists in adoption often have adoption in their personal histories.

Fact 3: Numbers of young women who were adopted
as babies become pregnant teenagers themselves, repeating the "sins" of their birthmothers.

One adoptee who has become a prominent figure in
search and reunion circles explains that the reason she became
pregnant at seventeen was that she was longing for some connection with her birthmother. "The only thing I knew about that
woman was that she had a baby when she was seventeen."
Repeating the birthmother's act was her unconscious way of
making the connection.

Among the birthmothers we interviewed, several discovered that their daughters were also birthmothers. (One
daughter searched for her birthmother immediately after having had an abortion, the issues of pregnancy and motherhood
very much on her mind.) Additionally, two of the women indicated that their sons went through unplanned pregnancies with
their girlfriends. Surely, these experiences helped the daughters
and sons understand the pressures their birthmothers had been
up against a generation ago, but the mothers were understandably distressed to discover that their children had recreated the
same dilemma.

Marcie, the birthmother in the Prologue, is one of these.
Lee had become pregnant at sixteen and decided to marry—
"which I was glad of," Marcie says. "But she's now divorced,"
Marcie continues, "and it's not been easy for her. When you
think that you surrendered your child because you thought she
would have a better life, and then you see that it's a repeat
performance, that's a big disappointment."

People like Marcie have learned that an assortment of
unhappy discoveries may lie in wait behind the adoption blur.
As reunion and post-reunion bring adoption into clearer focus,
it is becoming apparent that what adoption participants expected and what they got were frequently two different things.

Many writers have pointed out that the terms associated with the subject of adoption are likely to be negative ones

—orphan, foundling, bastard, illegitimate, unloved, unwanted, rejected, abandoned. The whole subject of adoption often elicits pity. It also makes us uncomfortable.

For many years, adoption was a taboo subject in this culture. As one adult adoptee points out, "People do not know how to respond or react to questions, so they ignore them whenever possible," a coping mechanism we also often use in dealing with death.[6] Adoption has not traditionally been something you talk to your friends about, particularly if they happen to be the parents of an adopted child. In society at large, adoption has been a matter of inattention, not an issue of public consequence, despite its enormous importance to the individuals it touches. There is an unspoken belief that adoption is a second choice, the option one chooses when all else fails, certainly not the preferred way of creating a family.

Recently though, the taboo has begun to break down. Adoption is discussed, its shroud of secrecy less impenetrable. During the course of writing this book, articles kept appearing in newspapers and magazines about various aspects of adoption—including assorted stories about adoptees being reunited with their birthmothers or with other members of their blood families. Much of the printed material is heartwarming: a story in the *New York Times,* for example, about five siblings put up for adoption years ago by parents who were "unable to feed them," tells of their reunion "over a Thanksgiving feast."[7]

Television talk shows have all featured adoption and/or reunion stories as their subject. Some have returned to the topic several times. As a result of the media's attention, stories about adult adoptees who search for their biological parents, rare ten years ago, are now familiar. Stories in which the birthmothers do the searching are fewer, but still beginning to be heard.

Much has changed in a short period of time. Three of the founding figures in the adoption search movement—Jean Paton, Florence Fisher, and Betty Jean Lifton—wrote biographies of their own searches in the late 1960s and the early 1970s. Stirred by this awareness, adoptees all over began searches of their own. As Florence Fisher happily observes, "In seventeen years, it's gone from 'Why are you searching?' to 'Why *aren't* you searching?' "

The inherent drama and often heartwarming quality of reunion stories is not the only reason that adoption has captured the public's attention. The spotlight is being thrust on adoption for two other reasons. First, because prospective parents are currently looking to adopt babies in record numbers and, second, because the evils and hardships that used to be obscured in adoption are beginning to come to light.

As for the first, it's not news anymore that the rate of infertility in this country has become a serious problem. Ten million people, or one out of every six couples of childbearing age, are defined as involuntarily infertile. There are not enough "desirable" (white, healthy) babies to go around; one hundred seekers compete for every such one that is available.[8] In a society that believes in every person's right to reproduce, the plight of the infertile elicits quick and widespread sympathy. Add to that an element of scarcity, and adoption becomes a veritable triumph.

But adoption is also coming into public awareness via stories in the media which shatter the view that adoption is always a happily-ever-after situation. We hear about "baby selling"—one of the abuses connected with the supply and demand equation. We read in the newspaper about a mother who has important medical information to give her son: he may have the same, possibly fatal, heart problem that is plaguing her. But she is thwarted in her ability to locate him by the adoption laws of the state.[9]

We hear reunion stories in which adoptees reveal startling details about their adoptive upbringings—an alcoholic parent, an experience of sexual abuse—and we wonder how this could have happened. We hear wrenching disclosures about birthmothers who never wanted or intended to relinquish their child to adoption at all. (There is one in our sample.) In late 1987, we all became familiar with the case of six-year-old Lisa Steinberg who was abused and died while under the care of adults who, it turned out, had never legally adopted her. In August 1988, a suit was brought by adoptive parents in Texas, demanding that the state turn over the background files about their children and assist in providing the psychiatric care which these children, all defined as having "special needs" and adopted as toddlers, now require. Cases like these stir the collective conscience, making adoption an issue that grips us all.

However, for all its newfound visibility, the cloak of secrecy has not been fully removed from adoption; it's just been raised a bit, allowing the public a hint of the many kinds of adoption stories that exist behind the screen. But to large numbers of those whose lives are personally connected to adoption, their adoption-related status remains very much as it always has been—an intensely private matter and not easily discussed.

When we told people we were working on this book, almost everyone volunteered that he or she knew someone in the adoption triad. The details of *what* they knew about the situation or the feelings of the people involved, though, were typically limited. It was clear that we were treading on highly sensitive territory, and that probing too deeply would constitute an invasion of basically private material.

Secrecy has been mandated by the legal structure. It has been promoted by adoption agencies and social workers. Society as a whole has generally respected its mantle. Public concern and curiosity may now be belatedly aroused, but the door has a way of swinging shut again.

In keeping with the silence that is adoption's frequent companion, one rarely hears the names of famous people who have adoption connections. There is, of course, the son of President Ronald Reagan and his first wife, Jane Wyman, Michael Reagan, who announced what his adoptive history meant to him in an autobiographical *On the Outside Looking In.* Christina Crawford, the adopted daughter of Joan Crawford, is another adoptee who publicized her story in *Mommy Dearest.* Although the playwright Edward Albee prefers not to discuss his adoption, at least one article has appeared in a psychiatric journal interpreting several of his plays in the context of his adoption.[10]

All these people are middle-aged. Today, the world is different from the one in which their birthmothers became pregnant. Because adult adoptees are becoming more comfortable with letting the rest of us know what it feels like to be adopted, birthmothers are able to admit their children exist and meet them in this lifetime.

A Social Revolution

"I don't think adoptees can possibly comprehend what the world was like then—the times, the attitudes. I was scared. I was desperate. I can remember hating the pregnancy. What I wanted to be rid of was the shame, the stigma, the problem of being pregnant. I don't think I thought of it in terms of a baby. My first inkling of baby was when they tried to take her away from me."

A birthmother who relinquished in 1959

"The home for unwed mothers was difficult—like white slave labor. We were there and you had to do certain things, like clean, and then you sat around and watched television or knit or listened to records. I don't remember any discussions or counseling about childbirth. We used first names only. We were told not to use last names, not to exchange addresses. We only existed for each other in that space. We were specifically told that if we ever saw each other again on the street afterwards we were not to recognize each other. It was like you lived in a cave for a few months and when you came out you had amnesia."

A birthmother who relinquished in 1964

The women surveyed in this book have lived through a time of extraordinary social change. When they surrendered their children, mainly during the 1950s and 1960s, there was no greater disgrace than to become pregnant before marriage.[11] The very term "unwed mother" hissed with social disapproval and the label stuck fast until the permissive 1970s, when the less accusatory "single mother" worked its way into our vocabulary. So shameful was the condition of being pregnant and unmarried that the unfortunate young women who found themselves in this position were usually forced to interrupt or terminate their education. Whisked away from the security of their homes and families to guard them from the wagging tongues of neighbors, they were sent for months to homes for unwed mothers or to relatives in distant locations. There, their identities could be hidden, and they could be convinced by their elders that adoption was the best, indeed the only, possible course of action. Shame fell not only on the pregnant mother, but her family as well. For the sake of all concerned, this "mistake" had to be covered up as quickly and as fully as possible.

By the time these "mistakes" had grown into adults themselves, a sexual revolution had shaken society—a change of such magnitude that it's difficult, even for those who lived through it, to believe how harsh and punitive the "old ways" had been. By the mid-1980s, society had become so open-minded that even pregnant, unmarried teachers were successfully fighting off morally indignant parents and school board members who were trying to get them fired.[12] A generation ago, unmarried, pregnant teachers would have been cast out; now they could remain in front of the classroom.

The idea of single motherhood by choice is a relatively new concept. According to one source, in fifteen years the percentage of out-of-wedlock babies placed for adoption has plummeted from eighty percent to four percent.[13] In some places, the percentage is miniscule. In 1985, for example, there were 9,340 births to unmarried women in Connecticut, but only seventy of these babies were legally adopted by unrelated residents.[14] In some high schools, pregnant teenagers have become part of the landscape.

The birthmothers we interviewed are aware of these changes. The impact of the "old ways" mores will remain with them for the rest of their days, yet none of them embarked on a reunion relationship with a sense of entitlement. All were keenly aware that they had relinquished the right to their child, and that whatever right they might have to a relationship would need to be conferred by other parties: either the adult adoptee, the adoptive parents, or both. But, by relaxing its stance, soci-

ety has made it harder for these women to live with their relinquishment decision because, today, society does not extract
the same price.

In explaining the adoption decision to themselves and
to the offspring with whom they have been reunited, many
birthmothers have come to the conclusion that it was not a free
decision at all. They were pressured into it by the people whose
help and advice they sought. They were given no options, and
could see no options for themselves. They and their children
were "separated by society," many of them are saying. It is a
conclusion that many adoptees, raised in a less repressive era,
have finally come to accept.

The change in social attitudes is one of the reasons
reunions have sprung forth and people are talking about them.
Still, of the three parties in the adoption triad, society remains
the least sympathetic with and the most judgmental of the
birthmother. Because many are still in hiding, it is a group that,
in some sense, does not even exist. "Birthmothers are supposed to go away," one of them tells us angrily, "No one wants
to hear that there's pain."

As if to prove her point, the birthmother admits that the
first question people ordinarily ask about a reunion is, "What
about the adoptive parents? How do they feel about it?" As if
to underscore the moral superiority of the latter group, they
often assert, "My sympathies are with the adoptive parents."
Many birthmothers reported that these were among the first
questions put to them by even their closest friends, and a few
verbalized being grateful to friends who held their tongues on
this issue and concentrated on the birthmother's feelings instead. "I've been worrying about the adoptive parents all these
years," Debora, one of our interviewees, explains, "For now, I'd
like to worry just about me. I really needed to feel that someone could at least hold me in their gaze, in their arms, in their
thoughts, in their compassion for two seconds and not force
me to think about somebody else."

Even in today's more accepting social context, the prevailing view is that the birthmother made her bed years ago and
she just better lie in it. Another common judgment is that

adoptive parents want no part of birthmothers. But the truth of the matter is both variable and complex. Birthmothers are not the "bad guys" and adoptive parents the "good guys." As a group, the former have been dismissed too thoughtlessly and too harshly. The average person rarely stops to think about the pressures these women were subjected to years ago. Nor does the average person realize that, rather than being an event which the birthmother would rather "put behind her," the act of surrendering a child to adoption often left a wave of consequences in its wake, influencing her future life in ways no one expected.

By focusing on the birthmother in this book and highlighting her perspective, we hope to redress the balance of ancient grievances and chip away at an unfortunate stereotype that serves no one well.

The Consequences of Secrecy

Nearly all the birthmothers interviewed had kept their pregnancy and adoption history a secret throughout the years. Even when family members or close friends knew, the adoption was almost never mentioned again, often at the specific request of the birthmother or one of her parents. The few women who did not make a point of preserving the concealment lived with the same silence. "Even though it wasn't a secret, it was never discussed, so it might as well have been," one explains.

After their reunions, some birthmothers became aware that, occasionally, information had leaked out during the years, despite the overwhelming conspiracy of silence. Maybe a relative had leaked the news and then sworn the person to secrecy. Maybe the word had slipped out over drinks, when confidences were being shared and inhibitions were let down. But, generally, with few exceptions, the cover stories remained secure. The stories that had been invented by parents to explain the noticeable absence of a daughter ran the gamut. Several were sick (even including infectious hepatitis and tuberculosis); a few were visiting or attending relatives in distant cities; one was having a nervous breakdown; a few were declared married.

Many of the birthmothers broke the pattern of silence with men whom they subsequently dated, especially if they thought the relationship was leading to marriage. These men had a right to know, they felt, and the woman wanted some assurance that this history would not change the man's desire to marry. However, a few birthmothers waited to tell their husbands until after they got married, a strategy that produced its own complications when the couple began to think about having children, and/or at reunion time. (We will have more to say about husbands and reunions in Chapter 11.)

The central trait of secrecy is hiding—intentional concealment, according to Sissela Bok.[15] Secrets are powerful agents, and we sense their mystery, attraction, and danger even from early childhood. As adults, we all know from experience that to keep a secret requires a healthy dose of will power; that keeping a secret can make us feel guilty, duplicitous, or unauthentic; and that, over a long period of time, it can have a powerful influence on character and personality. Often, we are offended and angry when we find out that we have been the objects of people's concealment. Secrecy suggests distancing at best, cover-up at worst.

Secrecy is associated with shameful acts, immoral behavior, illegal activity and negative thoughts. One common response in discovering a secret is to want to break through it, but also common, Bok points out, is the cautious inclination to leave it alone. Both in our personal lives and in society at large, secrecy triggers a conflict between the desire to respect what's hidden and the desire to unmask it. Keeping things hidden, however, can extract a heavy price. Secrecy can impair communication, cause fantasies to flourish, and let wrongs go unnoticed.

The concealment built into adoption law and practice has produced a host of unfortunate consequences, both in terms of the kinds of unseen evils we were discussing earlier[16] and in terms of hardships inflicted upon people in the adoption triad.

Birthmothers, who were advised that they could "go on with their lives" after the adoption, were expected to live with a socially sanctioned denial. As one veteran social worker writes, "It not only interferes with the resolution of grief, but intensifies the birthparents' poor self image by reinforcing the idea that what they have done is so heinous that it must forever be concealed."[17]

Like Marcie in the Prologue, almost all the birthmothers we interviewed described the damaging effects of denial. Lila remembers, for example, that her mother and father made a pact that they would go to their graves carrying the secret of her pregnancy. Such a pact intensified the guilt and shame she already felt by transmuting her pregnancy into an unspeakable sin. Faye, a seventy-seven-year-old birthmother whose twenty-month-old daughter was adopted in 1938 against her wishes (she believed the child was still in a foster home) says, simply, "Keeping it a secret was terrible, not being able to tell anyone for fear of their thinking ill of me. I thought about it a lot. I just kept it to myself."

Several women call attention to the toll that was taken in energy which would otherwise have been available for more constructive pursuits. Some even worried about being fired from their jobs. Many report that their relationships with other people were impaired because of their inability to share themselves completely. "I never got anywhere close to where the pain was," explains Constance. Living with a lie is also described as living two lives, "the 'me' who lived outside and the 'me' who was someplace else, that nobody knew about." In some cases, serious psychological disturbances occurred years later—depression, for example—but the women were not necessarily aware of the connection between their pregnancy/adoption history and the symptoms they later experienced.

Birthmothers, living with a lie, describe how uncomfortable they would become when a new acquaintance asked the innocent question, "How many children do you have?"[18] Confronted with the question by an obstetrician she was seeing for the first time, one answered, "This is my first." In the same situation a few years later, the same woman changed her answer, responding this time, "Well, I had three, but one died." She's still not sure why she said either.

Adoption and Reunion

Throwing off the burden of secrecy can be one of the most healing and exhilarating aspects of reunion for birthmothers. "It felt wonderful, very liberating," Debora recalls with a sparkle in her voice, "It was like bubbly, like champagne, like that first rush when you drink alcohol. You just feel so powerful, like nothing's going to hurt you. I felt so light. I guess it's the closest feeling to feeling whatever they say is reborn. You just feel blessed."

Most would agree with Emily Sue, a birthmother whose one-year-young reunion has already accomplished a liberation: "I feel free now to be who I am; I don't have to pretend to be someone I'm not. I feel much better about myself now that everybody knows about Pam."

However, even after reunion, the question, "How many children do you have?" can still be unsettling. "It's sometimes hard when someone asks," Emily Sue says. "Well, I really have four but I don't have four; I have three," she answers, because "it's still a little confusing to me that she's my daughter but I didn't raise her, so I don't feel I can claim her as my child like I claim my other children."

In the same manner that secrecy saps birthmothers, it affects adoptees as well. Being able to disclose one's adoption can be equally liberating for the adoptee, "It's a very good feeling to be out of the closet," one tells us, "I truly know what a homosexual living in the closet feels like, and I'm not a homosexual. But there was a big segment of my life, a big segment of who I am, that I kept quiet about. There were people who would ask mundane questions that I would not answer honestly because it related to my adoption, and I felt as though, because I was evading the question, I was being unauthentic. I can't express enough how liberating it is for me to talk openly about who I am now, who I was then, and what my history is."

In addition to the adoptees and birthmothers who verbalize the ill effects of secrecy, some adoptive parents share their viewpoint, despite the popular assumption that it is the adoptive parents who prefer the cloak of concealment. Clearly, however, large numbers of them still prefer concealment, since few adoptive parents express negative feelings about it. A study of write-in mail about a proposal to open adoption records, for example, revealed that birthparents and adoptees were almost unanimously in favor of opening the records (more than nine out of ten) whereas the adoptive parents who wrote in were generally opposed (eight out of ten).[19]

Adoptive parents who have given their blessing to search and reunion have come to understand that openness, not secrecy, is in their child's best interest. Even if they wish this was not the case, which some freely admit, they want to do what's best for their child.

Of course, openness can serve their own best interests as well. While their children were growing up, many were confronted with questions which they could not answer. Many found themselves parenting youngsters with personalities or talents quite unlike their own, with traits that seemed unfamiliar, even alien. They wondered where these learnings originated. Some adoptive parents had sons or daughters who became "quite a handful." What many couples expected from adoption was not necessarily what they got. They learned the hard way that bringing up adopted children entailed stresses for which no one had prepared them. We'll deal with adoptive parents and the post-reunion drama in Chapter 12.

Thus, it should come as no surprise to learn that adoptive parents, too, can profit from reunion. Many, indeed, feel a measure of relief when the mysterious birthmother emerges from obscurity and becomes, finally, a real human being.

2

The Adoption Structure: Figures and Facts

Adoption Numbers

We live in a society that worships numbers, that frequently values the quantitative over the qualitative, the collective fact over the individual truth. A politician can be elected in this country by a small margin, and commentators can be heard interpreting the results to mean that the wishes of everyone else—tens of millions of people—no longer exist.

The inclination to cite numbers and then to proceed on the assumption that the bigger they are the more deserving they are of attention, extends no differently to adoption and reunion. But even more than usual, attaching statistics to these phenomena is both difficult and, from a humanist perspective, somewhat beside the point. The one thing that can be said with certainty is that adoption is a big subject—in numerical, as well as emotional, terms.

Because of the secrecy surrounding adoption, and the sealed records which maintain it, no one knows for sure how many people in the population are adopted, what their current ages are, how many women in the population have relinquished a child for adoption, or how many adoptions take place in a given year. The federal government has not kept track of adoptions since 1975, two years after the Supreme Court declared abortion legal. In 1986, however, federal legislation was passed to establish a National Adoption Information Clearinghouse, so better information should become available by the end of this decade.

The most widely accepted figure is that five million Americans, or two percent of the population, are adoptees. One source estimates that two out of every one hundred children in the United States are adopted.[1] On a year-by-year basis, the number of adoptions between 1952 and 1973 ranged from a low of 85,000 to a high of over 171,000.[2] The highest number of adoptions ever was recorded in 1970. Numbers were on the high side in the late 1960s as well. After abortion became legal in 1973, the annual numbers declined.[3] In 1982, the most recent year for which statistics are available, over 141,000 adoptions took place.[4]

One problem with quoting adoption statistics is that there are different kinds of adoptions that any aggregate number obscures. In the case of the annual figures above, for example, the figures include both adoptions by relatives and by non-relatives—types which are vastly different because the birth family's identity is masked in one, but not in the other. Similarly, adoptions by step-parents, adoptions of foreign-born children,[5] interracial adoptions, and adoptions of older or "special needs" children each constitute a separate and distinct segment of adoption experience. They should not all be lumped together. Estimates are that there may be closer to five million than two million adoptees in adoptions which have resulted in reunion activity.

Any number, however, understates the magnitude of adoption's reach. The world of adoption extends beyond the adoptee to include the adoptive parents, the birthparents, the siblings (both birth and adoptive), the grandparents (both birth and adoptive), and the host of aunts, uncles, cousins, etc., that make up the extended family. Even restricting the calculations to two sets of parents, an absolute minimum of four other lives are involved, which amounts to a minimum of twenty-five million people who are intimately "related to adoption" (assuming five million adoptees). Add to that eight grandparents for each adoptee and the number increases by another forty million. Add to that the siblings and the extended family members and the number soars again. In fact, adoption's reach is so tremendous that at least half the population is probably touched by it personally, without even counting the social workers and other adoption professionals who necessarily become involved.

Adoption is as old as the story of Moses in the bulrushes. It will surely remain with us, despite the disposition of today's unmarried mothers to keep their babies instead of surrendering them and despite the proliferation of abortion. Large numbers of couples want to adopt. Unplanned babies are born every day and some percentage of their mothers will decide on adoption.[6] There are about one million teenage pregnancies each year and nearly half a million of these teenagers give birth.[7] Our country has one of the highest out-of-wedlock birth rates in the developed world, and the bulk of adoptions come from this source. But the proper assumption that adoption flows exclusively from unmarried teenage birthmothers oversimplifies the facts. Out of the thirty birthmothers whose stories we tell in this book, eighteen had indeed been teenagers at the time of adoption, but the rest had been twenty or over.[8]

The numbers of unmarried pregnancies is rising. One out of every five births in 1983 was to an unmarried woman, compared to one out of fourteen about twenty years earlier.[9] In 1985, a government publication made a dramatic statement when it said that "childbearing by unmarried women increased substantially between 1984 and 1985, to levels never before observed in the forty-five-year period for which national statistics are available".[10] The number in 1985 was edging toward a million (828,000, to be exact) and a growing fraction of these nonmarital births were to comparatively older women. Unlike the birthmothers we interviewed and their counterparts from the early 1970s, most unmarried mothers today, older and younger, are keeping and raising their babies.

The adoption numbers, questionable as they may be,

provide some other interesting insights about social attitudes and adoption.

> Fact: America is particularly adoption-prone compared to other countries. There are more adoptions in America than "in the rest of the world combined."[11]

> Fact: Adoptions are more prevalent among the white population than among blacks. Babies born to black women unable to raise them are more likely to be "informally" adopted—that is, raised by relatives, friends, neighbors—than placed for formal adoption with strangers.[12]

> Fact: Other Western countries, as well as many foreign cultures, handle adoption quite differently. They respect the concepts of lineage and birthright more than we do, give the child some kind of position in both families, and are more open about the adoptee's dual identity or connection.[13]

Search and Reunion Numbers

Statistics on search and reunion are no more reliable than those on adoption. Data is currently being gathered, but nobody really knows how many adoptees launch a search for birth relatives or how many birth relatives launch a search for family members missing-in-adoption. The estimates range from two hundred thousand to two million.[14] On a percentage basis, one expert in adoption and reunion issues believes that the number of adoptees who search probably lies between fifteen and twenty percent of the adoptee population.[15]

When it comes to knowing how many searchers have been successful in achieving reunion contact, the going answer is "tens of thousands," but how many tens is anybody's guess. The organization known as ALMA (Adoptees' Liberty Movement Association), which is the largest of the organizations devoted to helping people search, has been involved in 30,000 reunions over the course of its seventeen-year history.[16] The leader of one search group in the Northeast estimates that she personally has been involved in about 2,000 reunions, and, though hers is a particularly active group, there are a few hundred such groups operating around the country. One of the largest of the reunion registries, the International Soundex Reunion Registry, headquartered in Carson City, Nevada, takes credit for 1,600 reunions through May, 1987. There were over 44,000 active registrants as of the same date. There are also search and reunion initiatives taking place privately, uncounted, outside these structures.

It's a safe assumption that reunion numbers are climbing, if only because search and reunion have achieved greater visibility and sanction in recent years. Publicity catalyzes a desire that often lies dormant. There are numerous accounts of people who initiated their own searches after having read about the successful reunions of others. The registries, too, experience an increase in inquiries after any media attention to reunion. Several of the women we interviewed, like author Linda Brown, initiated some kind of reunion attempt after seeing something on television or reading something in a magazine. If Linda had not written in 1976 to the adoption agency she had dealt with in 1962, the agency might never have told her that Karen came to them in 1984, and Karen might still be searching for her birthmother.

As the barriers to secrecy fall, the number of people attempting reunions will doubtless continue to grow. Much has happened in a short ten years. It was only a decade ago that a landmark study first challenged the then-prevalent view that reunion was neurotic or harmful or both. The authors of the study described how beneficial search and reunion could be to *all* members of the triad and also concluded that "many (adoptees) harbor secret desires to search, but lack the strength to initiate action.[17] Their book, *The Adoption Triangle*, has become a classic in the field.

More than ten years later, we have reached a point where search has become more frequent and familiar. Though mainly conducted outside established channels, those who seek their relatives can find practical, knowledgeable, "how-to" help, more easily than ever before. "Everyone knows how to search now," one leader says. Searchers also find emotional support more readily available than ten years ago, both from like-minded individuals in the triad and from a widening circle of professionals who have come to believe that finding birth relatives is healthy and helpful. Still, not everyone searches, and it will be important for future researchers to try to discover the difference between those who want to and those who don't (See Chapter 3). But people who believe in search—including those who have lived in adopted circumstances as well as those who work with it professionally—find it impossible to imagine that anyone who is adopted does not, at some level, wonder about their origins. Adoptees who do not search, they contend, are inhibited or denying or fearful, but they do not lack interest. In the words of one search group leader, "I don't think there's a person who's been adopted that hasn't thought about this. I don't believe there's a mother out there who has given up a child and hasn't been affected."

Another local leader, a woman who assists with searches and is a birthmother herself, puts it this way, "I can't imagine any birthmother not having an undying need to have a reunion. They may never act on it; they may repress it. And I don't think I have an over-romanticized vision of motherhood. Even if they don't have the will or knowledge to search themselves, they would like to be found."

How Adoption Works

While pregnancy and adoption are personal and emotion-laden matters, society has always laid claim to exerting its influence on childbearing and family issues that affect the general social order. Both social attitudes and public policy profoundly affect our reproductive and parenting destinies. Abortion was not a legal option for any of these birthmothers, so all of them "chose" adoption, not because they necessarily liked or preferred the practice, but because it was the only route available.

Several of the birthmothers provide heart-rending illustrations of how ignorance of adoption procedures and alternatives worked against them. There was much they weren't told, options they never even suspected. More than one never received counseling about the ways that might have allowed her to keep her baby: the possibility of temporary foster care was never mentioned, for example, or the possibility of welfare. One birthmother, Betty, tells how she fought for months after her son's birth to keep him, but finally succumbed to the pressures of her family and the adoption agency. She signed the paper they all wanted her to sign and then, the next morning, realized she had to revoke it. She called the agency to tell them. "When we go to court, I'm going to tell the judge I don't want to do this," she announced, and learned, to her horror, that she would have no such day in court.

Like education, adoption in this country is an institution regulated by the states (hence, adoption agencies are licensed by the state), and great variability exists in all aspects of adoption law and practice. When you compare adult adoptees who have embarked on birth family searches, you discover that their personal journeys can take vastly different courses depending on the laws of the states in which all pertinent family members (birth and adoptive) live. A handful of states are more liberal in terms of providing adult adoptees with some opportunity to access the records they request.[18] Many state legislatures are reviewing new bills on the subject.

There is also a remarkable degree of variability within agency practices and as a result of the individual personalities and whims of the professionals involved. When dealing with something as basic as a human being's ability to know (or not know) the details of his or her birth and genetic heritage—a right that everyone but the adopted takes for granted—it is astonishing to realize how much depends on fate and luck: what state you were born in, which agency your birthmother dealt with, exactly what details about your birthmother (and birthfather and their families) the social worker decided to write down (or maybe even discreetly edit), how this same agency today handles search inquiries as a policy matter, and how the social worker you see today feels about all these things. Definitions of what constitutes "identifying information" (information that will not be released) versus "non-identifying information" (information that will) differ from agency to agency. Whether an adoption took place before or after a given year is another factor that determines which set of rules applies.

Despite these variations, certain common essentials have shaped the adoptions, hence the reunions, of the people we interviewed. We will describe them briefly here to prevent the reader from harboring mistaken beliefs, and to provide some important background against which these birthmothers' histories have been played out. What was standard adoption practice, it turns out, caused a good deal of pain. Substantial, often insurmountable, barriers were placed against any possible future contact between adoptees and birthmothers.

What are these commonalties and hurdles?

1. In order for adoption to take place, official "consent" of the birthmother was required and her "rights" to the child were terminated. The birthmothers we interviewed signed papers relinquishing their babies, and were given to understand that they would never see their child again. A few say they were tricked into signing, resulting in "involuntary relinquishment," a term that covers a variety of unsavory, even fraudulent, practices.[19] Hardly any of the women talk about—and, indeed, it seems that few actually remember—the *act* of signing. But this was the only ceremony. Society provided no other recognition or marker to commemorate the event. There was no ritual, like a funeral, to help the mothers acknowledge or deal with their loss.[20]

2. Adoption resulted in the substitution of another set of parents for the birthmothers' (and birthfathers') children—a second set of parents who would be subject to the same misfortunes that could beset any couple: sickness, death, accident, premature death. Thus, one of the daughters in our interviews was raised from the age of eight by her adoptive aunt because her adoptive parents died during her childhood.

3. Adoption involves official documents—papers that adoptive parents like to keep, or hide, in a safe place (assuming they have them at all, which some do not). It's not uncommon for adopted children to stumble across these papers, or inten-

tionally look for them, during either their childhoods or adolescence, when identity issues begin to loom large for everyone. Searchers need these official documents to begin their detective work. One of the documents is the adoption decree, signed by a judge. The second document, more important, is the original birth certificate, which was habitually sealed by the court when the adoption was finalized.

4. The birth certificate which adoptees routinely possess is an amended document. The birthparents' names were removed and the adoptive parents' names were substituted. (If Jill Jones was the birthmother and Sally Smith was the adoptive mother, the baby was born to Sally Smith according to the new birth certificate and no trace of Jill Jones survives.) In some states, the location of birth is also deleted. No one seems quite sure how the practice of obliterate-and-substitute actually started.

5. The original birth certificate is "sealed." Anyone who requests a copy of the adoptee's birth certificate, including the adoptee, receives the amended version, a document which many triad members consider forged. Adoptees are the only group in the country whose birth certificates do not contain the true facts of their birth and many maintain that the practice is an affront to their civil liberties. The amended birth certificate reinforces some adoptees' feelings that they were never born and they have no roots, a sensitivity which is problematic in its own right and which also sets them apart from everyone else.[21] Seeing the amended document can be painful for birthmothers as well, years later. What one birthmother saw on her daughter's birth certificate was white-out—the same white-out that typists use to correct mistakes. What it did, both functionally and symbolically, was to erase *her* as the person who had given birth. The state was actually saying, on a legal document, that some other woman had given birth instead.

6. All records of adoption (of which the original birth certificate is paramount for search purposes) are sealed, and usually found in the city where the adoption took place, not the city of birth. They are locked in the files of the office of vital statistics. Adoption-related records also may be found in the

agency of the state which regulates adoptions, in the agency that arranged the adoption, in the attorney's files, and in the court's department of adoption records. The laws of most states prohibit adoptees from having access to these records, which can be granted only by court order after the adoptee has persuaded the court that he or she has compelling reason (the statutory language is "good cause") to know the birthparents' identities. For their part, the courts have generally been unwilling to be convinced, even when medical need is offered as good cause, so search has basically become an underground enterprise.

7. There are two different kinds of adoptions: agency adoptions from public and private agencies, and independent adoptions which are arranged by third parties, typically doctors and lawyers. Among the adoptions we represent in this book, only three were independent cases; the majority were of the agency variety, and more were private than public. The pattern in the country today still favors agency adoptions, public more often than private, but adoptions arranged by private individuals account for a sizable proportion.[22] Independent adoptions, however, are not even legal in some states.

8. Agency and independent adoptions are different in important ways. Once an agency takes a child for adoption, the agency assumes legal responsibility for that child and, like a parent, is in charge of the child's welfare. In discharging this responsibility, agencies sometimes place newborns in foster homes before adoptive placement is finalized. In independent adoptions, on the other hand, the mother typically retains her legal rights to the child for a longer period, until such time as the adoption is finalized by court action. Independent adoptions also grant the mother a greater say in choosing who the adoptive parents will be.

9. In agency adoptions, the decision as to who adopts the child is the agency's. Birthmothers can and do express their wishes about the kinds of people they would like the child's adoptive parents to be, but there are no guarantees that such wishes can or will be honored, despite any assurances to the contrary. Several birthmothers we interviewed were sorely dis-

appointed to discover after reunion that their children's adoptive parents were not the kind of people, or did not provide the
kind of upbringing, that the women hoped they would have. In
addition to poor matches in terms of values, interests, etc.,
several found that their children had "a rough time" because
they were raised in homes with economic problems, alcoholic
problems, emotional problems, and the like.

10. Adopted children generally have all the rights of
natural children, including inheritance rights. In some states,
adopted children retain the right to inherit from the
birthparents unless they are specifically disinherited. (How the
birthmothers we interviewed plan to handle the inheritance issue is discussed in Chapter 8.)

11. The decision to relinquish a child for adoption
mainly resides with the woman and her family. The birthfather
was largely absent from any adoption legalities in this country
until the mid-1970s.[23] That situation remains, but changes in
the law point in the direction of giving birthfathers a greater
voice in what will happen to the child. (The historical involvement of the birthfathers in our cases, and the men's current
response to the appearance of their sons and daughters, is the
subject of Chapter 9.)

The Search and Support Movement

*"At the meeting, my husband and Barb and I went together
and he sat there and cried, he was so upset at what he was
hearing. He has never gone to another meeting. I was asked
to get up and tell our story, something I had never done, and
I stood up there, and I was so scared. There were about two
hundred people there and I hung unto the podium, I shook
so. Then we had questions from the floor. It was an
icebreaker for me. I just seemed to open up more and more
after that. Normally, I don't have much to say."*

Nell, a birthmother

A loose federation of hundreds of search and support groups
around the country constitute a grass roots movement some-

times referred to as the adoption reform movement.[24] In its political agenda, the movement supports opening records for adult adoptees and birthparents, and a more open style for future adoptions. Past adoption practice is something these people know intimately because almost all of them have lived with old style, closed-record adoptions either as adoptees, birthparents or adoptive parents.

As a rule, the search and support groups are heavily concerned with the search aspects of reunion, and they welcome anyone in the adoption triad. Groups composed primarily of adoptees predominate, but there are also groups made up of mainly birthmothers, and other groups which mainly address the adoptive parent perspective.[25] Whether a given group can genuinely serve all members of the triangle equally well is an issue which provokes some disagreement. Some individuals frankly admit that they feel free to be fully honest only in the company of people who occupy the same position in the triad that they do. One support group leader, for example, will not allow anyone but birthmothers to attend her sessions.

The support group structure is particularly active in the search process and less involved in the later stages, after contact has been made.[26] It is a support system that tells searchers that what they are doing is okay and helps them get the job done. Group members become very involved with one another's situations, call each other at times of need, and share one another's successes and failures. Betty, for example, called a young friend from her group to join her when, in high anxiety, she was about to meet her son for the first time. It was this same friend—a young man and an adoptee—who sat with her into the early hours of the next morning after her reunion meeting was over, going over and over the details of what had happened. No one else in her life could have understood it all so well.

When a reunion has been accomplished and has turned out to be difficult or disappointing, birthmothers often turn to one another for support, not to husbands or family or others in their "regular" lives. Conversely, Adrienne, a birthmother whose reunion and post-reunion relationship was positive right from the start, withdrew from a group almost immediately because she felt uncomfortable displaying her good fortune to women whose situations were painful. Others we spoke to were equally careful not to flaunt their blessings, consciously playing down the positives in front of counterparts with pronounced troubles. Indeed, the trauma they share goes a long way in explaining the dynamic of birthmothers who remain close over years when their search and reunion outcomes are less than happy. Says one: "Almost all my friends are birthmothers. I only want to be friends with women who have had the same experience. I'm happy other women can have a wonderful Christmas or Chanukah with their kids, but I don't want to be with these women. I'm not having wonderful times. I want to be with my birthmother friends. And that's what happens with birthmothers. We become very tight."

Because adoption support groups mark the end of an individual's psychological isolation, substituting a social environment for what was solitary confinement, the groups begin to combat the damage that prolonged secrecy has inflicted. The groups are exhilarating to birthmothers because they are an antidote to secrecy, and permit a unity and strength, which obviously helps people heal. Adoptees who have searched for their birthmothers frequently encourage their found mothers to come to support group meetings as a way of helping *them* deal with the emotional convulsions that accompany reunion and early post-reunion. Similarly, when we asked the women we interviewed if they had any advice for the unseen thousands who will be found by their sons and daughters in the next few years, one resounding suggestion was "get them into a group."

Debora recalls her own "coming out" as a peak experience, a time of exuberant emancipation: "Within one week I went from an ALMA meeting and a birthmother meeting in New York on Wednesday to a birthmother meeting on Long Island on Thursday, and another the following Saturday in White Plains, so I was swept in with all these birthmothers and it was incredible. It was the first time I was in a public place where I felt totally unafraid and I could look anybody in the eye."

When people confess to previously concealed matters,

the relief is enormous. In the support group setting, they are also getting reinforcements against forces which, in the past, were too powerful to combat alone. The sense of unity, and strength, is a healing experience.

The benefits of the group environment are not restricted to birthmothers or adoptees. Adoptive parents can also welcome a similar sharing. An adoptive father to whom we spoke recalls the impact of accompanying his very nervous teenage son to the first search group meeting and listening to a stranger, an adoptive mother, address the group about her own family's experiences with search and reunion. She had been through it twice, on behalf of her adopted son *and* her adopted daughter. The fact that she was so "open and unruffled" about it, the father says, helped him dispel his own very considerable discomfort at finding himself in these unexpected circumstances. She ended her presentation, he recalls, with "a wonderful story" about how "the whole family" (birth and adoptive) was present at the daughter's wedding.

More than any other resource, support groups offered needed assistance at the time of reunion to the birthmothers we interviewed.[27] A couple of individuals turned to a religious leader or a therapist or a counselor. A few indicate that social workers or adoption agencies provided helpful advice. A few agencies even offered to provide a place and a person to serve as an intermediary for the first reunion meeting. In the main, though, these birthmothers relied on the support group, an institution existing outside the social mainstream, to assist their meetings, and/or their subsequent interactions, with their children.[28]

The groups clearly fill a void. If they had sought help from other sources prior, or during these reunions, what the birthmothers would have discovered is that unless adoption has become a professional specialty, those in the medical and the mental health professions frequently have little or no experience with the kinds of problems reunion can produce. Also, many clergymen have no experience with adoption situations. Counselors of all types probably learned about adoption, if at all, when someone in the adoption triad appeared in their office for help. Several birthmothers visited professionals over the years who failed to recognize or deal with adoption or reunion issues appropriately. Happily, we also heard the reverse on occasion, from birthmothers who received help they considered invaluable.

Regardless of whether they've sought help before, once they reach reunion and post-reunion, just about everyone says they would, or did, benefit from outside support or assistance of one kind or another. Post-reunion isn't easy and participants are looking for guidance.

This book, which documents the post-reunion experience, reflects a natural evolution. The birthmother perspective could not exist as a focal point for a study until enough birthmothers were ready to come forth and reveal their identities and feelings. Post-reunion is healing. As one of the birthmothers we interviewed explains, she wants the world to know, "I don't feel any need for secrecy or confidentiality. I think it's important to document the experience we've had and to use it for change for the better. Closed adoptions are so damaging. Thank God, some of us have been able to repair a lot of the damage in our lives by being reunited."

3

Why Reunions Happen

"The adoption didn't ruin my life in any major or visible way, but it numbed me. I never felt quite as happy as I had before then. I never felt quite as successful. I felt more frightened. I had never felt frightened before then, and I felt sort of tentative and hesitant about doing things and getting involved in things. In retrospect, I think I was really worried that I was a big failure, that a man didn't want to marry me, that I had to give a baby away, that I had disappointed my family. I didn't want to fail again so I was numbed in a lot of areas."

Lila, a birthmother

Like other subjects being newly aired in public, adoption is a subject laced with myths. Rose-colored tints go along with the mythology and with society's inclination to romanticize adoption. The real experiences of these birthmothers indicate that there is a variety of reality and that the shading goes from pale to deep.

The myths include:

1. The distress birthmothers feel at relinquishment will go away. They will be able to go on with their lives as though nothing ever happened. They will forget about the child. They will not feel guilty.

2. Adoption workers will honor the mother's wishes regarding the kind of family (e.g., religion, education) in which the

child is placed. A "good" home will be found. An appropriate match will be made.

3. Adoptees will feel no ties to their birthmothers or to other birth relatives. The separation will be complete. There will be no feeling of connection. There will be no feeling of loss.

4. The predictable questions which adopted children will ask about their origins or about the circumstances of their adoption can be answered satisfactorily by the adoptive parents. Only a little information will be required.

5. Adoptees will get everything they need for healthy human development from the loving adoptive homes in which they are raised. Growing up adopted will be no different from growing up non-adopted. When adolescence comes, it will be no more difficult for adoptive parents than for biological parents. In the final analysis, the adoptee will be better off having been raised by the adoptive parents.

6. Adoptees who seek their birthparents are indulging a "curiosity." It can only hurt their adoptive parents.

What the common myths add up to is that adoptees and birthmothers have no reason to find one another, much less to continue in a relationship once initial contact has been made. The evidence says something quite different. Only in rare cases did we learn that things had indeed turned out, both for mother and child, pretty much the way the birthmothers had hoped and predicted years before. What usually happened instead is that the ensuing life of one or the other, or both, was affected in some negative fashion.

Birthmothers' Realities

Living with false beliefs is always dangerous, but when the birthmothers we interviewed were sold Myth 1—the myth of putting it behind you—they got a particularly bad bargain. In some cases it wasn't until many years later that the women discovered that the assurances which had been presented were false; for some, it happened almost immediately after the relinquishment. Contrary to what they had been advised, most discovered sooner or later that the fact of being a mother did not

35

Why Reunions Happen

disappear with the surrender of the child. The maternal attachment was not severed, and the decision to give up their child typically resulted in pervasive, life-affecting, often unhappy results of one kind or another.

The large majority of these women classify the experience of giving up their baby as the most stressful event of their lives.[1] Describing their feelings at the time of surrender, they recall feeling exhausted and beaten. It was "like a nightmare." Several focus on feeling angry or bitter; others talk about feeling frightened. Still others remember confusion or numbedness. Many talk about feeling a lack of control. Several remind us that they felt they were doing the best thing or the only thing that was possible. Marion remembers, "I was frightened to death. I definitely felt that I was bad. I had to get punished for this. When I think about it now, I just had no concept of the consequences, the price forever and ever."

The large majority also reveal that, as the years passed, they did *not* become comfortable with the decision; they continued to grope with unresolved feelings about it. One woman, both a birthmother and a support group leader, compares the bargain she made to selling her soul to the devil. "You're buying into something worse and you don't even know it," she contends, "You think you're going to go back. You honestly believe it. But motherhood is a rite of passage, and you never go back from a rite of passage."

Instead of being healed by time, the feelings of suffering usually remained, or even intensified, a condition that nobody seemed to recognize or heed until the mid 1970s. At that time, the first research studies were published, suggesting that birthmothers were not all proceeding satisfactorily with their lives.[2] A national study of over two hundred birthmothers in Australia, a country where the historical mores surrounding unwed pregnancy appear to have been very similar to our own, found that the effects of relinquishment were negative and long-lasting. Over half the women reported an increasing sense of loss over periods of up to thirty years. Among our survey, only four said that their feelings of loss diminished over the years. The child's birthday and holidays were particularly difficult times for some, just as the anniversary of a loved one's death would have been.

In addition to having suffered the loss itself, many birthmothers failed to grieve. Neither alerted to the need nor allowed to give vent to their feelings when the hushed and hurried separation took place, many birthmothers carried their unexpressed grief across the years. Often, years later, they were afflicted by severe depression or other psychological impairments even though they were unaware of the connection between the adoption and their symptoms.[3] One woman talks about being in a "state of shock" for thirteen years. Many accounts remind us of the Rip Van Winkle story, as birthmothers, awakening from a deep sleep, discover that they have been repressing grief, guilt or anger, for five, ten or fifteen years. One, a "found" birthmother, did not understand what was going on until she was hypnotized. She shared her amazement with a support group, "My guilt at leaving my daughter had never left me. It's continually been shoved down my subconscious mind as something bad I did, and it's left its mark ever since. Now that it's out in the open and it's something I can talk about without guilt, you have no idea how it's changing me."

Others we interviewed were hit by noticeable ailments quite soon after the relinquishment took place. Some found themselves indulging in what they recognized as self-destructive behavior or "a bizarre lifestyle," but without understanding why. At least two women experienced suicidal periods. In Vivian's case, the suicide attempt took place two years after the birth, at age eighteen, and the reason she gave her parents was that she missed her baby. The explanation was dismissed by her disbelieving father, who challenged her to tell him the "real" reason. In support groups, revelations of drug and alcohol abuse, as well as indiscriminate sexual activity, soon after surrender are not uncommon.

Regardless of how the distress was manifested, a recurring theme among birthmothers is not having been able to figure out "what was bothering me," "why I was acting this way," "why I was crying all the time," or "why I was falling apart" until they read or heard something about adoption or "birthmotherhood." Sophisticated as many of these women have since become about adoption and relinquishment, they often preface their accounts with wonder, "I don't know how I could have been so stupid." But it's easy to understand; they were still living under the influence of Myth 1.

Similarly, although over half the women had some experience with counseling or therapy prior to their reunions, many *failed to mention* their pregnancy and adoption history to the professional counselor or therapist, either because they failed to recognize its relevance to their presenting problem, or because they repressed thinking about it, or because it was just too shameful. One birthmother, Thelma, announces, "It was none of his business." A therapist who specializes in adoption tells us that she has seen clients who were diagnosed by other practitioners as clinically depressed. Once properly treated for their "birthmotherhood," these women were able to reduce medication and move on with their lives, finally freed of the psychological paralysis which had gripped them.[4] Other therapists compare birthmothers they have counseled to victims of post-traumatic stress syndrome.

Like Lila, who talks about being "slightly numbed" ever since relinquishment, and Marcie, the woman described in the Prologue, birthmothers also suffered damage to their self-esteem and self-confidence. They translated society's negative opinion into negative feelings about themselves. Many could not forgive themselves for "abandoning" their babies, and some translated their wounds into a state of generalized inhibition, a fear of reaching out to the world and becoming an active participant. They remained "stuck" in the psychological space they inhabited, functioning below their potential and unable to advance. "I'm finding out how much wounding there was by how much healing there is." one says.

Not knowing what happened to the child she gave away is one of the most agonizing consequences of being a birthmother. It keeps the hurt alive.[5] The desire to know is extremely widespread, quite possibly universal, and does not disappear over the years. A birthmother's conscious thoughts about the child often swell as he or she reaches the teenage years or the age of majority, a point at which contact becomes more acceptable. An escalating desire for information usually accompanies a birthmother's initial decision to search for her child. Search experts tell us that people come to them saying, "I want to find out if my child is still alive, period." Having passed that barrier, however, their need to know more quickly progresses.

Woman after woman talks about the pain of going through life not knowing. Is her child alive or dead? Is he well? Happy? What kind of life has he had? Where is he? Not knowing is compared to having a loved one missing in action—a limbo loss that is never resolved. One birthmother explains, "It's a death with no body. There is only the not knowing, and the not knowing became an entity unto itself." Countless birthmothers find themselves looking, involuntarily, at every age-appropriate boy or girl they pass on the street. The enormous void of not knowing produces a perpetual, if not always conscious, search. "I used to sit on the porch with my dog, looking up at the stars and say, 'She's somewhere out there sitting under these same stars, but where?' You don't know where," one woman anguished, "She could be living in the next town." (Among our interviewees, around one-third of their relinquished children actually were.)

It is also extremely common for the birthmother to worry about what the child must be thinking of her. Is she hated for not having kept him? Does he understand that she gave him up in the belief that he would enjoy a better life than she thought she could provide? She hopes the record is straight, but, she has no way of knowing. She cares about what the child has been told and what he thinks.

One of the most poignant images in these stories was the occasional instance of a birthmother who, knowing where her child was and watching her from afar, kept her silence and resisted the impulse to come forward. Suzanne, whose daughter's adoption had been privately arranged, was one of these.

Suzanne had married Kim's birthfather four years after giving birth. The two parents, who never felt they had the right to make contact, would occasionally ride by Kim's house, fifteen miles away, in the hopes of catching a glimpse of their child. They remained silent for twenty-five years until their first-born was finally successful in *her* repeated attempts to locate them, attempts which were impeded for three years by Suzanne's sister-in-law, whom Kim had reached on the phone, and who kept trying to "protect" Suzanne. We spoke to Suzanne three years after their reunion. She now feels the "total contentment" of finally having all her questions answered and all her explanations delivered.

In addition to the kinds of distress we've already seen, giving up a child for adoption can influence birthmothers' lives in other areas as well. There are birthmothers whose subsequent romantic relationships are affected by the woman's impaired ability to trust. There are those whose subsequent childbearing is affected, some of whom quickly become pregnant again in an attempt to replace the lost child, others who consciously refrain from becoming pregnant again out of loyalty to the child they relinquished. Betty is an example of the latter:

> *"I would never have kids because I felt how could I raise another baby when my first child was out there, and I didn't even know where he was and who was taking care of him. Here I'd be raising another baby and going 'goo goo I love you,' when my first baby was out there. And if I ever did find him, how would I look him in the face and say, 'I have other kids that I took care of.' I didn't realize I'd feel this way until I was married for a while and my husband started talking about having kids. I became hysterical and I wouldn't have sex with him. I was just panic-stricken. And then I realized."*

Secondary infertility is also found to be higher among women who have surrendered children to adoption than among other populations.

Giving up a baby can also cast a shadow on the kind of mothering a woman gives her subsequent children.[6] Both over-protectiveness and emotional distancing are possible effects.

Geraldine, for example, a birthmother who still has young children at home, expects that her reunion will have a positive effect on her youngest, a ten-year-old, because she will be less "smothering" of that child now.

Wanting to Connect

Given the multitude of unresolved feelings and problems that so many birthmothers share, the idea that they need or want to be protected from the unwanted "intrusions" of the children they relinquished is clearly fallacious. They never asked for anonymity, many of them like to remind us. It came with the territory as a condition of the adoption.

Virtually every one of the birthmothers we interviewed declared, many emphatically, that she had wanted information about or contact with her child over the years, despite the conviction that she did not have the "right." Only two had not fantasized or hoped or actively considered the possibility of reunion. One of these two immediately invited her daughter over when she called. Constance, the other, took longer to find a positive response. She had spent her life being "scared" and trying "not to think about it," avoiding articles or television shows or other external reminders of the "deep dark secret" which would be so very difficult to tell her other children. "I had my head in the sand," she now says, and has come to understand, four years after being found, that a powerful repression was at work. "In order to survive, I separated myself from my feelings." The pattern persisted for several years more, into her post-reunion relationship with her daughter.

Other women describe their desire to connect with their children as having taken a variety of forms: trying not to think about it too much because it was too painful; becoming "weepy" around the child's birthday and confronting selected family members with the question, "Do you know what day this is?"; fantasizing that the doorbell would ring one day and their child would be standing there; having dreams about hiring a detective; wanting a reunion, but never thinking they could be that "lucky"; writing letters to their children that they never mailed because there was no place to send them; and writing letters to the adoption agency. Norma, a birthmother who surrendered twins twenty-six years earlier, was talking to a friend about "my babies—they were still my babies" the night before one of her sons called. In another variation, Marion tells us, "I remember so strongly the sense that I would never be able to look for him and yet, at the same time, feeling somewhere deep in my gut that I was going to find this kid or he was going to find me." Over the years, several stumbled upon the information that some adoptees go searching for their birthmothers, and the news turned them around from "not the slightest hope that we would ever meet again" to the beginnings of hope. Others clipped information about search and reunion from newspapers and magazines and filed it away until the pages yellowed with age.

Several birthmothers specifically remember whispering into their baby's ear that they would meet again someday. One of them did so on the suggestion of the social worker who came to take the baby away. The new mother felt silly talking to a baby, but she hugged her anyway and whispered. Thelma is another birthmother who spoke to her newborn about meeting later as adults. Her daughter later claimed she "doesn't know why she found me" and Thelma has considered the possibility that somehow *she* is responsible for implanting the thought in her newborn:

> *"For the two weeks that I had her, every day when I held her I said only one thing to her, over and over again, 'When you grow up you will find me.' That's all I said to her for two weeks. I said, 'I love you, I'm doing this for your own good. I know you don't believe me now, but it's true.' And I just repeated it endlessly, 'When you grow up you will find me.' I really believe that's the reason she felt compelled, when she turned eighteen, to come and find me."*

Faye, one of the oldest birthmothers in our sample, and in poor health at the time of our interview, said that she kept herself alive knowing a reunion would happen, even though the agency had told her years before that her daughter, along with the girl's adoptive mother, had been killed in a car accident. It was a lie. Faye died a little more than a year after she and her grown daughter were reunited. (Hers was a case of involuntary relinquishment. Her child was two years old and in a foster home when the adoption took place.)

Debora's story illustrates how healing the reconnection between birthmothers and their children can actually be. Even when the post-reunion developments prove to be a new and different kind of trial, reunion can do its mending work.

Debora's Story

The act of searching for and finding her grown son, Teddy, has "given myself back to me," says this forty-one-year-old birthmother. Approaching three years, her reunion with her son, age twenty-two at the time of our interview, has proven to be emotionally liberating in terms of the past, but complicated and hurtful in the present. After frequent and intense early contacts which she describes as very loving, very comfortable, very connected, Teddy, crying, announced one day that he wanted "to slow everything down." The relationship promptly lost the quality of openness, excitement and celebration that it had at first.

Debora does not know what happened to precipitate her son's announcement, but she suspects the adoptive father is pulling the strings. The man was abusive to her on the phone when she first called trying to make contact. It is a phone call she now regrets making. (She also knows that the adoptive parents have refused giving search assistance to their adopted daughter, a fact she points to as signaling their disapproval of reunions generally.) Debora is abiding by the ground rule she offered Teddy early in the reunion. She would not call or write his home again. Since she has no way of reaching him when he's not working, (He was not employed at the time of our interview.) any contact between them must be initiated by him.

The invisible walls that stand guard at this reunion are

further buttressed by Teddy's understandable discomfort at having learned, from Debora, his birthfather's identity. His father is a man whom he has actually known casually for many years—a neighbor in a summer community. The man even dated Teddy's adopted sister. It is upsetting enough that his adoptive father looks disapprovingly upon Teddy's relationship with Debora as "unnatural" and sleazy, but Teddy's knowledge of his birthfather's identity is making the young man even more uncomfortable.

The cool acquiescence into which her son has settled, and his lack of further interest in his history, is a disappointment to Debora. "He checks in with me but he doesn't really want to spend time; he has no energy for me the way I want it," she says, and she wonders why he comes back at all. She became angry with him once, for which he punished her by disappearing for five months. When she expressed her frustration about her limbo status and asked him to define "what my limits were, or my privileges," he retorted, "What am I supposed to do? I can't invite you home for Sunday dinner."

Debora's two other sons have responded poorly also. So far neither of them wants a connection with Teddy, and she suspects that Teddy feels the same way about them. It has become so uncomfortable for her to discuss the fact of her first son with these two that "I have to rehearse it several times in my head before I even make the simplest, slightest, remark. But every once in a while I force myself to say something to remind them that this exists, and for my own good, not to allow their feelings to totally dictate how I'm going to handle it."

Far from being depressed or embittered by the post-reunion difficulties, Debora has blossomed from the experience of search and reunion. The immensity of what adoption did is staggering, she observes, and she reflects on the consequences of being unable to forgive herself all these years, "I was such a wisp . . . I never felt I had the right to have anything, even feelings," she says about her pre-searching self. Still, her guilt persists and the ability to forgive herself remains. "No one was holding a gun to my head," she insists, "I still don't feel at all comfortable. When I say to myself, 'You gave your child away,' *it is the worst thing anybody can do. When I saw **Sophie's Choice**, I cried like everybody else, and yet I felt that she had an incredible excuse and I didn't."*

But Debora is rebuilding her life now. She is enthusiastic about the future and making plans to return to school, change jobs, launch new projects—all a result of feeling more consistently positive and optimistic than before. "I've realized now that the search I was on was for myself. I found that person, that little girl, and have joined her back to me."

Debora is going through a mending time. It seems very much akin to what expert Dr. Phyllis Silverman describes as the process birthmothers must pass through in order to develop a better self-image and to resolve feelings of rage, bitterness and guilt.[7] The birthmother must "build a coherent bridge between her past and her present," she advises. This includes examining "honestly and without accusation, of herself and others, just what her circumstances were at the time" and also examining her feelings about adoption. Attempting to find out about the child is another step that forges a necessary link with the past. As for reunion, Silverman sees it as "the ultimate resolution of the birthmother's grief, the final link in the chain between her past and future."

Adoptees' Drive to Search

Psychiatrists such as Freud tell us that there is a time in every child's experience when the child has the fantasy that his parents are not his parents, that he is the child of others. Freud calls it the "family romance" and explains it as the child's way of separating from the parents and experiencing his or her own identity.

In the case of adopted children, however, the idea of other parents is not a fantasy at all. For the adopted, the knowledge that there are living, breathing people out there—another mother and father—is a basic and very real truth, and one that must be dealt with. What usually happens is that, in the absence of specific or detailed factual information, adoptees turn to fantasy to conjure up these parents. Fantasy fills the informational void, and adoptees are known to spend vast amounts of emotional energy exploring and living with their fantasy creations—not just in childhood but as adolescents and adults as well. The fantasy parents that most of us fleetingly encountered, then left behind, years ago, become a prominent part of the adoptee's psychological landscape, all the more powerful because there really is another, unknown set of parents somewhere.

It is probably impossible for those of us who are not adopted to fully appreciate what it means to know that the parents with whom you grew up, the people whose name you bear, are not your natural parents. The idea that we could just as easily have been someone else—a person with a different name, a different set of parents, in a home with different characteristics, different siblings, different traditions—is not an idea that most of us dwell upon because, in some fundamental way, we accept the fact that we are who we are. When an adoptee, Janet Povar, told us that, according to her original birth certificate, she was really Jane Marie O'Rourke, we began to sense how profound the duality really was. When a man named Dan Hauser told us several months later that it had never occurred to him that he had another name during the two years of his life before being adopted, it no longer surprised us that the discovery that he was Kevin Palmer sent him reeling.[8]

When people are not personally involved with adoption, they rarely think about it's "might have been" nature. Adoptees do. There are times in the lives of some when they can think of little else. If the word curious implies a desire to know "what is not properly one's concern," curious is surely a misnomer for this particular desire to know. Listen to Kate, the twenty-one-year-old daughter who found Lila, who makes it clear that nothing can be *more* properly her concern:

> *"You need to have basic information about yourself that other people take for granted, and knowing that other people take it for granted only adds to the horror of not having it. When*

you wake up in the morning and look in the mirror, you ask "Who is that person? Where are other people who have that same face? It's your whole life you're looking for, it isn't just eye color. It's where did that eye color come from? How many other people have that? What happened to those people? It's all of that; it's all connected. If you don't know where your eye color comes from, you don't know where you're coming from or what your potential is in life."

At least the word curious, unsuitable though it may be in this case, is a word we can all understand as we begin to think about why adoptees want to find their birth origins. We can imagine what it would be like to look in the mirror, close our eyes, try to conjure a person into focus. If all we conjured on our mental screen was nothingness—if what we got was nameless and faceless, with no physical images, no personality traits, no identity of any kind—wouldn't we be "curious," too? Wouldn't we seize upon any information that presented itself, holding it close as a precious prize?

We'd be less likely to explain our motives in terms of bonding or attachment theory, but the impulse to reunion is analyzed in these terms by many professionals. The question of how much bonding occurs between a mother and a developing fetus is a subject at which researchers are looking, and the fact of mother-fetus bonding may well have an impact on the desire for reunion. There are studies which indicate that some mothers-to-be begin to experience love for their child during pregnancy (though others do not experience these same feelings until birth, or in the first week, or after the first week).[9] In our interviews, many birthmothers talked about having feelings of love and attachment to the baby they placed for adoption. Many also spoke of feeling "incomplete" in the years following the placement. "It's like you lost a part of yourself," says one. Similarly, when adult adoptees describe *their* motivations for search and reunion, they too frequently speak of a lack of completeness. As one reunioning adoptee remarked to her birthmother, "I've read about mothers feeling bonded to their babies, why can't a baby feel just as bonded to its mother?" According to some current psychological thinking, the baby can.

Recent research supports the theory that most babies form a specific "mother attachment" by six to eight months after birth, and there is a substantial body of evidence indicating that separating a baby from its mother can leave a lifelong legacy of emotional injuries.[10] Adoptees would presumably form this attachment with their adoptive mothers, assuming they are adopted as infants, but it doesn't always work that way; either because they are adopted later or for other reasons. In the cases we investigated more fully, at least six of the babies were adopted at the age of six months or older. At least eight of the birthmothers believed that their child had not "bonded" or felt "attached" or "connected" to his adoptive family[11]—a disturbance some associated with their son's or daughter's need to search. More generally, adoption specialist Annette Baran cites the influential work of British psychoanalyst D. W. Winnecott on bonding and attachment to explain why she thinks just about every birthmother and every adoptee is emotionally disadvantaged. According to Winnecott, mothers bond with their babies over time, starting at a point *before* the birth and completing the process a few months *after,* which means that every birthmother-child pair who is separated around the time of infancy is being interrupted in the midst of this essential process.

Whatever its origin, the feeling of incompleteness is one theme that distinguishes adoptees from the rest of us.[12] There are many other themes as well. People who have studied adolescent and adult adoptees frequently point out that, as a group, adoptees are disproportionately prone to show up in psychological or psychiatric treatment settings[13]—a vulnerability that would poke holes in the "happily ever after" mythology, even if no other information was available. The theme of adoptees as restless wanderers, always in search of something, never feeling rooted, is another prominent motif we heard voiced.

Other characteristics which assorted studies find to be associated with adoptees include a host of largely inauspicious traits, many stemming from the common root of low self-esteem. Based on a questionnaire study which reached thousands of adoptees in its membership, one search and support group gathered data indicating that adoptees are prone to such cheerless conditions as: fear of abandonment and rejection; attachments to superficial things; being underachievers or overachievers; love-me-at-any-cost relationships; lack of courage in life; and disturbances in sexuality—that is, questioning one's womanhood or manhood.[14] (This last concern was echoed by several of the birthmothers we interviewed who told us they were "wondering" about their daughters' "femininity" or their son's "masculinity.")

Other studies suggest that adult adoptees may be burdened in various other ways: shy and withdrawn or angry at the world, afraid of conflict, afraid of abandonment, embarrassed about their status, seeing themselves as unfinished or imperfect. Some live in fear of falling in love with an unknown birthrelative. Some have difficulty telling their own children they are adopted. (In our sample, a married man in his late twenties, and father of a new baby, had never told his own wife he was adopted until his birthmother located him and their ensuing relationship forced him to reveal it.)[15]

All these burdens help explain why adoptees seek their birthmothers or welcome reunions when their mothers locate them. The need to search can be a powerful one, and searching adoptees frequently find themselves in the grip of a drive which can become all-consuming. Like the birthmother Debora, they too are on a search for themselves, a goal that is difficult to verbalize. One young man describes the feeling of always wanting to know "how I came into existence" as a "burning". It is not unusual for people to spend years and years in search, perhaps retreating at points but then resuming again, pursuing their goal with a persistence that bespeaks great need.[16] Perhaps we can call it an identity tropism. Or, perhaps, like other species in the animal kingdom, adoptees are driven by a homing instinct, a basic quest that refuses to be denied.

Why Reunions Happen

Adoptees themselves are often hard-pressed to explain their motives to those who do not already share some understanding. With appropriate language in short supply, they have difficulty in expressing themselves even to sympathetic outsiders. Faced with hostile audiences, they may cling to the more socially acceptable replies to justify what, to their mind, should need no justification. According to Robert Andersen, an adoptee who is also a psychiatrist, asking an adoptee, "Why do you search?" is an absurd question because it is really asking, "Why are you interested in your mother, father, grandparents, brothers, sisters, cousins, nephews, nieces, ancestry, history, proclivities, aptitudes, liabilities—in short, why are you interested in *you?*"[17] Another adoptee has written that the desire to search is "like instinct. It feels right and necessary. It is difficult to explain. Something seems to be missing, and reconnecting presents a possibility to find that indefinable missing piece."[18]

What these people are saying is that there is a void in the adoptee's life that only the birthmother can fill, a void that has little to do with the quality of the adoptee's relationship with the adoptive parents. To call it curiosity is too weak; the need seems far more primal. Using himself as a case in point, adoptee-psychiatrist Andersen concludes that after all the socially acceptable reasons have been stated, the search is "most fundamentally an expression of the wish to undo the trauma of the separation." The central wish, he says, is for "contact and healing."

An adoptee's drive to search can also be understood as arising from identity issues (who am I?), informational issues (why did my mother give me up? what is my story?), and medical issues (what is my genetic history?). Medical issues is the most socially accepted rationale. Certain life events have a way of churning up these questions and precipitating a search—engagement, marriage, pregnancy, the birth of a child, the death of a parent, for example—events which bring the subjects of family, heritage, and biological continuity to the forefront of our minds. Late adolescence is a time when the meaning of being adopted often becomes a central concern, even if the individual has known of his adoption since early childhood.

When thoughts of finding blood origins begin in childhood, they can persist for years, well into middle age and beyond.

Once they've decided to initiate a search, adoptees look for a great amount of details about themselves—details with which the rest of us have grown up, take for granted, and that infuse our sense of self. They want to learn such things as exactly when they were born (time of day), where (town or city), the name of the hospital, how much they weighed, what kind of labor their mother had and what kind of birth it was. They also want a host of details about their birthmother and birthfather: whether the two were married to one another, their ages, their circumstances, where they lived, whether they had siblings and living parents. They want to learn the nationalities and religions of all these family members, as well as their occupations, interests, educational backgrounds, etc. It is a quest for understanding and roots.

Sometimes a simple piece of information can resolve a lifetime of wondering, as in the case of the woman who grew up in an affluent New York suburb and constantly felt that she didn't belong there, she belonged on a farm instead. When she discovered, in her thirties, that her birthmother's parents were from the West Virginia hill country, something clicked. "That's what I felt all along, that I was raised in the wrong place." Other minds are put to rest upon learning that they are Italian (or not), or Jewish (or not), or Irish or German or Dutch (or not).

With respect to medical information, adoptees particularly want to find out whether they come from a family with a history of any hereditary disease such as diabetes, heart disease, or breast cancer, especially since many of these are preventable or controllable. When a suspicious lump appeared and a doctor asked one woman, "Is there a history of cancer in your family?" she answered with the practiced nonchalance of years, "I don't know. I have no history." But, at that moment, she decided to launch her search so that she would never again have to give that kind of answer to such a question. The adoption annals are filled with similar incidents, accompanied by adoptees' outrage at being denied such essential knowledge.

Who and what a searching adoptee will discover is unknown, of course. Attempts to dissuade adoptees from searching often point to the possibility that bitter truths may lie concealed behind the cloak of confidentiality. They may discover that their birthmother is in prison or in a mental hospital. They may discover that she has died. Their origins may turn out to be quite humble; they can be pretty sure they were born out of wedlock. Relatives may deny or reject them. Despite whatever fantasies they have about "coming home," acceptance is not guaranteed. Instead of reaching out with open arms, a birthmother may say, "Go away and leave me alone." She may be persuaded to grant one meeting, but nothing more. She may refuse to tell her husband or her children. She may insist on remaining anonymous. All these things are possible.

The conviction among adoptees-in-search, and among those who have completed a search, is that knowing is better than not knowing. Embarking on the search must mean being willing and ready to give up one's fantasies—good or bad—and to replace them with whatever truths may surface, for better or worse.

Considering all the uncertainties, it wouldn't be surprising if an adoptee-in-search admitted that what he hoped to find was a birthmother who had suffered as much as he had over the years and who, out of her own need, wanted to connect with him as much as he wanted to find her.

Being welcomed by a birthmother, however, does not necessarily depend on finding one who was hurt or damaged by the adoption experience. For Adrienne, reunion and post-reunion have provided not healing, but enhancement. Post-reunion is bringing a unique life embellishment to a woman who was content and well-adjusted when her son found her.

Adrienne's Story

Unlike the many birthmothers who experienced grief and guilt at surrendering their babies, Adrienne, who relinquished twin boys in 1957, had been comfortable with the decision over the years. She had been twenty-four, living with her parents in a well-to-do Midwest suburb, earning minimum wages, and pregnant by a man who was married. It never occurred to her that she had any choice, and she didn't spent a lot of time afterwards second-guessing her decision. She got on with her life. Even so, Adrienne was exuberant at her sons' re-entry into her life twenty-five years later. A woman in her late forties, she had never married, had no other children, and had become a successful commercial artist. A piece of paper came in the mail one day with only a date—the twins' birth date—and the cryptic message, "Both doing well. Write if you can." She responded immediately.

The twins' interest in finding her was less identical than their history. The searcher, Josh, wanted the kind of "Mommy" he had never experienced. David was less needy, less "yearning" and "soulful" generally, and he "held back" for a few months until the impatient Adrienne "sort of pushed him" by asking if he wanted "in" to the relationship. He said he did.

Now, five years into post-reunion, Adrienne and both sons share a profound feeling of connection. The rapport, particularly with Josh, was instantaneous: "It was like we had always known each other. Our heads are really in the same place. It's like we knew each other in some other time." Adrienne can't tell you why they were extremely comfortable with one another right away, but it is, regardless, a fact.

All three of them are artistic—able to write, draw, act. At the time of their reunion, one of the sons was attending the same college Adrienne had attended and was studying scenic design—the same unusual major that Adrienne had pursued a generation before. These days, each family member has a computer, and they send each other electronic mail almost daily. They know each other well by now, and the initial intensities have transmuted into a feeling of being "comfy" with one another, the sons' new wives included. In-person visits are infrequent because Josh and David live in the Midwest, where they were born and raised, and are established in their paths. Adrienne lives in the West.

She has considered moving back. It appeals to her now that she's ready to retire and leave the city. Also, she can afford to buy a big, beautiful old house there, the kind of house she loves and can't afford where she lives now. But, in deference to the adoptive parents, who raised both twins, and whose home Adrienne happily describes as remarkably similar to the one in which she was raised, she is choosing to remain in the West. Her feelings about the adoptive parents are quite positive, but her stance is careful. She is taking "great pains" to respect their position, not to interfere. They have been so cordial. "We're very grateful to you for having these children and letting us raise them," they've said. "I'm very grateful to you for taking care of them for me," she replies. So, Adrienne observes, "we have a pact."

There are conflicts in this congenial history, but they have arisen not between mother and sons, but as a result of other people's discomfort. Adrienne's father could not bring himself to acknowledge these grandchildren to friends and neighbors, despite accepting them in private. "We'd all be at my parents' house sitting on the front porch, and someone would come by and Daddy would say, "These are our friends," Adrienne recalls.

Initially, her sister also refused to extend a warm welcome to the surprise nephews—an attitude that Adrienne confronted head-on when her sister, a mother of three, pronounced the opinion that Adrienne had given up all rights to be their mother. "We stayed up 'til five in the morning arguing this out, and I think I finally convinced her they were my real children. My sister is crazy about them now." Another resistance, this one to accepting Adrienne herself, came from one of Adrienne's daughters-in-law, whose early reaction was one of rude, cold dismissal. That, too, has changed with time and exposure. It is Adrienne's mother, however, who provided the most moving example of public disclosure. At a memorial service for her late husband, attended by two handsome young men whom nobody knew, she publicly thanked her two grandsons for everything they had done during his illness. In announcing their existence to the world, her mother, Adrienne recognized, was "very noble."

Despite having made an attempt to gain information about their whereabouts when the twins were about seven (she particularly wanted to know if they were together), Adrienne did not live her life in guilt, overcome with her sense of loss. For her, being found has produced new pleasures rather than the easing of old pains. The twins have given her a family, she says. "Otherwise, I'd be going through life sort of drifting around; they've given me a focus." They have also given her heirs ("Now I have someone to leave my money to") and the security of knowing that someone will take care of her in her old age. Josh, early on, wanted her to know he would; Josh calls her "Mother." David calls her "Adrienne," through he introduces her to others as his Mom.

Adrienne's is a story of a reasonably happy and successful woman who has been reunited with sons who developed into impressive young men. They are, says Adrienne, "just as they should be"— charming, talented, good-looking. "My women friends all fell in love with them." Happily, too, Josh, the one who set the search in motion, seems to have accomplished what he needed. His friends have told Adrienne that he's changed since he met her, and she is aware of the changes as well. His carriage is straighter; he's become more open, less shy. "Something was missing in him," Adrienne says, "I don't know how to explain it. It sort of made him blue."

David and Josh are not the only set of twins born to the sample of birthmothers to whom we talked. Norma had twins as well, also sons, and their reunion has also evolved into a close and lasting post-reunion. In contrast to Adrienne's situation, though, there were some stormy times with one of the sons, and the bad atmosphere did not clear up for six years.

An interesting aspect of Adrienne's and Norma's cases is that, in each, only *one* of the twins felt compelled to search. But it wasn't very long after reunion that the non-searching twin became committed to the relationship.

Who Searches?

The attitudes of the sets of twins suggest that there is some quality of mind that compels one adoptee to search, while another remains inactive. While various studies have raised the question of why some individuals search and others don't, there are no results concerning what causes some to feel the pull more strongly than others. Having another real set of parents somewhere doesn't seem to register full force until a child reaches roughly the age of eight, the first point in an adoptee's life at which he may "go underground" and begin to have fantasies about whom his other parents are. This is the time that children commonly begin imagining that the woman down the street could be their biological mother, or daydream about her whereabouts or about finding her someday.

It's been suggested that searchers may be generally more intellectually curious than non-searchers. Or less fearful. Or more sensitive. One survey suggests that searchers are more likely to come from the ranks of those who were given less information about their birth heritage as children; those whose adoption revelation was traumatic; or those who were adopted at older ages.[19] It's also possible that searching is more common among adoptees who did not feel connected to, or didn't bond with, their adoptive parents. In some way, they are attempting to repair this flaw in their development. What does seem clear is that, in one way or another, searchers feel personally incomplete.

What constitutes "the search factor" remains elusive, but approaching the question demographically makes it easier to deal with. Of the two sexes, women are more likely to search,[20] an occurrence often explained in terms of a woman's ability to be closer to her feelings. A number of theories have been advanced to explain why this occurs: one theory is that women express emotions more overtly than men. Another is that, since men are more inclined to suppress emotions, they suppress the rage they feel toward the mothers who gave them up. Still another theory is that the capacity for childbearing links daughters to mothers in ways which sons do not share. Daughters frequently experience this connection anew at the time of their first pregnancy.

Other theorists believe that women search in greater numbers than men do because relationship and attachment occupy a more central position in the female psyche than in male psyches.

According to Jean Baker Miller, an analyst of female psychology, for many women "the threat of disruption of an affiliation is perceived not just as a loss of a relationship, but as something closer to a total loss of self."[21] Because of the different male and female "voices," as psychologist Carol Gilligan calls them, a recent research study concludes that gender does indeed seem to be a major determinant of the degree to which adoption is a salient status for the individual.[22] A man's identity formation is based on *separating from,* not on *relating to,* and for this reason men may simply find it easier to integrate the fact of their adoptive status into their developing sense of identity. Changes in social and cultural conditioning can affect this. The more permissive atmosphere of the last twenty years may explain why one of the largest reunion registries reports a recent jump in male registrants, both adoptees and birthfathers.[23]

Age is another factor that affects searching. Adult adoptees in their twenties and thirties search more often than their older peers. Many have waited to take action until they left their adoptive home. Others will wait until their adoptive parents die. For those who never search, the fear of hurting their adoptive parents often is a central reason.[24]

As for birthparents, it is also a more predominant pattern for younger people in their thirties or forties to search than older ones, a trend matched by the birthmothers we interviewed. As a total group, it seems clear that birthrelatives are searching much more than they used to. There are even registry sign-ups these days by birthparents who have just recently relinquished their infants, and sign-ups by adoptive parents on behalf of recently adopted new babies. Both kinds of activity suggest that some individuals are having second thoughts about the practice of closed adoptions.

The quality that distinguishes the searching adoptee from the non-searcher is strong and compelling; an "identity tropism" or a "homing instinct," as we suggested earlier. It drives behavior and refuses to be denied. As long as records remain sealed, adoptees who feel its pull will, doubtless, continue to muster their courage, take a deep breath, and launch their own personal searches.

Many individuals will consume years of their lives playing amateur detective before they can complete their journey. Some grown men and women wait for one set of parents to die before they can meet the other set and complete themselves as human beings. Consider Kate, whose words about the birthparents she sought and found suggest the foolishness of pretending that a birthfamily doesn't exist: "I always had feelings about them," she says, "I just didn't know who they were."

4

Post-Reunion Basics

Fears of Rejection: Definitions of Success

The process of search becomes an entity in itself. It assumes a life and rhythm of its own. Still, at some level the searching mind is always worrying about what will happen when the quest is finally over. What will the other person do after you've discovered his or her identity and made contact? The basic question for adoptees is: Will my mother love me? It assumes many forms: Will she meet me? Will she accept me or reject me? Will she be able to overcome the past and welcome me into her life?

Whatever the conscious goal may be when an adoptee embarks on a search—wanting to see someone who "looks like me," seeking information only, or daring to hope that a relationship will ensue—no one wants to be rejected, especially not the (adopted) self who once experienced "primal abandonment" years ago and who generally equates being adopted with being rejected. For all he or she knows, the searcher may be risking rejection once again. As a veteran search consultant points out, "It's a big risk to say, 'Here I am, take me or leave me.' You're laying yourself out there for someone to either reject or to love."[1] The searching birthmother takes a similar risk.

It's no wonder thoughts turn to the extremes—love or rejection, all or nothing—when dealing with a subject as emotionally charged as how your mother or your child will receive you. The real world of reunion reception is complex. First, there are shades of welcome even from birthmothers. Second, even if your birthmother rejects you, other members of your birth family may not, which can eventuate in lasting relationships with siblings, aunts, uncles, even grandparents, whom you would not otherwise have known. In other words, you may not meet your mother, but you can still learn about yourself and make a connection to your roots. Another encouraging thought for searchers is that it is not necessarily the birthmother herself who is doing the rejecting; someone else may be advising or pressuring her behind the scenes—perhaps her mother or husband.

It should also encourage searchers to know that there is no such thing as a complete rejection. Repeated attempts to meet someone who is initially unwilling to meet you can pay off. Thus, many search experts advise those who have met resistance not to give up, no matter how rejected one feels. Keep those cards and letters coming, they say, in effect borrowing the wisdom of the salesperson who knows that the more contacts you make, the greater the chance of a sale. Early rejection is often driven by fear, especially among birthmothers who have kept quiet too long, or denied too well. They cannot overcome the repressions of a lifetime in a single phone call. They need time to collect themselves and adjust to the idea.

Another reassuring perspective is the body of opinion which holds that, once you achieve contact, there is no such thing as a bad reunion. Every reunion is good in the sense that it is useful, enabling adoptees to replace fantasy with reality, grieve if necessary, and then move on. Since Freud, therapists have taught us that we must confront our demons to be free of them, and adoptees are saying the same thing when, despite unhappy reunions which left them hurt or disappointed or shaken, they announce that they do not regret having searched. "We cannot speak of reunions as successful or unsuccessful," writes Betty Jean Lifton. "All of them, no matter whom one finds, are successful in that adoptees are given a feeling of being grounded in the human condition, of becoming autonomous people in control of their own lives."[2] A related, emerging view is that reunion is "closure" in adoption and some professionals anticipate that some day in the future reunion will constitute a more or less routine procedure in the process of adoption.

Search enthusiasts cite statistics showing that only small percentages of people who search are actually rejected by their birthmothers.[3] ALMA's Florence Fisher estimates that around three-quarters or more of those who manage to achieve reunions probably go on to develop and maintain post-reunion relationships, but it's admittedly an educated guess. Reliable statistics about how often searchers are greeted by acceptance or rejection would be enlightening to have, but it's important to understand, especially in their absence, that any reunion, even a one-contact encounter, can be a "success" in the sense of being useful: answering some of the why's and who-am-I's, replacing unknowns with knowns, helping the searcher become "unstuck." An adopted woman explained, "When my birthmother didn't want to speak to me again, I felt 'Well, that's done'—not rejected or disappointed. If she had opened the door, I would have been happy to get to know her."

In the sense of either refusing to meet at all or meeting only once, the concept of rejection doesn't apply to the birthmothers we interviewed in depth. Our focus, by design, was *post*-reunion, thus we sought out functioning relationships. But to conclude "once a relationship always a relationship" would be a mistake, although it does seem to be the pattern in post-reunion more often than not.

Jeanne's story, below, illustrates that rejection in the form of a break-up can lie further down the post-reunion road than the uninitiated might imagine. The relationship between Jeanne and her son has terminated. When the story has this kind of ending, regardless of the reasons, the birthmother's sense of failure can be particularly bitter.

Jeanne's Story

Jeanne is the only birthmother we interviewed who was found by her child, twenty-six-year-old Steve, and then eventually made the painful decision to sever the relationship again.

The break occurred about two years after their initial, happy meeting and was all the more unforeseen because Jeanne and her family were "ideal" for Steve. Her husband was his birthfather—the college freshman she loved in the 1950's and expected to marry; her three other children, Steve's full siblings, were all daughters, eliminating the possibility of same-sex sibling rivalries. It seemed an auspicious beginning: "When Steve first came to us I was ecstatic. I loved everything about him. I wanted him to immediately become part of our family, and mother him as if he had never been separated from us. I wanted the relationship more than anything in the world."

Deciding to end the relationship was devastating, even more painful than the original relinquishment, Jeanne discovered. She reached her decision only after a turbulent post-reunion history which eventually forced her to conclude that Steve was destroying their family. Jeanne and her husband don't know how long it would have taken them to come to the decision on their own, because they sought psychiatric assistance and came to understand that Steve was a pathological personality. "It's difficult to describe the first year without going into the psychological dynamics of the narcissistic personality disorder," Jeanne says, "but the diagnosis was made by professionals, and all Steve's behavior fits the descriptions in the psychiatric literature."

At the outset, though, no one suspected that the turbulence of the post-reunion was anything more than the normal emotional upheavals that often accompany these relationships. Jeanne remembers being "absolutely fascinated" with Steve at first. During their first visit, a five-day stay at her home, she felt that they "fell in love," (a post-reunion phenomenon known as "genetic sexual attraction," which we'll explore in Chapter 5). The attraction became a complicating factor in a reunion already headed for disaster. "Because of our limited knowledge of character disorders," she notes, "and because we were aware of the feelings that many adoptees experience, we had a difficult time sorting everything out." Episodes of rage and abuse had become frequent by the end of their first year together, and when it became apparent that Steve's pathology was the dominant force, the only options were to tolerate his destructiveness or to end the relationship. She fought the decision for many, many months.

The psychiatrists told Jeanne that her son's disorder was the result of faulty early development, so she can't help feeling great anger at Steve's adoptive mother, "even though I realize that her destruction of Steve was not intentional." In fact, "since he always had problems and she was unable to accept any responsibility for them," it was his adoptive mother's idea that he search for Jeanne "and perhaps find the magic answer for his life." (The court concurred with the idea; Steve is one of the few adoptees whose petition for his birth records was actually granted.) Ironically, though, Steve's adoptive mother, not unlike some other adoptive parents, was ultimately unable to tolerate Steve's relationship with his birthfamily despite having encouraged him to find them.

Three years after Jeanne has ended her association with Steve is "probably too soon to tell," she says, how to assess the trade-off between the good and the bad of her reunion and post-reunion experience. There were major positive effects for her—"I feel good about myself for the first time in my life, with the help of therapy"—but the negatives are equally powerful. She is heartbroken about Steve's condition and its bleak prognosis; she lived through the unremitting stress of the abusive and manipulative behavior that characterize his illness; and she lost him a second time.

Is Jeanne's reunion a success or a failure? From her perspective, it is neither and it is both. "While good things have come out of this, there is still a deep loss that will always be with me."

During the course of our interviews, a few of the birthmothers tried to convey how strongly they were committed to continuing their post-reunion relationship by trying to imagine what kinds of horrible deeds their children would have to commit to warrant expulsion from their hearts and lives. "If he were an ax murderer," one said. "If she tried to hurt my other children," another exclaimed. But those were hypothetical statements to make the point that the relationship was here to stay. In Jeanne's case, unhappily, and perhaps through no fault of his own, her child crossed a forbidden line, causing his mother to relinquish him again.[4]

Given the stresses of post-reunion, more than one specialist takes the position that a relationship between a birthmother and her adult adoptee can be considered a success "so long as they're still talking to one another." Perhaps it's not the most exalted definition of success, but it does serve as a realistic reminder that sometimes it's better to scale down one's expectations. The course of post-reunion does not run smooth. There is no comparable relationship in anyone's life, and no relationship which can prepare a birthmother for embarking on this frightening expedition with the familiar stranger who is her son or daughter.

Post-Reunion Turbulence

According to people who've been there, you have to experience it to understand it. Reunion is the kind of experience that sets off an explosion in your life. It's like being hit by an earthquake. No one feels in control. Everything is shattered, "rattled up." It can take years for the dust to settle and, when it does, the pieces of a birthmother's life come back together in new and different configurations. Reunions rearrange lives. In the words of one:

> *"The day a social worker from the agency called and told me that my daughter would like to meet me, my whole world changed. I remember thinking, my life will never be the same again."*

The emotional climate of reunion and post-reunion involves confused and ambivalent feelings (not just on the birthmother's part), with opposites coming fast upon one another. There are also extreme intensities of feeling. "Emotional indigestion," one conselor calls it. Many birthmothers talk about being on an emotional roller coaster, the metaphor they use to convey the strong polar emotions that are very natural, but very hard to live with nonetheless. Wanting to befriend their child does not preclude being "scared to death" about having a relationship or about what the relationship will mean in the broader context of the rest of their life.

Reunion often catapults a birthmother into experiencing "the loss piece"—the unresolved grief and mourning from the past—at the same time that it brings great joy.[5] That the two can come in rapid succession seems to make no sense. It is not uncommon for birthmothers to wonder if they are going crazy as they feel themselves ricocheting from "the heights of joy" to the "depths of despair" with frightening frequency. Even three years into a post-reunion history which she considered very successful and satisfying, Lila stated with great conviction that she never, ever, would be able to experience her relationship with her daughter as unequivocally pleasurable. There was too much pain in the past; the foundations were just too shaky.

In addition to feelings of loss and mourning, the sense of being thrust back into the past generally contributes to the overall emotional confusion. Every birthmother brings with her into these relationships her own tapestry of feelings about the pregnancy and adoption experience, especially the issues that remain unresolved. The relationship she had with her boyfriend, for example, will rub off onto the birthmother's feelings about her adult son or daughter, making it easier or more difficult— and occasionally just impossible—twenty or thirty or forty years later for the mature woman to carve out a relationship with her grown child. Vast amounts of emotional energy get spent reviewing and reworking the past, deflecting attention away from decisions about the here-and-now of their interaction. The nature of the relationship can remain in an uncomfortable state of ambiguity for some time before birthmother and adoptee are able to come to grips with the key questions they must answer eventually: Who are you to me? and How am I going to integrate you into my life? Being able to acknowledge the past, and deal with it constructively, is a critical post-reunion task for birthmothers who have not done so earlier. Unless the door on the past can be closed, the echoes will keep reverberating through the post-reunion space.

The volatility of reunion and post-reunion also arises from the fact that while reunion is an event between mother and child, reunion, and post-reunion especially, extends beyond the mother-child diad. We all have a "lifespace" and these events spill out all over it, churning up birthmothers' relationships, both intimate and more distant ones. Very few reunions proceed without angst of some kind, somewhere. There is almost certain to be a vulnerability or sore spot, either in the birthmother herself, in the response of someone close to her, in the adoptee, or in the adoptive parents' domain. The issues are fundamental and positions are strongly felt. Sometimes birthmothers find that other people "fall away" during post-reunion; "I stood alone in my healing," one said.

Even in cases without major blow-ups, the mere fact that reunion involves a cast of many, rather than being a one-on-one interaction between consenting adults, puts a birthmother on a delicate and precarious perch. Her antennae pick up the feelings of everyone around her, not just her own and her child's. Remember Irene, whom we met in the Prologue, and all the people who felt cut out when Rita commandeered Irene's attention? Irene was "pulled this way and that" trying to keep everyone's jealousies under control. Another birthmother calls it an "awesome balancing act"—a kind of "making nice" that women have been trained to do generally. It is especially common behavior among birthmothers.

How Comfortable Can You Be?

One of the most disorienting aspects of reunion and post-reunion is that nothing in one's repertoire of concepts or experiences applies. How do you describe a relationship with a person who is your flesh-and-blood child, on the one hand, but a stranger on the other? With what relationship do you compare it? What do you expect it will be like? What rights and responsibilities do you have? What rights and responsibilities does the other person have? What would constitute a good relationship? What would constitute a bad one? Who's to say that "as long as they're still on speaking terms" isn't "success"?

Post-Reunion Basics

Small wonder there's conflict in post-reunion. No one knows what the rules are. The timid—which many birthmothers tend to be, especially in the early post-reunion stages—tread cautiously, picking their way through the minefield of their own confusing emotions, their past history, and their present lives with spouses, children, parents, and the rest of the supporting troops. In the absence of the usual props we rely on to help us interpret our experience, just being able to talk to one other person who's been through a similiar experience can help bring clarity. It can assist in interpreting the storm of feelings coming from every direction, and the behaviors—both yours and other people's—that may be difficult to understand.

Birthmothers who are just setting out on post-reunion will be encouraged to find out that, according to our interviewees, it will probably become more comfortable with time. Comparing their own comfort level at the beginning of their relationships to how comfortable they were at the time of our interviews, the majority of women to whom we spoke indicated that it did indeed get better. Mainly, they described themselves as "somewhat" comfortable. "As comfortable as it can be when you're getting to know anybody," Norma reminds us, "and this of course had more overtones." But the majority had progressed to feeling "very" comfortable or even "extremely" comfortable in their relationships by the time we met them. Some were surprised at how little time it took—a few days, a week maybe. For others, the transition was measured in months or years.

A few of the womens' relationships, including Adrienne's with her twin sons, felt extremely comfortable right away and they continued to be so as time progressed: women who felt this ease of communication were surprised that their first days were not more awkward. "It was just like we were never apart," Adrienne marvelled. Others, though, found that their comfort level deteriorated: in one case, because unresolved feelings about the birthfather began to intrude; in another, because the daughter, in her thirties, grew emotionally distant from her birthmother after several years of closeness, leaving the mother hurt, confused, and dissatisfied.

There are also a few birthmothers who felt uncomfortable with their children almost from the outset. Marlene, who was uneasy in the beginning and who finds herself uneasy again six years later, describes her comfort curve as having changed direction twice:

> *"It got most comfortable in-between the beginning and now. It was uncomfortable in the beginning for one reason, and it's uncomfortable now for another reason, but there was a time in-between when it was pleasant."*

Thelma, the woman who suspects her daughter searched because she "implanted" the idea in the baby's head, has been uncomfortable with Sara almost since the day they met because of the limitations the nineteen-year old has imposed. For two years, Sara has professed to have no interest whatsoever in learning anything about their shared past. Thelma is "bursting" to tell her.

Factors that Affect the Post-Reunion Course

Observers caution that reunion and post-reunion are unpredictable. The tales vary enormously. Even so, it's possible to identify three common factors that influenced to some extent the shape of post-reunion.

- Readiness and mutuality
- Geography
- Time

Mutual Needs Or Wants for The Relationship. When Hamlet said "the readiness is all," he could easily have been talking about reunion and post-reunion. As we've seen already with respect to search, some mechanism clicks into place when a person is actually ready to take action, a readiness activator that, in some individuals, sputters off and on over the months or years a search may last.

Even with the stop-and-start pattern that characterizes so many of them, active searchers are the most reunion-ready of anybody. Those who have been more passive in establishing reunions show readiness of varying degrees. The more a birthmother allowed herself over the years to think about her pregnancy and adoption, and then to think about her child's growing up, and then to consider the possibility of obtaining information, and then to imagine that a meeting could really take place, the more reunion-ready she is. The individual who is less ready is likely to experience shock first. Then, shock worn off, she frequently holds back or draws back from her son or daughter as the emotional gravity of the past begins to exert its pull.

The case of Constance, sketched below, is a stunning example of a late-bloomer relationship whose growth was impeded by such dynamics. It could not begin to flower until Constance was finally able to uncover and experience the emotions she denied when Peg was born.

Constance's Story

"I had not even wanted the relationship before she found me," says Constance, a fifty-four year old Californian who did not start to discover the love, helplessness and anger she had repressed for thirty years until four years after being found. "In order to survive, I separated myself from my feelings," she says, a pattern that persisted several years into the post-reunion period.

In contrast to the experience of many other birthmothers, the appearance of Constance's daughter, Peg, age thirty-two, did not revive the trauma of the relinquishment immediately. It took over three years of time, a decision to contact the birthfather ("the hardest call I ever made") and two meetings with him to "unclog the memory channels." Amazed at how much he remembered and how much she had forgotten, her feelings and understandings started "bubbling up" after their second meeting. She now recognizes that burying her feelings became the pattern for her life, explaining, among other things, why it took her over four years to tell Peg she loved her.

Having moved beyond her initial shock and the reserve

that both women displayed at their first meeting, Constance is now profoundly grateful to this daughter who searched—a ten-year effort. She is on "the path to healing," and she is joyful in the experience of getting to know, and coming to love, her daughter. She expressed it in a letter to Peg this way:

> *"I was expected to make a sacrifice that no woman is created to make, and I could not understand the consequences for me or you when none of the adults around me knew the consequences themselves. . . . At a time when feelings were intense, I was expected to remain silent, and I know that I can let go of all that and just cherish you. I value you as a person, a daughter, and as a new dimension that has been added to my life. I know I'll never shut down emotionally like that again, and I rejoice in the years we have ahead."*

Being less than ready for reunion and post-reunion is not confined to birthmothers. When Betty located her twenty-eight year old son, Skip, he had little apparent concern for the meeting. He had never even told his wife about his adoption.

We met Betty when she and Skip were moving into the second year of their reunion. Skip was feeling connected to Betty by then—a result of numerous physical and temperamental similarities, she thinks—but he refused to open the relationship beyond the immediate foursome: Skip and his wife and Betty and her husband. Once Betty understood that Skip needed to position her as something other than his mother or his family (as his wife explained it one day, "He wants to see *you*, but his family is his family"), she recovered from her early "panic" at his restrictions and was happy to "flow with it the way it is." They've made great progress, she feels, and she's optimistic of more to come.

The fact that two people have complementary wants and needs from a relationship makes for better relationships; post-reunion is no exception. Birthmothers who found themselves in stronger, happier relationships tended to feel that what they and their children wanted from post-reunion was reciprocal. In the beginning, one or the other may have displayed greater need, but such imbalances worked themselves out over time or were considered unimportant—in the same way that people who are connected at some fundamental level can gravitate both toward and away from one another on a day-to-day basis without feeling that the relationship is in jeopardy. In these reunions, there is a joint desire to sustain the relationship because it is mutually satisfying. "We want to be close, we want to be part of each other's life," they say. The feeling of reciprocity is usually accompanied by a give-and-take that is the hallmark of closeness.

Birthmothers often indicated to us that they have "held back" in post-reunion so as not to "overwhelm" their son or daughter with needs or requests which the younger person might experience as excessive. But Joan, who is enjoying one of the smoothest post-reunion scenarios we came upon, was free of such concerns almost immediately:

> *"I was pretty tentative in our first few conversations, afraid to ask for much. I didn't want to push, didn't want to frighten her off. As soon as I felt comfortable that she wanted the same thing, I've been comfortable with asking whatever I want to ask, and I think she's been the same way. What we want is mutual. We want to have a relationship that grows, and is strong, and will be lifelong, and I have no reason to believe it's not going to be that way."*

Post-reunion associations don't usually seem to unfold along such secure mutual ground. Apart from the imbalances imposed by discrepancies in readiness, there are often differences in the intensity or in the nature of what both parties want. There would be no problems, for example, if an adoptee who was looking for a "mommy" found himself with a birthmother who was happy to assume that role, but problems arise when needs are out of sync. Role issues aside, incompatible needs or wants can lead to frustrating, discordant interactions.[6]

Thelma for example, whom we met earlier, is uncomfortable with her daughter Sara because Thelma's need to "unburden myself" and tell Sara about their shared past is at odds with Sara's need not to hear. Debora, and others like her, are distressed because their children have emotionally withdrawn or "backed away." Virginia wants a more steady and defined relationship than her college-age daughter seems capable of giving to anyone right now, her adoptive parents included. It's a lot easier when, like Ethel, a birthmother can say: "Our mutual needs appear to hold the relationship together."

The Impact of Geography. Finding a birthmother in Baltimore when you live in Seattle has different post-reunion implications from finding her in the next town, but there are advantages and disadvantages to each. A Maryland birthmother in her sixties, whose daughter is living in Australia, is painfully aware of the negatives associated with distance. Found by her daughter three years ago, their interactions to date have mainly consisted of exhausting let's-meet-all-the-families dinners and travels, scheduled around the daughter's annual trip back to the States. Mother and daughter have had almost no time alone, so a multitude of questions stand unanswered. The relationship is still in its infancy.

Most birthmothers don't have to travel halfway around the world to see their children, but it's not unusual for birthmothers to be situated halfway across the country from their children,[7] and distance can be a very real force in slowing the post-reunion pace. It's true, for example, that Constance's relationship with Peg could not begin to thaw until Constance could access her buried feelings, but it's also true that one lives in Kansas and the other in California. They have met in person only three times and are getting to know each other slowly. "Getting to know someone by mail is very difficult," Constance finds.

But distance has advantages as well. While it's responsible for the slow pace that Constance now decries, it also makes it possible for their reunion to "take root" without throwing any disturbing offshoots into the lives around it. Constance's three other children—all grown, two of whom have moved away—are essentially unaffected spectators, as is her husband, who was told about the baby before he and Constance married. Constance is beginning to experience the emotional upheavals of opening the door to the past, but the external realities of her day-to-day life have not changed.

Geography didn't appear to be a critical factor in terms of post-reunion quality, but in our study it inevitably affected the post-reunion character. People who have to get on an airplane to see one another must rely on mail and phone to keep the relationship going. In long-distance situations, visits become events that require logistical planning and money. Imbued with a vacation-like aura on top of all the other emotional overtones, they become removed from the realm of everyday life even further. A few birthmothers talk about their post-reunion experience in terms of the number of "reunions" they've had, suggesting by their language that, where long-distance is involved, post-reunion can feel more like an intermittent series of events than a continuous process.

But long-distance keeps the "rotten spots" less visible too, as one birthmother put it, and gives people a chance to assimilate what's happening. It calls a temporary halt to things. It forces reflection, and that can be helpful.

If the disadvantages of long distance are the slowed pace, the sense of wanting more, and a position someplace outside of everyday life, the troubles with being nearby include too fast, too much, and the feeling of being intruded upon. Proximity encourages a more casual, less special event, kind of interaction, but frequent or surprise visits, or endless hours on the living room sofa can be ill-timed, conflicting with a birthmother's other responsibilities and putting her in the distressing position of needing or wanting to be somewhere else but not wanting to seem as though she's rejecting her child (again). Irene, the "smothered" birthmother we met in the Prologue, recalls:

BirthBond

> *"It was mind-boggling. I was dealing with my feelings, and her feelings, and her feelings about her birthfather, and my feelings about her father, and worrying about my husband's feelings and the boys'. I felt much more comfortable after she moved away; I was able to open up to her more because I knew she couldn't drain off me. Once she moved away, I was able to say what I had to over the phone easier. Her last visit was probably the best we've had in the entire 10 years."*

If they can manage to avert the pitfalls of proximity, living within driving distance of one another is desirable, because it is easier for the birthmother and the adoptee to get to know one another. Being nearby also facilitates the entrance and continued involvement of the rest of the birthmother's family into the post-reunion scene, enabling relationships to root and grow between the adoptee and these other individuals. (We'll explore these relationships in Chapters 10 and 11.)

Taking proximity to its ultimate, some adoptees actually move into their birthmother's homes, though the stay is generally temporary. A few adoptees in our interviews came to live with their birthmothers for a couple of months or a school semester; one went to her birthfather's; one went for an extended stay with a birth sibling, and one lived in her married birthparents' home for a month while the couple was vacationing at a summer cottage. There is also the example of Helaine, a birthmother who refused her twenty-three year old daughter's request to move in, because she believed the young woman was "only looking for a safe refuge and a mother substitute." The daughter became very upset, but apologized the next day and admitted that she had been manipulating Helaine, which she realized she shouldn't have done.

A couple of these birthmothers toyed with the idea of moving closer to their grown children, but resisted the impulse. Like Adrienne, they were concerned about the "pressure" their presence might create on the adoptive family. There is safety, and non-intrusiveness, in distance.

The Impact of Time. Some reunion and post-reunion experiences are fortunate from the beginning. They start well, without awkwardness, and get better. More commonly, though, post-reunion relationships seem to benefit from the calming effects of time. Time, however, won't resolve all post-reunion problems, and the effects of continued association can produce new stresses, years into the relationship, that were not there in the beginning. How time affects post-reunion over the long haul (more than fifteen or twenty years) is still unknown. There's not enough history yet.

In the post-reunion timeline, less than a year is practically nothing, and three years is still rather new. Two or three years can be consumed, easily, in working one's way through the terrain—the emotions, revelations and introductions—that is the foundation for what can become a mutually satisfactory and lasting relationship. Five or six years, or more, may be required before significant turning points are reached or major problems are resolved. Consider Helaine and her daughter, for instance: "In six years we are finally able to be honest with one another. I don't walk on eggshells anymore." Or Norma, who didn't feel comfortable writing the words "Dear Son" until seven years had passed.

"I'm seeing that this is something that's going to go on for years, and it's a slow, slow process," one birthmother says. The discovery often comes as a surprise, though it shouldn't. Faced with the necessity of dealing with any major shock or stressor (a birth, a death, a serious professional failure, etc.) almost no one is able to absorb the effects and reorient their lives in the space of a few weeks or even months, and reunion, no matter how joyful, is surely a major stressor.

Whether "settling in" takes two years or seven years or more (and geography, as we've seen, can have an influence on this), enough time must elapse to enable a birthmother and her son or daughter to pass through all the events that constitute post-reunion "firsts," many of which involve members of the respective families. To traverse the whole course, the principals must get through a collection of stumbling blocks which family life and the calendar inevitably present. These include:

- adoptee's first birthday after reunion
- first Mother's Day together
- first set of holidays
- first visit to the birthmother's home
- first meeting between the adoptee and the birthmother's family (spouse, parents, children, siblings, extended relatives)
- first meeting between the two mothers (and their spouses)
- first meeting between the birthmother and her child's adoptive siblings
- adoptee's attendance at the first major ceremonial event (wedding, graduation, etc.) in the birth family
- adoptee's first meeting with the birthfather.

There are also the emotional firsts: the first big disappointment with one another, the first fight.

Some reunioning pairs won't continue their relationship. Some, like Betty's son, have established limits defining what they will and will not do, and their restrictions indicate that they need to keep the post-reunion relationship in a tightly lidded compartment of their life rather than attempting to integrate the pre- and post-reunion components. Some reunioning pairs test the limits of their comfort zone and conclude afterwards that they won't do whatever it is again (e.g., getting the two families together), either because it's unnecessary in their opinion or because it was too painful or difficult. But the more hurdles a post-reunion pair overcomes, and the more their first forays are followed by seconds and thirds, the more the birthmother and the adoptee will have completed the full agenda of tasks to work through that post-reunion presents.

Time is helpful in post-reunion because, one by one, the parties experience the "firsts" and pick their way through what one adoptee calls the "little landmines." Over time, the issues that belong to the past get resolved, the emotions that were put on hold can get dealt with, everyone who is going to meet finally does so, birthmothers and their children cease being strangers to one another, and the emotional highs and lows begin to level off. Wariness or suspicion are replaced by understanding, friendship, or love. A point comes when there are no more surprises.

There seem to be two periods in post-reunion—the early years and the later years—with the early years being the struggle years, the more stressful and volatile ones. Some of the "little landmines" get deactivated over time and the individuals come to an understanding of where they will, or will not, fit in each other's lives. In the early years, "everything gets turned upside down"; in the later years, the pieces fit together, some perspective is achieved, and life starts feeling normal again.

Human relationships being what they are, however, questions, emotions or dissatisfactions that are shoved under the table during early years of post-reunion later will be steady irritants, robbing the relationship of a good deal of pleasure for one or both participants. The least happy post-reunion relationships have a resigned quality of "putting up with each other". In describing their difficulties with one another, Marlene, for example, recalls her daughter saying something to the effect of, "I haven't worked this hard and long on this relationship, and on finding you, just to walk away from it now"—a hang-in-there style of commitment that's sometimes heard from other post-reunion players too. An adoptee in a post-reunion relationship which had soured after about eight years was overheard saying:

Question: "How's it going with your reunion?"
Answer: "Well, she's still my mother."

Just as adult adoptees have said that adoption is a lifelong process, birthmothers say that post-reunion is a lifelong process too. Discussing their thoughts about the future of their relationships, they state that they think in terms of "the rest of our lives" rather than some specific goal they wish to accomplish in time.

5

Patterns of Post-Reunion Experience

As we've seen, factors like readiness, mutuality, geography and time have a bearing on post-reunion, affecting how smooth the course will be and how quickly, if at all, various points along the route will be reached. Nonetheless, attempting to categorize or classify post-reunion experience along any set of dimensions turns out to be extremely difficult. In the absence of precedent, it's like trying to bring order to any complicated subject while struggling to invent the vocabulary and the grammar at the same time.

Because every post-reunion has been an "unchartered course," with the participants serving as their own guides, any attempt to put markers along the way may help those who are lost on their own by introducing some roadmap of normalcy into this extraordinary voyage. While it's risky to generalize, we have attempted to elicit patterns and consistencies in the post-reunion experience. We describe them in this chapter in the hope that these hypotheses will be useful to those who are enmeshed in their own personal confusions and speculations, to those whose interest in the subject is professional, and to the general public.

We'll look at the different twists and turns that post-reunion can take depending on (1) sex and age of the adoptee, and (2) adoptees' feelings of familial identification. Then we'll see how post-reunion can vary overall in terms of (3) the pleasure-pain ratio.

Sex and Age of the Adoptee

Since sex and age influence so many aspects of our behavior, it should come as no surprise that an adoptee's age and sex also partially dictate the post-reunion script. Some birthmothers were quite explicit about the ways in which their child's gender and life stage factored into the post-reunion scenario.

Reunions with Teens. Reunions with children in their late teens[1] are inevitably affected by the dynamics of the teenage years generally, a time which confronts the adolescent with a formidable developmental agenda and which produces behaviors that any parent, birth or adoptive, can find difficult to understand, condone, or survive. This is the time of the "identity crisis." There is a formidable body of professional opinion stressing that resolving identity issues is even more difficult for adopted adolescents than for non-adopted.[2] These birthmothers concur; listen to Irene on the subject:

> *"Adolescence is a terrible time. Identifying with your natural parents is bad enough, but trying to identify with people who are so extremely different than you, and yet knowing there's someone else, it must be as torturous for the child as it was for us."*

As part of identity formation, the tasks of adolescence include separating oneself from family, and dealing with a galloping sexuality. Both are fraught with special and disturbing overtones for the adopted.

It's not possible for a birthmother to know for sure whether the difficult young person she meets in reunion is a garden variety adolescent or one whose adolescent turmoil is being exacerbated by adoption. Birthmothers who were reunioning with teenagers, however, most often described their sons and daughters as troubled. Several say their children were immature for their years or "scattered." Others referred to adoptees who were in, or just came through, "the wild phase." Collectively, the birthmothers who met teens also found drugs, moodiness, depression, dropping out of school, troubles with the opposite sex, and a lot of crying or screaming.

These birthmothers also tend to report that reunion and post-reunion have been beneficial for their child, resolving identity issues and, as a result, helping him or her "settle down." In a few cases, as noted earlier, the children temporarily moved into these mothers' homes. It was a logical place to go at a time when young people are often eager to leave their childhood homes anyway, and it gave the birthmothers an opportunity to participate in their child's parenting. Sometimes, it also gave the adoptive parents a welcome relief from being totally responsible for a child who is experiencing serious problems.

The story of Carol and Joey serves as a particularly dramatic example.

Carol's Story

Carol is a birthmother who searched for her eighteen-year old son, Joey, and has known him for four years. "Even before he was born, I bonded with him very strongly," she explains. "I talked to him for hours and hours; it was just he and I together."

Carol made her initial contact with Joey through his adoptive parents; they lived a 2-hour drive away and she went there and introduced herself one day. Since then, she has been engaged in a "traumatic but good" post-reunion with her adolescent son, who had been experiencing severe identity confusion for some years. He was away at boarding school, his adoptive parents' most recent attempt to get him on track, when she first contacted them. He was wearing punk clothing, long shaggy hair, a mustache, long sideburns and an earring when they met, and she describes him then as "very mixed up emotionally." He had no direction in his life, and a history of drugs and juvenile delinquency. His anti-social behavior, his emotional neediness, and his manipulativeness were the kinds of problems that are a mother's nightmare.

Carol's love for Joey, however, was as instantaneous and unquestionable as his self-proclaimed need for her. He had dreamed of meeting her; he felt he could tell her anything and she would understand. "It was like an immediate, intense emotional bonding after years of separation," she recalls, and the feeling has persisted. He has shared his inner world with her, and he tells her she's the most important person in his life. Since the reunion, they have been in constant contact, including a one-year period when he came to live with her. "I never felt anyone loved me or needed me the way Joey has shown he loves me," she says, and they both attribute his disordered history to the fact of having been separated from her by adoption. "I never thought that he would have such strong emotional needs that only I could fill for him," she says wonderingly. Together, they grieved over their lost past.

Despite having been raised in a home with loving and intelligent parents, Joey often felt isolated, "in a house with strangers." For one thing, he didn't look like them. He has dark complexion and curly hair (like his Hispanic birthfather), and his adoptive parents don't. He is also different in temperament, and grew up believing that he would have enjoyed a better sense of who he was if he had been raised by his natural parents.

Carol, too, has come to feel betrayed by the adoption system, the system that said her son would have a better life being raised by others. (Ironically, she is one of those birthmothers who became a social worker, helping pregnant teenagers arrange adoptions for their babies for many years, prior to her personal reunion experience.) Although reunion and post-reunion have promoted a regenerative process—Joey's become more "normal looking now, less wild looking" for one thing—the process is far from complete. They must now separate from one another once again. "We have to let go of each other for the growth to continue in a healthy way, and that's very hard." Both are anxious about having to undergo another separation.

With Carol and Joey so intensely involved with one another, everyone else in Carol's immediate family resented the time they spent together. This includes her husband and four children: two daughters and two stepdaughters. Because Carol had continued to date Joey's birthfather after the adoption, *then married him a few years later when she found herself carrying his child yet again, the two daughters are Joey's full siblings. But the situation is complicated because Joey was grieved to learn that Carol and his birthfather—the man he so strongly resembles—were no longer married. He has established ties with his birthfather, and with his father's other children too, bringing to a total of 9 the number of siblings (all varieties) Joey acquired by virtue of Carol's finding him.*

Carol credits the strength of her current marriage for withstanding the abandonment her husband felt as she "made up for all that lost time" with Joey, trying to "catch up on the emotional bonding of eighteen years all at once." She and Joey "couldn't get enough time together . . . We desperately wanted to establish a normal relationship, he as a brother to his two sisters, as a son to his father, as a grandchild to his grandparents. He wanted to be my son and I wanted to be his mother." He wants to live with Carol next semester, but whether he will was undecided at the time of our interview. Her husband has "some problems" with the prospect, both because of feeling displaced already and because of Joey's drug problem.

The least trauma in this story has been on the side of the adoptive parents who were "helpful though cautious" from the beginning, and who appear to be experiencing some measure of relief now that another parent is on the scene who can help Joey develop in socially desirable ways. He was "quite a handful." The two families are in touch, and his adoptive mother has confided to Carol that she occasionally envies her the close relationship that Carol and Joey seemed immediately to enjoy. The two families split holidays.

In contrast to Joey, some of the teenagers these birthmothers met were surviving adolescence with fewer visible scars. Charlene, for example, was delighted with her son.

> *"He's smart, well-mannered, polite, talented. He'll be a very successful adult, and very wealthy one day. He's also very loving and warm, and he has*

> *a very good attitude about this whole situation*
> *—his two separate families."*

Nora, too, was enchanted with the son she discovered, who instantly reminded her of the handsome and sensitive lover she had known in Vancouver years before. Impressed with her son's talents, insight, and competence, she treated him as an equal. It was he, during their first year, who reminded her, in a difficult interchange between the two of them, "But Nora, you've got to remember, I'm only nineteen." It helped, she said; she needed to be told.

Birthmothers who reunite with adoptees in their twenties or thirties or forties sometimes speculate that reunions with teenagers must be harder than the ones they are having. "There's a big difference in maturity between eighteen and thirty-two," says Constance. A reunion with an eighteen-year old or even a twenty-year old is bound to entail different stresses from a reunion with someone who's older, for several reasons. First, because teenagers are in flux as people; second, because they're economically dependent on their adoptive parents and living under their roof; and third, because teenagers usually lack the wherewithal to become active searchers. There's a good chance their reunions were either initiated by the birthmother and/or helped along by the adoptive parents.[3] That the birthmothers in reunions with teens are younger in age themselves, possibly with young children still living at home, also affects the post-reunion script.

Adolescence can be tumultuous in any household, and people sometimes wonder whether adoptees use their adoption as a "scapegoat" for all the problems that anyone of this age would have. But at a stage of life when young people are separating from their parents and trying to consolidate their own identity, it's hard to dismiss the testimony that adoption, at the very least, complicates development. Nora's son, Colin, put it this way:

> *"Once you reach the middle of adolescence,*
> *you start reaching for your individuality. It was*
> *hard for me to find mine because I didn't know*

> *where to look. I was very different from the rest*
> *of my relatives. I'm an artist (his birthmother is*
> *an artist too) and I'm virtually the first artist in*
> *my family and that made things even more diffi-*
> *cult. I didn't feel as if I belonged, but I don't*
> *know whether that was because of adolescence*
> *or because of the adoption."*

Phyllis, who searched for her teenage daughter, understands that at least some of the traits that trouble her about Sharon are the result of Sharon's youth. But she's not sorry to have met her daughter at this stage of their lives. Summing up what the other birthmothers who reunited with teenagers mainly feel, she says:

> *"If I'd waited until she was thirty-five, say, maybe*
> *she would have been less of a crazy teenager,*
> *but that would have been seventeen more*
> *years."*

Reunions with Children in Their Twenties. One consequence of reunions with teenagers is that birthmothers sometimes take on a parenting or semi-parenting role like Carol did, helping adoptees make the transition into adulthood. Reunions with adoptees in their twenties, in contrast, can present sons and daughters who are launching adult lives of their own: starting jobs or employment training, establishing marriages and families. They are exploring adult options and making decisions that will affect their long-term futures. (One of these decisions may be the decision to search for their birthmother.[4])

In our sample, the assorted consequences of having a reunion with someone in their 20s included: the discovery that a son or daughter was married (thus, the presence of a son- or daughter-in-law with whom the birthmother had to forge a separate relationship); the discovery that the adoptee was a parent (thus, the birthmother was a grandmother); the discovery that the adoptee had either established himself in a career or was having trouble "finding himself"; the discovery that the adoptee was either financially able or had "money problems." Birthmothers express parental type concerns about these things, regardless of whether they voice them aloud to their children. One hears things like, "I wish she had an easier time financially" or "I wish he'd get married."

As post-reunion progresses, birthmothers witness their adult children reaching the various adult milestones—marrying, becoming pregnant, getting divorced. Not infrequently, the mothers attribute these events to the fact that a reunion took place. Because the reunion enabled the adopted adult to resolve crucial issues of personal identity and biological continuity, they explain, it then became possible for him or her to redo earlier decisions which no longer felt appropriate, or to become "unstuck" and move on. In several instances, a post-reunion adoptee terminated a marriage which had been entered into for the "wrong reasons" (it had been used as a way out of an unhappy adoptive home, for instance, or in the quest for another family). Several adopted women in their twenties and thirties have made the post-reunion decision to have a baby; now that they know their biological history, they're not afraid of bringing a child into the world.

Reunions with Mid-Age Adults. "He was older, which made it easier," says Millie, a birthmother who was reunited with a son in his forties:

> *"I think many times the eighteen to twenty-seven-year-olds aren't dry behind the ears yet and they're too worried about themselves, especially males. My son was stabilized. He owns his own home, his wife has a good job, he has two kids, he works for IBM."*

In addition to meeting children who are likely to be "stabilized," birthmothers who meet children in their thirties and forties are women in their fifties or sixties or seventies and the attitudes they bring to reunion and post-reunion were likely planted in their own conservative times. These were not the 1960s or 1970s when people "let it all hang out." These mothers were raised during the Great Depression and World War II; they were not part of the "me generation." The sheer weight of time is also pressing upon women whose relinquishments took place so long ago. "When someone holds a secret for 50 years, spontaneity is not one of our talents," Ethel reminds us. Birthmothers of Ethel's age are not the individuals who are likely to be out there searching.[5]

Another consequence of their older age is that mortality becomes an aspect of the reunion and post-reunion scripts. A search often begins when an adult adoptee fears that time is running out and her birthmother could die before she finds her. Mortality also becomes a factor in these situations because the reunioning pair do not have to contend with the presence of the adoptee's grandparents—the generation that played the dominant role in the relinquishment decision so often. Sometimes, the birthfather has also passed away by the time a reunion takes place. Arriving too late to meet him causes great sorrow for many adoptees, but his absence also removes another potential tension producer from the post-reunion proceedings.

Still, there are no guarantees that older mothers and children will have an easy post-reunion time. Serious tensions exist in two of the six relationships we heard about in which the adoptees are in their 30s or 40s. But the others in this age group seem to enjoy a mellow quality and sense of calm that is usually absent from post-reunion and which seems to come from these older mothers' more philosophical view of things generally. Compared to their younger counterparts, they seem to be more accepting of things and less angry about any negative ways in which the adoption worked out. It was all very long ago, and the reunion has brightened the years ahead with a new and loving relationship.

What happened to Ethel is a case in point.

Ethel's Story

Over a half century ago, during the depression, a fifteen-year old teenager hugged her eleven-day old baby and whispered in her ear that they would be together again someday. Never proud of what she calls her stupidity at allowing herself to be-

come pregnant, only now, two years after reunion and age 66, is Ethel shedding much of her guilt at "abandoning" her child. She is crying a lot but with "healthy tears," and she is able to interpret the pregnancy as a "tragedy waiting to happen" given her circumstances at the time: few friends, parents divorced, father gone, mother working long hours, and mother's boy-friend living in their home. He was the birthfather—a divorced man, twice Ethel's age. He was also helping with household finances, fulfilling Ethel's needs for a father, and providing the only elements of fun and affection in an otherwise heavy and dreary time.

He offered to marry her but she declined because "that idea terrified me; I was even less prepared for marriage than I was for motherhood." So she relinquished the baby as her mother instructed, despite her mother's own ambivalence about the decision. Ethel returned to school, joined the armed forces, and married four years later, revealing her secret to her fiance and extracting the promise that he would never mention it again. Four children and a career as a psychiatric social worker followed. She was retired for two years when her first daughter, age forty-nine, telephoned in the summer of 1985. They met two months later in the daughter's home territory— San Francisco—a city capable of providing enough tourist at-tractions to structure the visit, deflect some of the intensity, and provide the space which the two very nervous women needed.

Two additional visits and a stream of letters and phone calls later, Lucy has been made to feel welcome in Ethel's large family, not just by Ethel and her husband (the same one she told back in the late 1940s), but also by their now grown chil-dren and these children's families. The next scheduled get-to-gether will complete the introductions between Lucy and the out-of-town siblings she has not yet met.

Moving into Ethel's family circle is important to Lucy, now fifty-one, who has virtually no ties left with her adoptive family. The adoptive parents divorced when she was five and both died by the time she was ten, so she was raised by an

adoptive aunt in her late fifties. The aunt honored her obligation
to care for the child but was less committed, Ethel thinks, than
a loving parent would have been. Ethel has been impressed by
her daughter's strong need to belong and to look like other
people—a need that propels so many searching adoptees—but
believes nonetheless that Lucy would not have searched had
any of the key people in her adoptive background been alive. In
her imaginings, Lucy hears her adoptive mother saying, "But
darling, I thought our love for you was enough."

In spite of her difficult life, Lucy has told Ethel that she
"forgives" her and that she believes adoption was the best decision. But Ethel knows that there have been depressive episodes
in Lucy's life, and she is aware of Lucy's still active need for
nurturing. "I felt in the first call that she needed a mother,"
Ethel recalls. She wonders how much Lucy's early history and
upbringing account for the fact that her daughter now considers herself a lesbian—this, some years after divorcing her foreign-born husband, a man whom her aunt could never accept.
Trying to understand the "strange phenomenon" of her daughter's current sexual identification, Ethel muses, "She probably
needs to feel loved and has found a way of life that she can
tolerate." But she wonders if Lucy's sexual identification would
be the same if she had grown up in Ethel's household, and
whether Lucy will change in the years ahead as she is loved by
her family.

The relationship between the two women is developing,
"like we're good friends who share common interests." Ethel is
gradually able "to read her expressions." The two have encountered some of the rough spots that frequently appear on the
post-reunion trail (times that Lucy drew back, times that Ethel's
"obsession" with this new person disturbed her family constella-
tion) but the overall post-reunion character has been smooth.
Long-distance has contributed to keeping the pace relaxed.

Ethel looks forward to many wonderful years ahead.
The bottom line could not be more positive: "I feel I don't have
to hold secrets inside anymore, and I have another lovely
daughter to enjoy and share my love."

BirthBond

Reunions with Daughters Versus Sons.[6] Putting adoption aside for a moment, mother-son relationships are generally understood to be different from mother-daughter relationships. The conventional thinking is that mothers feel closer to their daughters, a bond based on shared gender and women's greater emotional openness.[7] The psychoanalyst Carl Jung describes mothers and daughters as being links in the chain of posterity. According to Jung, "We could say that every mother contains her daughter in herself and every daughter her mother, and every woman extends backwards into her mother and forwards into her daughter."[8] The thought is particularly poignant in the adoption context precisely because adoptees feel cut off from any link in the biological chain. Without knowledge of their natural parents, the chain is severed through adoption.[9]

Knowing that female adoptees search for their birthmothers more often than males do, it's tempting to predict that reunion and post-reunion experiences with daughters will be easier than with sons. Listening to the birthmothers in our sample, though, it's hard to say for sure. They can only speak on behalf of their own experience, of course, and, like the mother of a newborn, they are delighted to have had a reunion with whatever sex they got. Among the many birth families to whom we speak there are difficult situations that involve daughters and also difficult ones that involve sons.

Nonetheless, the mothers of daughters frequently stress that their shared female identity makes post-reunion easier and closer. Many believe that their daughters explored feelings more than sons would have, and were more empathetic about the position the unmarried birthmother had been in years ago, particularly if the daughter had had a pregnancy of her own or had watched an unmarried friend struggle with the same decision.
Listen to Phyllis:

> *"I think girls think more about their mothers and being biologically connected, and she's had two*

Patterns of Post-Reunion Experience

abortions. She said the first thing she thought about was finding me and giving me the baby."

Faye:

"The mother-daughter relationship is unique. A son wouldn't come and stay with me for three or four days and sleep on my couch."

Joan:

"I feel very fortunate she's a woman because I think women deal more easily with this, and it's easier for me to communicate my feelings to a woman, and it is for her too. I think more women can acknowledge their need to know their birth family."

Virginia mentions that she and her daughter share common ground in that both are single women and both are dating; in her case, it's one of the few connections binding the relationship together. Another birthmother tells of her special delight to be reunioning with a daughter because her other children are all sons. Being a parent to a daughter when all you knew before were sons, or vice versa, can be a challenge in its own right. Another birthmother maintains that her daughter is a "confidante" in a way a son could not be. Still another, who describes herself as a feminist and her life as "so woman-identified," believes that she would have been less impelled to find her child if it had been a boy.

Mothers of sons point to the pleasures that come with reunions with male children: pride in finding a handsome young man, or a settled and competent family man, or one who is talented, or one who is sensitive and caring. One birthmother feels that her child's gender made it easier for her because "I've always gotten along better with men than with women; I know how to talk to guys; I don't know how to talk to girls." A few comment, however, that their sons are "protective" of their adoptive mothers and wonder if a daughter would be different in this respect and would find it easier to admit or display the reunion relationship to the adoptive family.[10] A current idea in adoption circles is that sons are less forgiving of birthmothers: more apt to cling to feelings of resentment and rage, however denied or deeply buried such feelings may be.

One of the most troublesome aspect of reunions with sons, however, is the possibility of what reunion and post-reunion observers have come to call "genetic sexual attraction," a feeling on the part of the mother or the son, or both, that they are in a romantic relationship. Such feelings are extremely unsettling, and birthmothers who have found themselves drawn to their grown sons in this way are comforted to learn that they were not the only ones caught in the grip of these unexpected, intense and disturbing feelings.

Several mothers we interviewed spoke about having experienced this kind of attraction early in their relationships. Before they understood what it was or knew how to deal with it, they found themselves engaging in dating-like thoughts or behavior, even though they were confused and embarrassed about why and what they were doing. They would hold hands, for example, or dress up as if for a date. It can go on for many months or longer, before it becomes so uncomfortable that one or the other is finally forced to confront it verbally. If she's feeling it, he's probably feeling it too.

In attempting to describe what they felt, and what they thought it meant, several of the women vacillate between a motherly desire to have physical contact with their sons, like young mothers who can't stop fondling their new babies, and more womanly and erotic desire. The fact that their sons are grown men, not babies, makes even the motherly feelings disturbing. Complicating the situation still further, the sons sometimes resemble, and thus remind them of, their lovers from years back, hurtling them back in time to their younger self. One of the birthmothers talks about herself as "the twenty-three-year-old that I had become" when she and her son first met.

It is a fine line between the more acceptable motherly-like desires and those which are erotic and taboo, as the women's self-analyses indicate:

Patterns of Post-Reunion Experience

Debora explains her feelings now:

"I still haven't gotten over the feeling that I would love to totally undress him, but in the way a mother undresses a baby to count the toes, to see where the birthmarks are, to see what their backs are like. I would love to go to the beach with him. I can't get over that feeling."

In the early days, however, her feelings were more erotic:

"There was that sensual excitement. You're a man and a woman, you're not a baby and a mother. Luckily he didn't look enough like the birthfather. He seems like such a nice boy too— he's like me, he observes the rules, so I never felt threatened. But I found that his talk would be very erotic—like he finally found some woman to tell all these things that he probably would not tell another woman. He trusted me immediately. It would end up being some kind of sexual conversation, and I realized I had to stop it."

Nora recalls an incident in the first week of reunion when she couldn't differentiate mother-child from man-woman:

"We were on the river, tenting, and I said to him at one point, 'You know, I'd really like to hold you but I feel very confused because you're a grown man.' He said, 'Just hold me.' He knew there was a danger there but the child needed to be held. We were kind of comfortable with it. It was touch and go."

Charlene believes that the attraction and the desire to touch are associated with bonding:

"I'd like to talk about the bonding and feeling of sexual attraction I had to this nineteen-year-old good-looking kid at the beginning of the rela-

tionship. I felt like I'd like to take him and put him in my lap and rock him and get close to him like I still do with my three-year old. And I wanted to do this knowing full well that I couldn't put this 19-year-old in my lap. I was trying to bond with him.

I also had feelings of, not sexual feelings, it's hard to explain, but I'd like to touch him. Whenever I could, I would hold his arm or rub his arm; I would want to be as close physically to him as I could. I still love to look at him. When he's around, my eyes are glued to him, less now, though, than they used to be—and I'm always rubbing his shoulders, playing with him, tickling him, and he's tickling me. I think that's his way of getting that bond. We've talked about this, and we know these are feelings we have and that we'll work it out the best way we can."

Marion, like the others, was stunned and frightened by the feeling of "romance in the air." She learned that the way to deal with it was to declare—actively, loudly, by word and deed—her maternal role. According to one expert,[11] the best way to manage genetic sexual attraction is to do essentially what Marion did: avoid all behavior or situations that smack of romance (dinner by candlelight, for example) and keep asserting that you are his mother. In Marion's case, husband Dan (also the birthfather) was the voice of reason:

"When I met Allen there were a lot of sexual feelings that I refused to recognize, because I was afraid I was feeling them, and I wasn't sure why. I love my husband very much; we have a wonderful sex life; I wasn't clear what was happening. It's like you're seeing the father again when he was young, when everything was heightened. You just look at their bodies and you get turned on. Also that physical bonding that you have with the other kids isn't there.

Patterns of Post-Reunion Experience

When I talked to Allen on the phone I would say, 'Oh Allen I love you' and I would say it very passionately and he would say, 'Oh my God that sounds so raunchy,' and I wondered, 'Oh my God, what am I doing?'

Somehow Dan managed to do what needed to be done. Like when you have children that grow up with you, there's a sexual thing between children and the mother but the family, somehow, balances it out. Dan balanced it out when he had this talk with Allen and after that it seemed to be a lot more relaxed for both of us. Dan came in and said, 'She's your mother and you're going to respect her.' Other birthmothers I know didn't have anybody come in and set the limits."

Not all mothers of sons experience genetic sexual attraction. Those who do are often loath to talk about it, embarrassed or fearful that they are the only ones with such feelings. Judging from its frequency in our sample, though, it's probably very common, and experienced by sons as well as mothers. Birthmothers have also been known to have feelings of "being in love" with daughters, but one hears less about this phenomenon in the support group network than about the more disturbing version associated with sons. One also hears about genetic sexual attraction among siblings separated by adoption, and there are occasional newspaper stories of men and women who wanted to marry only to discover, to their horror, that they were brother and sister.

One current hypothesis explaining genetic sexual attraction centers on the theory that the feelings are associated with physical bonding, the view Charlene expressed. Because these mothers and children did not experience this bonding in the childhood years, they do so now, but it is colored by the fact that this grown-up male and female did not live together in a family environment and do not feel like mother and son, at least early in post-reunion. Because the child did not grow up in the household, the incest taboo that normally protects us from acknowledging such feelings, much less acting on them, is far less strongly felt.

Another theory to explain genetic sexual attraction connects it with intimacy, suggesting that the emotional intimacy which may be shared by a man and woman who have been reunited can easily ignite the desire for intimacy of the ultimate kind, sexual intimacy. Still another theory has to do with the concept of mirroring, namely, that there can be attraction to a person who looks very much like the self. Seeing the other person is like seeing yourself in a mirror; and, like the mythical Narcissus who fell into the water from admiring his own image, the element of self-love may be strongly involved in this attraction between mother and child.

For the birthmothers we interviewed who experienced it, genetic sexual attraction to their sons was something that made post-reunion more complex, confusing, and uncomfortable than it might have been otherwise, but it was not responsible for permanently ruining any of the relationships.[12] It needed to be acknowledged, understood, and handled. When it was, the feelings could begin to dissipate. But there are people in reunions around the country who are grappling with this issue less successfully, and for whom such feelings persist.

Feelings of Familial Identification

Post-reunion experience is profoundly affected by what we'll call the adoptee's feelings of familial identification. Which family, birth or adoptive, does the adult son or daughter come to feel, over time, that he or she belongs in? Can it be both?

What the interviews indicate is that it's possible, post-reunion, for an adoptee to become attached or bonded[13] to the birthmother's family, and that it's also possible for adoptees to reaffirm their attachment to the adoptive family by relegating the birthmother to some kind of non-maternal, non-familial, or tightly circumscribed role. What happened most often, though, is that these adopted adults became included in the birth family and participated in both families, moving back and forth with greater or lesser comfort depending on the personalities, feelings, and circumstances of all the individuals involved.

Allegiance to a Birth Family. Two of the birthmothers in our sample (both of whom, it happens, are married to the birthfathers), describe post-reunion scenarios in which their child has completely "moved in," figuratively speaking. The child identifies with the birth family, not the adoptive family, and it is the birth family to which they feel they "belong." By words and deeds they've announced, "I'm coming in" and the immediate family, in each case, has opened the door, welcomed them, included them in the family's life, and helped them become full-fledged members.

Neither of these birthmothers senses that her daughter actually switched allegiance from the adoptive family to hers. Rather, each believes that her daughter had been unattached to the adoptive family for many years, possibly since infancy. Lila's daughter, Kate, had married at age eighteen, mainly to escape her adoptive home. (Before meeting Lila, she and her young husband lived with *his* parents, and she became very close to them.) Suzanne's daughter, Kim, had also moved away from her adoptive parents at eighteen; she was living with a roommate when she was reunited with her birthparents seven years later.

The evidence that these particular daughters have cast their lot with their birth families is unequivocal. When Kate divorced, for example, two years into post-reunion, she decided to use neither her maiden name or her married name. Instead, she took her birthmother's maiden name for her own and plans not to give it up should she marry again. In the three years she has known Lila, she has also changed her personal style to more closely conform to Lila's. Her hair is cut differently, her clothes look like Lila's, she sends funny cards now instead of the flowery kind she picked in the first year, and she espouses the family's values with respect to education and careers.

There are also other indications that Kate and Kim are "in" the birth family. The daughters have reduced their contact with their adoptive family in favor of the birth family; they have become more distanced from the adoptive family emotionally;

they have moved physically nearer to the birth family, and they announce feeling more comfortable with the birth family than with the adoptive family. After three or four years in both cases, the sense of affiliation is virtually complete.

Suzanne's Story

Ignorant of the facts of life and pregnant at thirteen, Suzanne delivered her baby at home in pain and confusion. "Even being sick all night and in this horrible pain," she recalls, "my mother didn't tell me that I was pregnant or giving birth to a child. I remember looking at the baby and saying, 'It's a baby, it's a baby' and being so shocked, not understanding what was going on." Within hours, the decision to place the child for adoption was made by the two sets of parents, hers and his, and the curtain of secrecy descended. "I was a little girl who had gone through all these adult things, and had no one to talk to about them; my parents never mentioned it again." Suzanne and her boyfriend married four years later and had three more children. They were found by their first daughter in 1984.

Reunited for over 3 years, Suzanne believes that Kim "would take 100 percent of my time if she could." Kim never bonded to her adoptive mother, Sylvia, probably because she was a "replacement child" for a baby who died, and Sylvia may never have wanted this kind of replacement despite her husband's well-meaning urgings at the time. Kim never felt that Sylvia treated her the same as she treated her biological son, and "she bugged them all her life, from the time she was old enough" for information about her birth.

Since the reunion, Kim has moved to her birth family's town, and mother and daughter have been in daily contact since their first meeting. "We've never had a day go by that we didn't talk to her, and we've seen her not every day, but nearly." To Suzanne, Kim is "a daughter, like the other children" and she expects "for us to be a family for the rest of our lives." They feel like, and are functioning like, one big happy family.

Kim still talks to Sylvia quite often and sees her, but they're not close. But then, they never have been.

The most extreme version of an adoptee becoming "a member of the family" exists in the phenomenon of re-adoption, whereby the parent or parents who relinquished the child for adoption a generation ago legally adopt that child back, years later. None of the birthmothers we interviewed in depth did this, but several to whom we spoke in the course of our study had this experience.

Just Visiting. Some birthmothers we spoke to describe the exact opposite of what Lila and Suzanne have experienced. Their sons and daughters have indicated that they are *not* interested in being identified with the birthmother's family. Their interest in a post-reunion relationship is confined to occasional contact with the birthmother, and they display little or no interest in developing relationships with other members of her network. Because the child's behavior seems to say "just visiting," these mothers sometimes have the sense that *they* are the ones encouraging or propelling the association.

These children, some of whom we've already met, impose some kind of restrictions on the post-reunion relationship or scenario. One is Debora's son, Teddy, who told her he couldn't exactly invite her home for Sunday dinner and he's not interested in getting to know his two half-brothers. Another is Thelma's daughter, Sara, who rarely initiates any contact with Thelma and who shows no interest in hearing about Thelma's pregnancy or her own adoption. "She very definitely feels that her adoptive mother is her mother," Thelma says. "There's a very strong bond there. She doesn't feel that I'm her mother in any way that I can tell." Then there is Roger, who, seven years into post-reunion, is still avoiding questions about his adoption story and who only rarely initiates any contact with any of his five siblings, despite having been included in family occasions. His relationship with his birthmother, Hattie, is tense. She believes he is "stuck" in unexpressed anger at having been placed for adoption and that the anger is preventing him from moving ahead. Roger was her third child and he's struggling with the question, Why me?

In one way or another, each of these adoptees is sending the message, "I have a mother," "I have a family," "I don't need other parents," "I don't want other parents." Each is signalling the birthmother, "These roles are occupied," "I don't want anyone else to fill them," "I don't belong in your clan." These relationships also have a quality of being stalled—sputtering along but not blossoming. They lack the kind of genuine interactiveness that we think of when we use the word relationship. The women have no way of knowing whether things will go on this way indefinitely, even though they hope some kind of breakthrough lies ahead. For the time being, though, it's as if the birthmother and the adoptee have walked out on a dance floor but just keep standing there awkwardly—a post-reunion dance in which the music hasn't started.

A Member of Two Families. What's happened in most of the cases in our sample is something similar to what happens when the rest of us acquire a second family by virtue of marriage, divorce, or remarriage. In-law and step relationships present us with second families, and we begin to integrate the new affiliation into our sense of who we are and how we spend our time. From the moment marriage or divorce expands our familial base, we can expect to encounter occasions when divided loyalties will cause us conflict, but, generally, we'll work it out.

Most of the adopted adults our sample birthmothers met are not "transferring over" or becoming "fully rooted" in the new families, even when the adoptee did not bond with the adoptive parents as a child. Nor are most of the adult adoptees erecting the kinds of barriers to birth family inclusion that Teddy or Sara have presented. Instead, they generally continue to be a presence in their adoptive family and, at the same time, become a presence in their birthmother's family. They have a relationship with both, and, like the child of divorce who has a bedroom in both parents' houses, they belong in both.

This is not to say the relationship with each family is the same. It usually isn't. The point is they can move back and forth between their two families without feeling the need to declare which is "it," and without feeling a compulsion to choose.[14]

Patterns of Post-Reunion Experience

Once in a while, the two families become blended as well, creating a new, larger, entity.

One adoptive mother, for example, welcomed her nineteen-year old son's birthmother into their clan. She remembers her own excitement when the other woman was located:

> "I was excited for Cal. I thought this was important for him, and if it was important for him it was important for us. It was like when someone gets married, you add a member to the family. I felt that when Cal found whoever he found, she would be part of our family."

Most of the birthmothers in our sample did not find that their children's adoptive families opened the door quite so wide, but the adoptive parents, with one exception, did not slam the door either. We'll look at adoptive parents more fully in Chapter 12, but for now it's important to recognize that most open the door to varying degrees, and that their attitude about reunion and post-reunion makes a world of difference in the post-reunion drama, enabling the adoptee to move back and forth between his two families openly and with ease, or forcing him to do so furtively, with discomfort and guilt. Post-reunion relationships are driven by the adoptee and the birthmother but the adoptive parents either facilitate or inhibit the relationship by their attitudes. When post-reunion relationships terminate, a common cause is that adoptees were put in the position of being forced to choose.

Like citizens of two countries, it may not be easy for adoptees to manage their dual citizenship in two families. In some of the cases, the adoptee is so uneasy about his or her position that the adoptive family has not been told about the reunion (yet)—and these cases are up to four years old. In other cases, the adoptee moves back and forth between the two families openly but with discretion, because they perceive that their adoptive parents are uncomfortable, displeased, or disapproving. Adoptees in the latter situation can experience a good deal of guilt in maintaining a relationship with the birthmother. Ironically too, in trying to "protect" their adoptive parents, they are introducing a new brand of deception into the adoption script; years ago it was the birthmother who was living a double life; now it is the adult child instead.

How much easier and more humane everything becomes when the two families can acknowledge and be comfortable with one another. Then, both can be present at the same place, at the same event, rather than forcing adoptees to shuttle back and forth in a forced pattern of separate interactions with the two groups. Like the best of step-family accommodations, the ideal solution is when everyone accepts and is comfortable with the fact that the child has two families. Unfortunately, many people have trouble with this idea. It still feels alien.

Emily Sue, for example, believes her situation is unusual in the degree of acceptance which Pam's adoptive parents have extended both to her and to Pam's birthfather. "They feel so secure in their relationship with Pam that they can allow her to have a relationship with us," she thinks. Marcie also describes the mutual regard that exists between herself, her family and her daughter's adoptive family. Members of both families were present on the occasion of the daughter's second marriage; similarly, on a less happy occasion when the adoptive father was ill, "everyone worked together to do what had to be done." What's evolved is that "everyone is cooperating and sharing joys and sorrows as an extended family." The policy is fully open-door.

How different this is from Helaine's case, where the daughter's adoptive parents still refuse to meet Helaine after five years. Initially, she was furious at their resistance, but her anger has softened to a hope that they will eventually relent— an act which would not only assuage the loyalty conflict her daughter is experiencing, but which would also reassure Helaine that she will have an accepted place in Angie's life forever. "I'd love to be friendly with her parents so that if she gets married I could go to her wedding," Helaine says. "I know they can keep me from a lot of things."

Comparing reunion relationships to step relationships is a strategy which serves to normalize the post-reunion situation, bringing it more into the mainstream and rendering it more understandable. Joan, a birthmother who is also a stepmother to four, suggests that stepfamilies provide a useful analogy for post-reunion families. "If more people could look at reunions as similar to step relationships, we'd all be a lot better off."[15] But Joan herself hastens to add that the similarity is far from total. "It's different because Jenny (the daughter she gave up) is mine," she says. "She's my flesh and blood."

The Pleasure-Pain Ratio Overall

While all of the birthmothers whose stories are presented in this book are somewhere between happy and ecstatic that they have had a reunion, there is more variation in their feelings about how the *post*-reunion scenario is working out. Reunion is about reconnection: finding a missing piece. But post-reunion is about developing a relationship, *and* about how everyone in each person's sphere responds to the existence and development of this new entity.

Listening to birthmothers talk about post-reunion, one is struck by the fact that their relationships proceed not just because of the positives but in spite of all the negatives. The quality of post-reunion almost always seems to be a combination of bitter and sweet, pleasure and pain. Some birthmothers are luckier than others in terms of the objective realities with which fate presents them: healthy, stable children, for example, versus troubled ones; or welcoming adoptive parents versus hostile ones. Some birthmothers make it easier on themselves because they are the kinds of people who judge the proverbial glass to be "half full" not "half empty." Based on how they present their post-reunion experiences and relationships, the birthmothers convey situations which can be summarized as:

• Extremely happy, almost nothing bitter or painful about it

• Somewhat happy, a mixed bag; i.e., happy in spite of the problems, or with problems in the foreground reducing the feelings of happiness

• Mainly uncomfortable

Extremely Happy Situations. Some of the cases we heard about have blossomed into extremely happy situations. According to the birthmother no negative now exists on any front to mar the satisfying relationship she and her child have achieved.[16] The people in these reunions generally felt a loving connection to one another from the outset.

The good fortune in these cases is tied as much to the supporting cast as it is to the principal players. These are situations in which there are no troublesome ripple effects with which either the birthmother or the adoptee still needs to cope. The adoptive parents are supportive or geographically distant from the birthmother or deceased. The birthmothers' families were largely supportive from the beginning; or, if they presented resistances, the resistances were either minor, short-lived, or had been overcome prior to our interview. (Alternatively, the birthmother may have decided that she just didn't care. Joan, for example, was disappointed that her own parents and siblings weren't more interested in establishing a relationship with Jenny, but they don't live nearby and it's just not important enough to diminish Joan's pleasure.) The birthmothers in these reunions also enjoyed a state of neutrality or equanimity about the birthfather; whatever action their child took or didn't take in terms of finding him did not set off a "little landmine" in *her* world.

The mothers in this group also seem capable of accepting their children as people, whatever flaws they have. They do not allow disappointments, or unappealing aspects, to serve as chronic irritants.

Happy in Spite of Problems. The largest cluster of birthmothers we heard from can be characterized as basically happy with their post-reunion situation, despite its blemishes and imperfections. Women who describe these kinds of post-reunions are dealing with, or aware of, some important problem or problems stirred up by post-reunion. Whatever it is, though, the problem is not inhibiting their personal relationship with their son or daughter, and it is not undermining their happiness about maintaining a relationship. Typically, the principal players are pleased with one another and the distress is located outside the mother-child diad, somewhere in the larger environment of adoption or reunion. In evaluating how satisfied they are with their reunions, these mothers tend to focus on the value of the relationship, not on the troubles.

The thorns and thickets they've encountered include such things as: intense grieving that was never expected and won't seem to abate; uncovering detail after detail about the disadvantages of a son or daughter's childhood and coming to the conclusion that she could have provided a better home herself, even as an unwed mother; having relationships with adoptees who are caught in the vise of divided loyalties between their adoptive mothers and their birthmothers; and feeling uncomfortable and deceitful in their relationships because adoptive parents have not been informed.

We've mentioned some of the other trials in different connections. Carol, whose teenage, dark-skinned son is struggling with identity issues, acknowledges that his social development has become her problem too. Norma admits to a genetic sexual attraction which lasted year after year. Emily Sue is coping with her husband's long-standing inability to forgive her for having become pregnant before they met and never telling him about it. (He discovered it when he was "poking around" in her diary one day, years after they married.) And Geraldine, raped at age seventeen, has not yet disclosed this information to the daughter she's known for one year. (Despite the circumstances of the conception, Geraldine wanted to keep the baby when she was born. Now, her post-reunion relationship is warm and strengthening.)

Another group of birthmothers describe post-reunion scenarios in which the problems, whatever they are, occupy a more pervasive place. Post-reunion seems to have brought them pleasure and pain in about equal proportion. And so, unlike the mothers whose bottom line can be summarized as "happy despite the problems," these women tend to convey their situations with the emphases reversed: "big problems, but I'm committed to the relationship regardless." Although the

troubles themselves aren't necessarily different from those encountered by their happier counterparts (what could be worse,
after all, than the memory of rape, or the discovery that your
child never felt loved), what differentiates this group is that the
problems have become more consuming, as salient in the
women's consciousness as the satisfaction of maintaining the
association.

Irene, the woman with the "smothering" daughter, is an
example of a birthmother who experienced post-reunion as an
exquisite combination of pleasure and pain. Millie and Virginia
did as well. In Millie's case, post-reunion revived forty-year old
feelings of hurt and anger occasioned by the birthfather:

> *"Even now I can't seem to get over the hurt, not
> just from losing the baby but from the rejection
> from the birthfather."*

Virginia is dissatisfied with her daughter (their needs are out of
sync) and uncertain what the future holds for the two of them.
She is the only birthmother to have expressed her own ambivalence about the relationship quite so clearly:

> *"This isn't a voluntary relationship in a way. . . .
> I'm not sure I'd have somebody like that as a
> friend unless she were my daughter."*

Mainly Uncomfortable Situations. The post-reunion situations
that appear most strained are those in which birthmothers
can't reach a state of acceptance about the relationship; the
problems, whatever they are, are just too upsetting. Sometimes
these birthmothers freely state that they are uncomfortable in
the relationships. Sometimes their unease stems from the dis-
crepancy between what they want and what the adoptee wants
(with the mother usually being the hungrier party). Sometimes
these are cases in which the son or daughter is "just visiting" or
where communication is so poor that the woman constantly
feels she's "walking on eggshells." Sometimes the specter of
the birthfather stalks in the background. Sometimes the mothers are disappointed in their children. Common to many of

these women is a feeling that they are not in control of what's happening.

Perhaps the most significant commonality in these cases, though, is the difficulty the birthmothers have in articulating exactly what is wrong. It's clear to them that all's not well, but their vision is cloudy when it comes to identifying and naming the problem with anything approaching certainty. And since they can't identify the problem, they're not sure what to do about it either.

When we asked them, "How satisfied are you with the post-reunion outcomes overall?" these are the birthmothers who take the cautious position: "somewhat."

6

The First Meeting

"It was like a thousand emotions in the space of one minute."

Betty, a birthmother

Like those milestone events we never forget, the reunion meeting between a birthmother and her child is climactic. Everything that happens afterwards, no matter how tumultuous or how joyous, is an anticlimax because that meeting is a culmination—the point on which all energies are focussed. One adoptee refers to it as "the moment of my birth." A birthmother describes it as "the greatest, grandest day I ever lived." Everyone conveys its matchless excitement. It is often referred to as a miracle.

Occasionally, this first meeting also represents the first contact between mother and child, making the shock of the reconnection an element of the interaction. More often, though, the first meeting is preceded by a telephone or letter contact and it is not infrequent for such contacts to go on for weeks or months before the individuals actually get together, especially when a long distance is involved. Having to wait can be a source of impatience or relief, but this pre-meeting period can be extremely valuable. It is a time for exchanging photographs, asking and answering questions about the past, getting acquainted with the here-and-now's, becoming more comfortable with the idea of reunion and post-reunion generally, and beginning to develop a shared history. Those who experience such pre-meeting communication typically view it as a helpful, and calming, launch. By the time they meet, many of the information gaps are filled, and feelings about the other person can begin to be disengaged from inquisitiveness. The other person is no longer a total stranger.

Some birthmothers and adoptees who are anticipating first meetings discover that they are fearful about the event beyond the natural uneasiness that comes with the prospect of meeting a stranger. They worry or fantasize that the other person may hurt them or wish to do them harm. Their family members are often quite suspicious too, asking over and over, "What does he or she want"? Norma's husband, for example, insisted on accompanying her to the restaurant where she was scheduled to meet her son and remaining there "in case I needed help"; he stayed in the room, discreetly hidden from view, until he was satisfied that Jerry's intentions were aboveboard. Kate remembers driving with her husband to meet her birthparents and asking him, only half in jest, if he thought they would want to kill her. Beverly was "freezing cold" from fear. Possibly it is the taboo against such a meeting that causes such irrational fears. The unconscious mind apparently expects some kind of retribution—for giving up a child, for exposing a birthmother.

The women we interviewed met their sons and daughters in a variety of public and private places: at restaurants and hotels, at parks and on the street, in front of public buildings, at airports and train stations. The largest number met at the birthmother's home. A few met at the adoptee's home.

Hardly anyone suggests that physical environment *per se* makes any difference in terms of how smoothly that meeting went, but it does affect whether third parties will enter in. Some birthmothers wish to meet their children alone,[1] but others include their husband, a close friend, or (less often) their other children. Married adoptees frequently wish to include their spouse, and some adoptees, younger people especially, wish to include their adoptive parents. Desired third parties definitely provide moral support.

The presence of others affects everyone's comfort

level, of course, which Emily Sue didn't discover until months after the initial meeting, once her daughter had made her first long-distance trip to Emily Sue's home. (The two first met, then visited for several days, at the adoptive parents' home.) "Having her out here, away from her family and her friends, has made the relationship more comfortable for me," Emily Sue found.

But the tone of first meetings is never comfortable, because birthmothers are overwhelmed with emotions of all kinds. They may feel elated, excited, or charged, but also tense and scared, or cautious and uncertain. They may feel loving, but also unexpectedly romantic. Often there is a mixture of joy at meeting one's child, accompanied by an indescribable sadness over the lost years. Tension is high from not knowing what to expect. Some are glad when distractions present themselves —the tourist sights of an unfamiliar city; a baby that needs tending; a meal to prepare.

Just laying eyes on their child has informational value for birthmothers who can finally answer specific questions they've had all along about the son or daughter as a physical being. Hattie, for instance, wondered for 21 years how impaired her son had been by his congenital club foot. Whatever concrete expectations they had about who, or what, their child looks like can now be confirmed or amended; and those who had only a diffuse wondering on this score, usually because "I never let myself think about that," now acquire a mental picture instead. Just by laying eyes on her child, a birthmother learns that her son or daughter looks like her, or like her other children, or perhaps like the birthfather and his family. This discovery alone, as we'll explore more fully in Chapter 8, can influence the complexion of her post-reunion feelings.

Seeing the other person for the first time is also an occasion for staring at the other person hard and long. Not unlike the way a new mother stares at her baby, reunion meetings are occasions when everybody stares intently at everybody else, even when they try not to be too obvious about it. Birthmothers' impulses are to "take her all in," and they are fascinated with the looks of someone who often is "both so familiar and so unfamiliar looking" at the same time. Adoptees are equally intent on looks, face to face for the first time in their life with a human being whom they may resemble.[2]

The conversation at first meetings is also intense, partly because many birthmothers and adoptees are anxious that if they don't say it all now they may never have another chance. They describe a sense of urgency in these meetings, "trying to cram a lifetime into a few hours." Norma refers to the interaction as "urgent exchanging," which, in her case, involved a son's pressing need to tell her about his life, but without a corresponding urgency on his part to hear about hers.

Granting differences regarding which person has the greater need to inquire and which has the greater need to deliver information, first meetings give birthmothers and their children the opportunity to talk about the circumstances of the adoption, and to piece together what happened afterwards. Openers such as, "Well, lady, at last we meet," or "So, how've you been?" are quickly obliterated by the urgent exchanging that follows the first awkward greeting. Informational catch-up will continue for months or years into the relationship, as the individuals become more familiar to one another and feel freer to reveal their private selves.

First encounters can last anywhere from several hours to a full week. When the interest is mutual and the meeting expected, the stories are wonderful. Here is Nora, who met her son at a house, borrowed from a friend, midway between their respective cities:

> *"I arrived two days ahead to prepare. I had gotten plants for the beach house, and sheets—my layette, I think. I nested that place; I knew I was nesting it. He walked in and we gave each other this long embrace. We knew each other so well from the letters. I came this close to kissing him on the lips, then I had to remember he was my son."*

Irene reconnected with her daughter on the telephone one day before they met:

> *"When she asked who is this, I couldn't bring myself to say, 'This is your mother,' so I said, 'I understand you're looking for information about your background, who you are, and this is the only person in the world who can give it to you.' She asked, 'Is this some kind of joke?' and I said no and she said, 'Well who is this?' and I said, 'Your mother,' and she started to scream, 'Is this true? Is this a joke? Is it really you?' We talked for three hours. We arranged to meet the following day in front of the public library. She opened the car door, jumped in, and said, 'Oh my God, I look like someone' and started to cry."*

Ethel met her daughter at the airport:

> *"My husband had the camera poised and ready. After we came up the ramp I looked at all the strange faces and then focussed on Lucy. Suddenly she was in my arms and we held each other for a long time. We didn't say much of anything, mostly small talk, but we kept smiling, looking at each other, searching for similarities. We held tight to each other's hand, almost fearful that if we let go we would lose each other again."*

Suzanne and her husband went to the mobile home their daughter shared with a roommate:

> *"It was totally unbelievable, to see your child. First thing we did was hug her. We were there from 7 p.m. to 1 a.m. We stared at one another. I couldn't help but touch her face and touch her hands, and all the things that we had never done. When she was born she was in the same*

BirthBond

> *room with me from early morning to late after-
> noon, but I was afraid to touch her."*

Vivien and her daughter met at the adoption agency:

> *"I just immediately loved her. She knew that I
> was sixteen when she was born; she knew those
> circumstances. She didn't believe that I didn't
> love her, but I don't think she really realized how
> much. I had brought her a beautiful pearl eve-
> ning bag that had been given to me by a favor-
> ite aunt, and in it I had a pair of booties that
> Cindy had worn as an infant, and I had a medal
> that she'd worn for her baptism in the hospital,
> and I gave them to her. It was an emotional
> moment and I started to cry a little bit and I
> think she realized how much I cared. Booties
> and a medal—I had cherished them for eighteen
> years."*

Even if the meeting is unexpected, the result can be positive, as
it was for Marion:

> *"I found his address in Queens. A guy comes
> out of the house in sweats. We reach the same
> point at the curb at the same time, and I say,
> 'Excuse me, are you Allen?' He said yes. Then I
> said, 'I knew you a long time ago. Do you know
> you're adopted?' He said yes, and I said, 'My
> name is Marion. I'm your birthmother,' and
> shook his hand. He's thrilled; I'm ready to pass
> out.*
>
> > *Then I said, 'That's your sister in the car,'
> and as she was coming out, I said, 'She's the
> youngest,' and he says, 'You mean there's
> more?' That was the perfect line, because then I
> took out all the pictures. I kept looking at him. I
> was seeing him but I wasn't. I was totally over-
> whelmed. He kept saying, 'Why don't we go up
> to my apartment,' and I kept saying 'No, that's*

okay.' I was frozen. It started to rain very lightly
and he said, 'Well, now you have to come up' so
he escorted us to his apartment, made me tea,
and kept trying to reassure me it was fine and I
should relax. We proceeded to talk. I told him
everything."

Before Marion ever appeared on that curb, her son had made inquiries about finding her too, which helps explain his easy grace. Betty's son, on the other hand, had not, and he was, and continues to be, less receptive. First, she talked to him several times on the phone hinting each time about who she was; finally, she presented herself in person and revealed her identity. His response was devastating: "I don't want to hurt your feelings or anything, but I never gave you a second thought." Still, he didn't want her to leave and they talked briefly. "I just wanted you to know that from the second I found out I was pregnant, I have always loved you," she told him. "He just looked at me and said, 'I knew that.' "

When first meetings are over and the time comes to say goodbye, birthmothers often experience great difficulty and sadness. It reminds them of having to leave their babies years ago— "almost like the feeling the day I left him at the hospital," says Bonnie. Nora, who had spent a week with her son, felt "ripped open" when he drove off:

"I have never ached in my life like I did at that
moment. I didn't know how I would take my
next breath. That was the letting go—the sec-
ond time. I wasn't prepared for that."

The pain of letting go becomes a recurrent aspect of early post-reunion experience for many women, as Charlene also discovered:

"When Rich left that night, I felt really good. I
was so excited, but I was a little saddened be-
cause I didn't want him to go, I wanted him to
stay here. I kid him to this day that I would like
to have chained him to my bedpost. I didn't

*want to let him go. I wanted to keep him and
hold him and get as close to him as I possibly
could. I felt that way for a long time. Every time
he would leave, I would have that same feeling."*

In the world of search and reunion, one meeting does not ensure a future. Reunioning individuals quickly learn that each of
them has to make continuous decisions about what kind of
relationship, if any, theirs will be. But some enjoy an almost
instantaneous certainty that a mutual future lies ahead, and
some enjoy an instantaneous closeness that provides the same
assurance. In Faye's case, "I knew I would keep up contact the
first time I saw her at my door. I knew it would continue for our
lifetime." In Geraldine's, whose shiny face in all the reunion pictures reminds her how heavily she perspired from nervousness,
"I knew when they left that she would always be in my life." In
Carol's, "We both knew we wanted to be in each other's lives
forever from the moment we met, and we both worked very
hard to accomplish that." In other cases, though, it can take
months or years before birthmothers and their children are fully
confident that the relationship will endure.

Making specific plans for a second meeting before saying goodbye at the first can be a helpful tactic. Emily Sue's
daughter, Pam, just came out and asked whether their meeting
would be a "one-time deal" or not. When the subject is not
addressed directly, uncertainty about what will happen next can
be a source of great anxiety.

People leave first meetings feeling totally spent. As
Beverly's put it, "When it was over, I felt absolutely exhausted. I
felt as if I couldn't have said one more thing or had one more
feeling." Reunion has been a watershed event—an end, but also
a beginning.

By the time the first meeting is over, important work
has been accomplished. Fantasy begins to diminish. People begin to know one another as people instead of fantasies, ab-
stractions or roles. Lila's daughter, Kate, explains:

*"I had this fantasy that I had to let go. This was
it; this was my life; there wasn't going to be an-*

*other one. I had to deal with that. There's no
more fantasizing it. It seems ridiculous but I was
very attached to that fantasy. It's what I turned
to when I was feeling unhappy."*

We are moving now into post-reunion, which begins at the point
at which birthmother and child decide that they will, indeed,
have some kind of future together.[3] The question becomes:
What kind?

7

How Post-Reunion Develops

"Our insights change and shift from day to day."

Nora, a birthmother

What the post-reunion future will be like can frequently be glimpsed in the first meeting. When the meeting is warm and open, positive feelings are likely to continue and intensify as post-reunion unfolds. Those who have feelings of instantaneous closeness find that these feelings deepen with time. "It was like we had always known each other; we've been close since the day we laid eyes on each other," they say. Or, "The more time we spend together the more I feel like he's my child." In other cases, a chillier atmosphere prevails and indicates a bumpier period of adjustment.

Regardless of how the people feel about each other, early post-reunion happenings are liable to be affected by whatever else is going on in each person's life. The birthmother may be coping with a traumatic divorce; the adoptee may arrive in the midst of wedding preparations for one of the birthmother's other children; a first meeting may occur when someone is gravely ill, or just before a baby is due. When the timing is inopportune in these ways, the found person may decide to delay announcements or family introductions until the other event is over. But such control is not always possible, as

Thelma found out. Ready or not, she had to tell the man with whom she was living about her daughter's existence:

> "My boyfriend's mother was dying in the hospi-
> tal. When I got the letter, she had been in a
> coma for three weeks, and he was totally
> wrapped up in that. The last thing he needed
> was information about my child. But for all I
> knew she could show up on my doorstep to-
> morrow, and I couldn't let that happen without
> telling him. So I took him out to dinner and told
> him, and I apologized."

Even with the best of timing, post-reunion relationships between birthmothers and their children are disjointed relationships, inescapably marred by a past that was not shared. The
history that is taken for granted in other family relationships
does not exist. There are no shared memories or family traditions. Everything is strange in the beginning. "There's so much
in the future for us to talk about," one birthmother said during
her first year of reunion, "but right now there's just a lot of
observing going on."

The Stranger Who's Not A Stranger

Getting to know their adult child is frequently characterized by birthmothers as "getting to know someone that you
already know." They struggle to describe the peculiar combination of familiarity and strangeness they feel, but can find no
analogy. Listen to Joan:

> "It was so strange because I felt so comfortable
> and felt that I knew her so well, yet she was a
> total stranger. It's so strange to feel that this is a
> person you've always known and yet you have
> no idea whether she likes mustard or pickles or
> chicken or potatoes or green beans. Or what her
> home would be like. Or what her taste in any-
> thing is."

And Marcie:

> "There's a stranger and yet she's not a stranger.
> She has always been a part of my life, of me. I
> don't have the history with her, yet she's mine.
> There's a closeness and yet a strangeness. It's
> weird."

And Beverly:

> "You're strangers when you start and yet you're
> as close biologically as you can be. It's how to
> get those two together that takes years of expe-
> rience."

While just about every birthmother probably feels some sense
of connection with her grown child, there are dramatic differences. Some women, less disoriented than others by the time
and role confusions inherent in the reunion phenomenon, experience a primal sense of mother-child connection immediately.
Others focus more on the years and histories that separate
them, initially experiencing the adult adoptee as essentially unfamiliar. Constance, whose story we told in Chapter 4, is one of
the latter. She was caught in a time warp from the moment she
was contacted by her daughter until many months later.

> "I had difficulty with the fact that I had the expe-
> rience of giving birth to a baby, giving her up for
> adoption, and then, many years later, having a
> phone call from this adult woman telling me
> about her master's degree. There was too much
> space in-between those two events for me to
> even fathom at the time."

In a similar vein, another birthmother recalls feeling angry at the
adult adoptee because she wanted her *baby* back.

Other birthmothers, however, are amazed to discover
how close or attached they felt almost immediately. As Nora
put it, "It was a mystery to me that I could love him so much,
this person who was supposed to be a stranger. We were so

connected." When Bonnie experienced it, "I looked into his eyes and I felt like I was looking into a mirror. I thought we were almost one and the same."

Frequent, Intense Contact

A common dynamic in post-reunion experience is frequent, intense contact. In its ultimate form, the adoptee moves in with the birthmother, and, as we mentioned in Chapter 4, several in our sample actually did.

Like Carol and Joey, birthmothers and their children can become obsessed with one another, visiting and talking so frequently that neglected family members begin to pressure the mother for a return to normalcy. As with Carol and Joey, the behavior is often felt to be a kind of bonding or delayed bonding, triggered by the adoptee's need for a kind of mothering he or she had missed. They are trying to fill a gap.[1]

Marlene is another birthmother who came up against a particularly importunate individual:

> "She was so needy. She would plop into my house any time after I got home from work. It would be 2 o'clock, and then my kids would be coming home from school, and then it would be dinner time and I wouldn't know whether or not to ask her to stay to dinner, or to postpone dinner. She wouldn't see this or, if she did, she was ignoring it. She just needed to be there with me."

Some birthmothers view the frequent contact they have after reunion with their son or daughter as a simple desire to make up for lost time. They describe high phone bills, visiting several times a week, spending overnights or weekends together, restaurant lunches or dinners, joining a health club together, shopping expeditions, long walks, watching a son play sports, etc. — all accompanied by endless talking. Some explain that they were impelled to express the mothering or nurturant feelings which post-reunion elicited in them by giving gifts—like a doll or a teddy bear or a copy of *Little Women*, for example,—which mothers ordinarily give their little girls or boys. Lila's analysis is that early post-reunion was a time of attempting to raise her child, symbolically and in compressed form:

> *"Instead of having her for, say, fifteen years, and over that time buying toys and taking her to the theater and traveling with her and having family occasions, we did it all in six months. We bought fifteen years worth of toys and goodies and clothes. We did fifteen years worth of 'meet the family'; we did fifteen years worth of bringing up Kate."*

Nora suggests something similar when she reflects on the progress of her week-long meeting with her son. Her idea is that, in some sense, reunioning birthmothers and their children repeat the developmental stages that children normally pass through as they grow up:

> *"We did go through the maturation process of a child. The first couple of days he was the adoring toddler, the next few days he was the older child. At one point I said something and he went in and wrote it down. He was like a sponge. By the time he left he was the alienated youth."*

Paula, an adult adoptee, had essentially the same interpretation about her changing stance vis-a-vis birthmother Marlene. Marlene remembers her saying, "When I came to you, I was like in infancy, and I've grown up to be like the rebellious teenager, and now I'm moving on. I'm moving away from you, Mother."

Another aspect of this early, intense contact is the same difficulty saying goodbye that was encountered at the first meeting. One of the recurrent themes of post-reunion is how difficult it is to "cut the cord," because the original separation continues to resonate:

> *"She and I spent the first six months on the phone, unable to break the connection. It oc-*

> *curred to me at one point as I was unable to
> hang up that it was really very symbolic. Here I
> had this connection with this daughter—literally,
> this cord, we were connected by a cord—and I
> was no way going to let go again."*

These early post-reunion days are reminiscent of "falling in love," and many reunioning pairs talk with one another about the parallels: the headiness, the obsession, the fact that they don't want to share the other person with anyone else, "the need to have this person adore you, and the way your life seems devastated if they wrinkle their eyebrow wrong at you." What they mainly conclude is that, strange and frightening as the feelings may be, they are somehow related to bonding.

> *"I remember the first time Rita came over—and
> it kind of scared me—she'd lay her head on my
> shoulder and she'd say, 'Ma, can you scratch my
> back?' And I'd think, 'Wait a minute, this kid is
> nineteen-years old.' What this is, I believe, is just
> a kind of bonding—trying to get close to what
> they've missed."*

As in other human relationships, the challenge facing many of these reunioning pairs is to connect but not merge, and a problem with their concentrated contact is that it becomes overwhelming. In their fervor, one or the other may push things too fast, violating the other's comfort zone and provoking a withdrawal for "space." Early post-reunion can be a case of too much too soon, with birthmothers either romanticizing the possibilities of the relationships or acting out of guilt and attempting to "make up" to their children "abandoning" them. Birthmothers often engage in what one calls "symbolic gestures to undo the past." Another confided that she'd go slower if she had it to do again; she recognizes now that by her effusive welcome, she was trying to hasten the day that her relationship with her daughter would feel "normal," but that the attempt was destined to fail.

The Honeymoon and After

The early elation of reunion is like a honeymoon, and some reunioning pairs continue to be in a honeymoon phase for many months. They may want to tell the whole world about their reunion. They may feel a kind of magic: that everything's for the best in this best of all possible times. The pleasure of getting to know the other person is intense—and this is no ordinary someone. Some people suspend judgment and see only the good in the other person. The most ordinary occurrences of daily life hold special pleasure and meaning, as this birthmother indicates:

> "I remember one moment I was walking through the living room and he was coming in with a glass of milk. I was filled with such an incredible sense of joy that here was this son that I haven't seen in twenty years just doing the everyday thing of walking into the living room with a glass of milk. How very normal, but how absolutely exquisite."

Another aspect of the honeymoon period is that people are on their best behavior, trying to impress one another and, in this way, seeking to ensure that the other person doesn't leave them a second time. Birthmothers reminisce about the days when "I was still cleaning the house before he came" and "worrying about what I cooked when she first came to dinner." Some went on diets or tried to get rid of grey hair. Most "take the lipstick off" later and become more relaxed as they get to know the adoptee. But wanting to do everything right, and wanting everything to be perfect, puts additional effort and anxiety into a period that is already highly charged. As several point out, no soap opera could compete.

Cautious about giving offense, reunioning pairs often display an exquisite concern with one another's feelings. They engage in lengthy ruminations with themselves or their behind-the-scenes advisors about what they should or should not say or do; many try to curb impulsive actions. But no matter how much time is spent second-guessing how the other person is likely to react, the possibility of being misunderstood remains high. One birthmother decided to reduce her letter-writing to her son so as to convey the message "no pressure," but the fewer letters were misconstrued to mean that she was "pulling back." Post-reunion is filled with such ironies, until and unless the parties learn to communicate honestly with one another. Learning to do so may not be easy, though, especially if it goes against a person's usual grain.

It is the nature of honeymoons to end. Many birthmothers and adoptees experience an unexpected sense of letdown after the honeymoon highs vanish. Often, this is when a feeling of unresolved grief returns. Unfinished grieving can remain as a post-reunion backdrop for a long time. Added to postponed grief about losing their baby, many birthmothers also grieve over the years they missed raising the child—not having been there for the first smile, the first tooth, the first step, the first day at school, and the like. Confronted with a grown person, all they've missed is suddenly, painfully apparent.

At this point many birthmothers and adoptees sink into depression. Norma's son, for example, thought reunion would solve all his problems; he awakened to the realization one day years later that his post-reunion life was still fraught with difficulties. This is the time one must integrate the realities and give up the fantasies that have been such a central presence in one's psychic life, and their departure can be felt as a significant loss. Adoptees' letdown states can also be the result of loss, sadness, guilt, or anger associated with other aspects of their adoptive condition or history. Phyllis' daughter, for example, feels guilty that her birth caused so much pain. Many adoptees feel guilty about betraying their adoptive parents. Some mourn the self they think they could have been.

Among the birthmothers we interviewed, a few have been lucky. Good feelings of the honeymoon persist and there have been "no crises" in their post-reunion relationships. The majority, however, describe major or minor crises that broke the spell—from something which was resolved as easily as Adrienne's sitting up all night with her sister arguing about her "right" to be a mother, to something as difficult as Vivien's post-reunion experience, described below, which sent shock waves throughout her marriage and family life.[2]

Vivien's Story

Only one-year old, the reunion between 34-year old Vivien and her eighteen-year old daughter Cindy has already had explosive consequences. As a result of helping Cindy find her birthfather, Vivien and the boyfriend she planned to marry years ago "fell in love all over again"; they were close for months, emotionally parenting the child of their joint past. Vivien and her husband almost divorced, and, though divorce has been averted, her husband's feelings of betrayal have been the worst aspect of post-reunion to date. But there is a wistfulness in her voice when she acknowleges that she still has "a lot of deep feelings for the birthfather which I have to deny"—a defense strategy she regards as perverse necessity. It is necessary if she wishes to preserve her otherwise happy marriage, and the birthfather's too (they have a total of seven other children between them), but it is perverse because "I know what denial did to me for eighteen years."

The reunion is also responsible for what may or may not become a more permanent rupture with members of Vivien's own family—her parents and her older sister—none of whom accept the daughter she went searching for or comprehend the depth of her need to reconnect. Everyone just assumed she had no feelings about the adoption, she recalls, and they continue to be insensitive to her pains and joys now. Her mother's reaction to Cindy is "cold" and unfriendly. A letter of reproach from her sister was "the last straw" in what had become an unsatisfactory association anyway. "For my own wellbeing," she has concluded, "I need to be apart from my family."

A third dislocation caused by this reunion occurred with Vivien's seven-year old daughter, who was jealous of Vivien's love for the new older sister. To make matters worse, Cindy reciprocated with jealous feelings of her own, because Vivien had been "supermom" to the younger child but not to her. It *took an incident at the younger one's school—Vivien "went to bat" for her by challenging a teacher who wanted to discipline the girl—to reassure the little one that "I was still her mother and loved her very much."*

All the hurt and tangles notwithstanding, Vivien is unequivocal in wanting and expecting the reunion to continue. She and Cindy have become close friends and confidantes. They love and accept each other, and Cindy feels a powerful sense of connection. Vivien also credits the reunion with her own development into a whole, feeling person. "The intensity of feelings that I've experienced this past year I've never experienced before in my life." Freed from the restraints which denial imposed for so long, her capacity to care for her husband, she says, is stronger now than it has ever been.

Expressions of Negative Feeling: Anger, Fights, Testing, Retreat

A year or more often passes before a birthmother and her child feel able to disagree or to argue. The first fight imposes a risk in any relationship, but the risk is especially grave in post-reunion. The prospect of fighting raises the specter of repeating the earlier loss. However, being able to risk a fight (hence, risking the loss of the relationship) can be a turning point. It often produces more secure feelings on everyone's part.[3]

Although most reunions go through "a honeymoon period" there are also reunions with a lot of yelling and screaming right from the beginning. Marlene's reunion, for example, has been intense and stormy, with lengthy, fervent contacts interspersed with arguments and silences—all with a daughter who said she was closer to Marlene in a matter of months than she ever was to her adoptive mother. "She wanted to have this ongoing relationship; she wanted to sit on the sofa and curl up with me like she wanted to be a little child." There were times when "just surviving it" was a victory, but Marlene was trying to "make up" to her daughter "for all the years she was so un-happy," a stance that lasted several years.

> *"I remember one time when we had one of our great arguments. We had been out and had left the restaurant. I was angry. She drove me home and I got out of the car and she left. Then she came back and said, 'I'm not going to go home this way' and I said, 'I don't have anything to say.' Two or three nights later, it was pouring rain and there was a knock at the door—and I wondered, did she wait for the rain? She was standing there, soaking wet, with this little plant in her hand and said 'Can I come in? I haven't been able to eat. I haven't slept.' Later she said, 'I can't think of losing you again; I just can't handle that.'"*

Just about every birthmother expects her child to be angry about having been given up for adoption. Because so many of the women are angry at themselves, they are certain that their sons and daughters must also be harboring or "sitting on" angry feelings. Occasionally, it may be a case of birthmothers' projection: ascribing to the adoptees feelings that are really their own.

Over half the women we interviewed reported that they were surprised their children have *not* expressed anger or rage at any time during post-reunion. Many keep prodding these sons and daughters into revealing hidden emotions in the certainty that feelings of anger or rage must surely exist, however deeply buried or disguised. Time and again, they give the adult adoptees permission to admit their anger or show it. For the birthmother, one of the benefits of post-reunion seems to be receiving the child's "pardon" or relieving herself in some other way of the nagging fear that the adoptee must hate her. Marion is a good illustration:

> *"For a long time I tried to pull out of him whether he hated me, hated what happened. He*

*said, 'You know, I think you're sick. I think you're
neurotic. I'm telling you it's okay, I understand. I
don't know why you're doing this to yourself.' It
took a long time for me to trust that—that he
understood, that it was okay."*

One adult adoptee, cognizant of her birthmother's likely state
of mind, told her almost immediately upon meeting: "I don't
hate you. I did that before and I'm done with that." The message, she says, alleviated a lot of fear.

Birthmothers whose children have not been visibly angry offer various explanations. Several believe that their children vented their anger in adolescence and don't need to do so
again. Some note that expressing anger is not their children's
characteristic style: they're the types who turn anger inward
instead; "She doesn't confront, she cries." Some report that
their children did not specifically express anger at adoption, but
point to "bad tempers" or angry outbursts. One woman wonders if anger is something her daughter "hasn't gotten in touch
with at all or if she can't express it to me." Another asserts that
her daughter just isn't angry. She thinks that her adoption
worked out for the best.

Years into post-reunion, some adoptees can still be
found "sitting on" their anger to protect the relationship—a dynamic that occurs in many relationships, especially among
women. In these relationships especially, fragile and fraught
with pain on both sides, people are even more inclined than
usual to suppress angry feelings because building and sus-
taining the union occupies a higher priority. Instead of anger or
rage or provocation, what a few birthmothers see in their children is precisely the opposite: "If anything, she's too protective
of my feelings;" or, "She goes out of her way to make me feel
comfortable."

Suppressed anger, though, can also stall a relationship.
You may recall from Chapter 5 that Hattie's problem, seven
years into post-reunion, is that Roger is "stuck" in what she
perceives to be unexpressed anger about having been placed
for adoption, preventing them from having the honest dialogue

they need to have before they can become comfortable or close. He was not her first child (she already had three young "mouths to feed" and a disappearing husband when he was born), and he has yet to resolve his angry feelings about her decision. "Why me?" he asked one day, but in circumstances where he knew she couldn't answer. "We haven't really talked," Hattie says, and their relationship is strained:

> *"I'm comfortable with him but I know he's not,*
> *so that makes you walk carefully; you don't*
> *want to step on his toes. I still feel that I don't*
> *have the right to make advances, so I don't. I*
> *still wait for him."*

Another frequent behavior in adoptees' post-reunion repertoire is testing. They test their birthmothers by behaving in ways that ask, in effect: Will you be there for me this time? Will you reject me? What if I let you into my life and you walk out on me again? They seem to seek symbolic evidence that the bond is secure and that they can trust the birthmother.

Sometimes the birthmothers do the testing. The question they seem to be asking of the adoptee is: "What do you *really* want from me?" As we've mentioned before, the same question comes easily to the lips of onlookers too, though it's usually asked in the absence of any knowledge about what motivates reunion and post-reunion, as though the adoptee had a hidden agenda which he was intentionally concealing for some dark purpose of his own. At subsequent meetings, a certain amount of testing can occur between birthparents and adoptive parents as they too struggle to invent the nature and the rules of their unprecedented relationship.

Like Marlene, who was fully aware that she was trying to "make it up" to her daughter for all the unhappiness which the younger woman attributed to adoption, the common birthmother response to being tested is to be understanding, giving, and to turn the other cheek. Depending on the personalities of the individuals, they can wind up doing "the provocation dance," with the adoptee testing and the birthmother "walking on eggs" until she becomes upset enough, or feels secure enough, to set limits and force a halt.

The majority of birthmothers we interviewed did *not* encounter adult adoptees who were frequently provocative or whom they had to handle with kid gloves. Mainly, such behavior was rare, or confined to the early days, or "not just with me." But for those who faced it more routinely, post-reunion has been volatile. Helaine's daughter, for example, is like Marlene's. Helaine, too, needed to stop dancing the provocation dance:

> *"It feels like a roller coaster. It's been difficult. One time she called me on the phone screaming and yelling and I told her, on the advice of someone I trusted, 'Angie, I'm not going to take this anymore, I'm going to hang up.' I was able to be angry with her and I hung up on her and I thought, 'Well, that's it. I'm never going to hear from her again.' And ten days later she called me up and said, 'Well, I decided I need all the friends I can get.' Whenever I have actually spoken up for my rights—which I never thought I had the right to do—she has always come around."*

Even if they're not walking on eggs, many birthmothers are careful about what they say. They are concerned about overstepping their "rights" (a word which comes up time and again in the post-reunion vocabulary) or overstepping some limit which they or their child specifically imposed. According to Thelma, the birthmother whose daughter is conspicuously uninterested in hearing the details of her adoption story, "I have to be really careful that I don't blurt out something about the past, and it's so hard not to think about those things when I see her." More routinely, being careful is equated with trying not to take over the parental role. Sometimes, being careful translates to staying away from the subject of the adoptive parents entirely.

In addition to the characteristic caution and tentative-ness in post-reunion interactions, retreat is integral to the post-reunion scenario as well. Besides "holding back," reunioning in-dividuals describe periods of "pulling back" or "backing off," which, translated, means less frequent contact and less emo-tional involvement with one another. Sometimes, withdrawal is precipitated by a fight or by the adoptee's suddenly expressed anger. Sometimes, the adoptive parents' distress or pressure (chronic or acute) prompts adoptees to pull away from their birthmothers. Sometimes a need for "space" precipitates the hiatus. Sometimes, a person is taking the time to absorb and integrate what's happened, concentrating on the meaning of it all and deciding what he or she wants in the future. Sometimes, withdrawal is the defense mechanism of habit, the one that occurs in all one's relationship, not just in post-reunion. ("I'm working on that in therapy," a daughter told her birthmother.) The swing between moving toward and moving away may be a habitual pattern; many adoptees make and break dates, or make dates and then do not show.

Retreat can last for months. It can occur towards the beginning of post-reunion or years after. One son, who was engaged in a steady and congenial post-reunion with his birth-mother, hasn't been in touch with her for five months. All she knows is that his adoptive mother died. For her, the silence is especially threatening, because it echoes the original separa-tion, raising anxiety that the loss is repeating itself a second time.

There may also come a time when birthmother and child need or want to separate, in the same way all children eventually leave the nest when they develop into adults. To call *this* kind of separation a retreat would be inappropriate. What it seems to signify, rather, is that whatever healing needed to take place has been accomplished; whatever correction needed to be made has been made.[4]

In the case of Nell and Barb, at which we look next, we see a long term reunion in which a daughter's need for her birthmother diminished over time.

Nell's Story

By the early 1930s when Barb was born, seventeen-year old Nell had already enjoyed more fortunate circumstances than most. Her family had lived in an eighteen-room home on Chicago's Lakeshore Drive, her father had been a lawyer; she had been dating her boyfriend for four years. At the time of her pregnancy, though, the family's good fortune was just a memory. Her mother was widowed, there were teenagers to raise, no income to speak of, and the Great Depression outside. Forty-seven years later, in the late 1970s, sixty-four-year old Nell was found by the daughter she had been forced to give up. In 1987, when we met her, the reunion was nine-years old. Nell was in her early seventies and her health had been poor for some years.

At the time of our interview, the association had lost much of its early warmth and luster, primarily, Nell said, because of Barb. Nell described her daughter as strong-minded, selfish, intense, and a loner, but also a person who "doesn't hold her feelings in," and who "can cry." Barb was also "very masculine when I met her." In many of the particulars, Barb reminds Nell of her own mother, whom she still has difficulty forgiving.

At this point in their relationship, both parties are experiencing certain drawbacks. "We're both more sensitive about things we don't care for in each other and treatment we don't like," Nell says. She is one of the few birthmothers in our sample who are less comfortable in the relationship now than she was earlier in its history, in her case "because we can't get to the root of whatever it is that's causing this."

Nell and her immediate family (husband, children) are the only family Barb has. The adoptive parents are deceased, and Barb has no adoptive siblings, or husband or children of her own, which is one of the reasons, Nell speculates, that their association continues. Still, she's mystified. She doesn't understand why the relationship has become strained and distant, or why it lost the "loving give and take" it used to have. "It used to be that we could hug each other, kiss each other. Now it seems it's a strain for her to do even that."

How Post-Reunion Develops

Nell is committed to working towards an improved future anyway. "I'll never let her go again if I have my choice. If she wants to go that will be her choice." Nell feels that Barb might break things off with her half-siblings if she weren't around. "If I died tomorrow, I'll bet you Barb wouldn't have seen them in a year from the time she went back home. I don't think she really truly cares that much; I think they do."

The fact that the two women have different temperaments accounts for at least some of the difficulty: "I hold everything in and she doesn't." Nell had to learn to deal with her daughter's more heart-on-the-sleeve kind of personality. Shortly after they met, they went to the seashore together for a week to "find out who we both are," and the second morning Nell discovered that she had hurt Barb's feelings because she had gone for a walk after awakening. "When I came back she was furious, and I asked her what was the matter and she said, 'You went without me!' I had no idea that it would bother her." But Nell has always been glad they shared that week. Barb was "so full of love and so thankful that she had found somebody." Her adoptive parents had died by then.

Another lesson Nell's learned about post-reunion is to try not to be judgmental of the returning adoptee; or, if that's not possible, at least not to express negative judgments too quickly or too openly. Her operating guideline became, "hold everything in; be as calm and cool as you can"—the result, she says, of being burned by her daughter's reactions time after time, but also the stance that comes more naturally. "I love her, but I don't love everything she does."

Trying to adjust to Barb's behavior, Nell altered her own in various ways. She stopped writing letters, for example, because Barb would frequently pick out some line and come back interrogating, "Now exactly what did you mean by that?" Also, Nell hesitates to buy Barb gifts now, because she returned them so often; "Nothing seems to suit her, and the fact that I gave it to her doesn't seem to mean a darn thing." And yet, Nell is aware that she's putting herself in a bind by accommodating her daughter in these ways; she knows it's important for birthmothers to be honest about their feelings. You can almost see *her throwing up her hands in defeat when she complains that adoptees like Barb "tell you to open up and be honest, so you are—and then they criticize!"*

For all its recent tensions, her post-reunion experience has also stretched her world view. "I've learned to accept a lot of things that I wouldn't accept before, in spite of the fact that Barb thinks I'm still very close-minded, I'm sure." In this connection, she refers to Barb's not being married as one of the things she's learned to accept, adding by way of explanation that "she isn't what I would call real normal."

Nine years into post-reunion, the women were split geographically, visits were becoming less frequent, and Nell had been hurt many times by Barb's hurt or displeasure over a myriad of incidents. Nell's inclinations to give were, in her words, "drying up." She had learned wariness.

A downward spiral for sure. Whether things would have turned around can not be known. Some weeks after our interview, Nell died peacefully in her sleep. Barb and another daughter were at her side.

When we interviewed her, Nell's analysis was that Barb must have gotten whatever it was she needed, but Nell was deeply hurt anyway. The pulling away felt like a rejection, and regardless of what it may have signified about Barb's development (healthy separation or something else), Nell didn't understand it, wasn't ready for it, and was uncomfortable in the relationship as a result. Her daughter's recent visits seemed motivated by obligation, not love or genuine interest, and Barb either couldn't or wouldn't explain why the rift had taken place. "I have a feeling that she must have had a limitation on what she wanted, and she got it and that's that," Nell concluded.

People who are familiar with the therapeutic process often talk in terms of the "work" that needs to be done in therapy, and the concept of work is applicable to post-reunion as well. Both birthmothers and adoptees have work to do, both on themselves and jointly on their relationship. Most fundamentally, the work of reunion is freeing oneself, insofar as possible, from the unfinished business and related emotional baggage which adoption produced. However, some experts maintain that scars will always remain, no matter how diligent the efforts.

By the time a birthmother and her adopted son or daughter are able to forge a genuinely adult-to-adult relationship—the kind of relationship a "regular" mother might have with a grown-up child—they have probably completed a scope of work that includes:

• Filling up the informational vacuum—i.e., finding out the story (birth heritage, adoption circumstances) and what's happened since in each person's life

• Resolving the psychological issues (to the extent possible) and coming to peace with the past—for birthmothers, whatever issues are associated with relinquishing their children; for adoptees, the issues associated with being given up

• Catching up present relationships—i.e., informing family members and others about the past; integrating the new relationship into other existing relationships

• Growing a shared history—accumulating experience, which will enhance feelings of connectedness, warmth, and closeness; putting pages in a joint book of memories

• Negotiating and inventing a mutually acceptable relationship—that is, deciding how to relate to one another in the post-reunion "ever after"

No one puts it exactly in these terms, of course. Even outside adoption, the nature of the relationship between mothers and grown children is imperfectly understood—an area which has largely escaped scholarly attention.[5] But it seems fair to say that post-reunion develops along two paths more or less simultaneously: the tangled path that leads backward to the past; and the newly laid track that is carrying birthmother and adult adoptee into their future. New opportunities are released by virtue of reunion and post-reunion, and their futures include possibilities for personal growth, and for relationships that did not exist before.

8

Post-Reunion Themes

Once they are set upon the post-reunion journey, birth-mothers and adoptees will inevitably discover several areas that command their attention or decision-making energies. We'll look at four of the most recurrent ones in this chapter: (1) genetic ties; (2) invisible history becoming visible information; (3) labeling each other; and (4) money matters.

Genetics At A Glance

Recent studies investigating how heredity and environment affect human development seem to point to the conclusion that the influence of genetics is far more powerful than previously thought. In addition to all the physical characteristics that are genetically transmitted, some personality traits which were once thought to be learned are now thought to be genetically-based or genetically "mediated" as well. Some of the new data involves studies of identical twins reared apart.[1] Some involves children reared in adoption.[2]

The researchers seem as surprised as anyone that earlier views about genetic versus environmental influences are being turned around by new data. "The biological children of a family and their adopted siblings didn't resemble each other at all in anything" says Sandra Scarr; it was "not what we expected to find." Yet, many adoption professionals who have observed adoptees after years in their adoptive homes have made similar observations, noting how often the children display talents, traits, and interests which nobody else in the adoptive family possesses.

Birthmothers' reunion experiences echo this finding about the strength of genetic influences. Because of the grown child whom they met as a stranger, nearly every one of the birthmothers we interviewed assigns greater weight to the role of hereditry than she did before her reunion. In the words of one of the husbands, "If you never believed in genetics before, you certainly will now." Many of the adoptive parents in this study also see it, as Carol's story about Joey and his adoptive mother illustrates.

> *"She said that when Joey was in kindergarten and early grade school, she spent many many tearful sessions with the social workers and the school teachers trying to understand what she could do to get him to be more like they were, and she finally decided that he was just a bundle of genes that came to them, that they were going to raise, but they could not change. She saw that he was very much who he was, from birth."*

The interest which two people share often forms a bridge on which they can meet. Imagine then the strength of the bridge constructed of shared genetics. Discovering that you look like this other person—that you have the same kind of hair, or hands, or facial structure, or that your interests or habits are similar—is an amazing experience. Discovering that you have the same sense of humor, or walk or smile the same way, or that your houses are furnished in the same style, or that you both have the same e e cummings poster hanging in your living room, are thrilling signs of commonality. Constance, who calls the numerous resemblances between herself and her daughter "fun little things," goes on to explain that they "add to the fact, or define the fact, that we are connected, that we are related, that at one time we were one." Some birthmothers and adoptees describe the experience of seeing the other person for the first time as "looking in a mirror."

Almost all the birthmothers in our sample report definite, strong, sometimes "uncanny" resemblances between their sons, daughters and themselves (or, in a handful of cases, between the child and someone else in the birth family); the resemblances are often confirmed by other, more "disinterested" onlookers.[3] Many also see likenesses between the child and the birthfather. This can be a potential source of ambivalence. If he hurt or angered the birthmother years ago, even if it was just a casual affair, she can be dismayed to encounter his presence in the child. One says:

> *"It reminds me of the hate I have for him. In the back of my mind, I'm thinking, 'Why did he have to have <u>any</u> influence on her?' "*

Another, also conveys her dismay:

> *"My son's voice reminds me of his birthfather's —that bothers me sometimes when he calls. It's the first thing that comes to my mind and I don't need that!"*

The evident commonalities which many birthmothers and adult adoptees share with one another provide a potent sense of connection. They would feel attached even without these manifestations, several assert, but the commonalities enhance the feeling.

> *"We have an ease of understanding and rapport because of our commonalities. . . . Having these things in common makes our connection with each other stronger. We have more to talk about that's interesting to each other. The relationship would be there without these resemblances but the similarities enhance it."*

Even before they meet, a photograph can be the proverbial picture that's worth a thousand words. One of the birthmothers tells how her teenage daughter's feelings about reunion changed from bad to glad just on the evidence of seeing their physical likeness:

"When she was thirteen or fourteen, the agency contacted her adoptive parents and said that I had written and wanted some information. She said, 'What does she care? What does she want to know about me now? She didn't keep me' . . . But she said that once she saw a picture of me and the kids, all those negative feelings left. . . . I guess one of the reasons she felt negative about me was that the agency told her I was short and fat and that I had long black hair. I'm actually 5'4" and fairly thin and I have brown hair, and I look almost exactly like her. I guess, thinking of somebody short and fat and with long black hair, she couldn't really relate to me. Once she saw the picture of me, things were a little bit different."

In a culture where reunion is not socially sanctioned, physical resemblances provide reunioning individuals with the validation that, in some sense, they belong together. (Perhaps this is also the reason that picture-taking, as well as showing the photos to anyone who will look, is a common reunion and post-reunion activity.) Early in reunion, the focus on genetic similarities also helps to make both adoptees and birthmothers feel more famil-iar with each other, easing the awkwardness and discomfort their meeting generates.

The power of these resemblances is so profound that some of the birthmothers feel that they never fully recognized the significance of having relinquished a child, or what adoption meant, until they saw their child in the flesh. Hattie, whose an-gry son bears a striking resemblance to his siblings, is one of these. "He belongs to his brothers and sisters. I watch him and I think, 'Oh my God, my genes must be pretty strong.' " She is no longer sure that his interests were better served in a good adoptive home (which his was) than they would have been with blood relations.

Betty was also "totally blown away by genes," as she puts it. "When you see an adult acting exactly like you, almost like a clone, it's almost scary. . . . Sometimes I actually think I'm in the twilight zone. This kid got into this other family and yet he's exactly like me." Norma too calls the similarity between herself and her twin sons enormous, "not explainable except through genes." They talk about it all the time. When Norma first met one of her twins, in fact, he announced to her, astonished: "My God, you look like Peter in drag!" In Geraldine's case, "The physical resemblance is pretty strong; when I look at her it's pretty touching."

Birthmothers simultaneously delight in enumerating their physical similarities with their children, and regret the unhealthy conditions they've transmitted. Generally speaking, though, it is the non-physical resemblances—the emotional similarities, common interests, and the like—that evoke a singular pleasure, partly because they were unexpected but also because these are the kinds of affinities on which close relationships thrive. An adoptee whose interests were always a mystery to his adoptive family, for example, may respond especially warmly to a similarly inclined birthmother, and she to him. Creative abilities such as art, music and writing, in particular, may produce these ties; several women in the sample discuss them.

Many adoptees, as we've discussed before, come to feel less "different" from other people by virtue of finding their biological roots. They begin to feel more natural—just like everybody else. As explained by Lila's daughter, Kate: "Seeing resemblances makes you feel like you're a regular person. It makes you feel real, normal, regular, average." The benefit may be even more pronounced when the resemblances with the birthmother (or other birth relatives) turn out to be especially striking. Faye's daughter thinks so and describes the discovery of commonalities as a kind of rebirth:

> *"The supreme pleasure for me was that when I found her, I found so many similarities that confirmed for me that I had not in fact made myself up, that I was and am who I am because of what*

*I had inherited. After thirty minutes of meeting
her, I was truly liberated."*

Another adopted woman explains that the discovery of similarities was confirming and validating; it helped clarify her own personality traits and claim parts of her identity in a way that was not possible before:

*"Every once in a while someone tells me I'm a
good writer. It somehow verifies me if my
birthfather has those same talents or interest.
When I learned, recently, that he was a corre-
spondent, something inside me jumped up and
said, 'Wow, that's right!' Pieces of the puzzle fell
into place. It's like someone giving you permission to be what you naturally are. It has to do
with my identity."*

One of the major commonalities that birthmothers and their children fasten upon is similiarity in their emotional styles—that is, whether the other individual expresses emotions openly or is more inhibited—especially if there was a difference between the adoptee and the adoptive family in this area. Several birthmothers point to common emotional styles as bulwarks of their relationships, though any common characteristics (temperament, interests, career choice, interpersonal style, etc.) seem to strengthen the bonds.

Consider Emily Sue:

*"She feels a real tie to me because, emotionally,
she doesn't cry a lot or show her emotions a lot,
and I'm like that too. Her parents are the exact
opposite and she has never understood her parents, and they've had a hard time understanding
her. They think that because she doesn't show
her feelings she doesn't have any feelings. I, of
course, know this isn't true. . . . Since she was
so different emotionally from her parents, she
really was interested to see how I was emotionally. It made her feel real good that we're alike. I*

think it's made her mother feel better too because she sees that I turned out all right. I think it helps her mother understand her better to have me around."

Consider Lila:

"Her personality is very close to mine—outgoing, friendly, we laugh a lot. She wants to be a social worker and her birthfather is a psychiatrist. And she has a real sense of people—she's very tuned in. As women, she and I are very much alike. Our favorite activity is shopping. We both enjoy sitting around, talking, and shopping. And we also both have a sense of trying to improve the lives of people who have difficult lives. Before I met her, she worked as a rape counselor, and I've done a lot of volunteer work too."

There are also instances when mother-child similarity turns out to be less than helpful to the post-reunion alliance. "We both need our independence," for example, or "we're both stubborn," or "we're both reserved," or "she has a terrible temper; she inherited it from me." Expressed by Helaine, both the best thing and the worst thing about her reunion is the discovered similarity between herself and her daughter:

"I'm pleased there's someone else like me, personality-wise. But I didn't want her to be like me because I didn't like me. I wanted her to be all the things I wasn't."

Additional examples of similarity abound in our interviews, including common likes and dislikes of both the weighty and fanciful variety. From Thelma: "Her favorite color is my favorite color (red); her favorite animal is my favorite animal (dragons)." From Constance: "We chose the same wallet style; we both have the same imported glass cups from Germany; my dog's name was Tasha, her cat's name was Sasha." From Marlene:

"We could have these deep long discussions about things; she's very much like me that way." From Phyllis: "We're both phone-aholics." From Adrienne: "I studied scenery design in college, which is a fairly obscure field, but that's where I found David, in the same college, studying scenery design." From several birth-mothers, mannerisms of various kinds: the way he glares (like his brother); the way she stands (like me); the way we cross our legs.

The birthfather's genetic presence is also cited time and again. By Bonnie: "He's very interested in forestry and his birthfather was very interested in that when he was his age." By Virginia: "I thought she was very much like my ex-husband and she worried that she was; she drinks too much sometimes when she's depressed, and he has an alcohol problem." By Marion: "My husband received a football scholarship and that's Allen's love too." By Charlene:

> "He looks a lot like his father; he stands like him, he points like him, he laughs like him. It's absolutely amazing how similar he is in a lot of his personal characteristics and idiosyncrasies. His ability to paint, his ability with music is like his birthfather. Neither of them is very physical or sports-minded. It really amazes me that he could be so much like his birthfather in so many ways without every having met the person."

Overwhelmingly in our sample, the physical similarities that people immediately saw, coupled with the other similarities they came to know, added up to what the birthmothers considered their common heritage. "My experience has given me a new respect for genetics" is the way one birthmother expressed it. In many adoptive families, there has been a corresponding realization that traits in their adopted children which puzzled them may have emanated from the birthmother or father. As one expressed it: "I always wondered why Johnny was so athletic when we're all couch potatoes."

Processing Information: Learning the Truth and Coming to Grips With It

The work of post-reunion, as we suggested in Chapter 7, includes filling in the informational vacuum. It is a task that belongs on the adoptee's agenda, of course, but it is also an important post-reunion activity for the birthmother. What she learns about her child's adoptive home, and about how the child has fared over the years, has important bearing on her post-reunion state. Such information has the power either to affirm her adoption decision (and its wake of associated consequences) or to deny its validity.

A few of the birthmothers in our sample concluded that adoption worked out "for the best" both for their child and themselves. Beverly is one of these.

Beverly's Story

Beverly and Lil were reunited as a result of each one's having signed up with a reunion registry, five years apart: Beverly in her mid-40s, Lil in her late 20s. She is amazed to be "one of the lucky ones" since neither she nor her daughter was required to undertake a long or arduous search. Neither of them, she guesses, would have done so.

Into the second year of post-reunion, Beverly presents the relationship with her daughter as largely conflict-free. The one difficulty lies in the strain placed on Lil. Her adoptive parents supported the idea of searching in the abstract but became threatened, her adoptive mother especially, after a reunion actually took place and Lil chose to maintain the contact with Beverly beyond the "give me my information" inquiry. Reflecting on the progress of their relationship, Beverly believes that Lil's feelings about her adoptive mother have sometimes caused her "not to draw back, but not to go forward as much as I think Lil would like." As it stands now, Lil and her adoptive mother just don't discuss the reunion. Beverly wishes the other woman could recognize that she has no wish to usurp the maternal role.

This concern notwithstanding, Beverly is thrilled at hav-

ing found her daughter, and in fortunate circumstances. Lil is enjoying a full, happy life and has a loving childhood behind her. According to Beverly, "She is better off than I could have believed in terms of being physically and mentally healthy. She is happily married. Her life is really pretty good. She had wonderful parents; she was very loved, and is still loved by them." Beverly judges that Lil's upbringing was better than she could have provided, especially in the early years, and believes "our lives have probably both turned out better in some ways" as a result of the adoption. (She never married, never had other children, and pursued a business career.) If she had it to do over, she would probably do it again, even though she was pressured into adoption by her parents and calls it "the worst thing that ever happened to me."

The fact that Beverly and Lil live in different parts of the country—mother in the Northwest and daughter in the South —enables their still young reunion to move at a gradual pace. The roots are deepening via letters and phone calls, in which both women feel more comfortable expressing their feelings than they would face-to-face. After their last visit, Beverly felt "such a bond" growing between them, but is cautious "not to overwhelm" Lil. "Although I know she wants a relationship with me, I try to hold back because I don't want to lay a lot on her. I think what we want is pretty similar—just a good, very special friendship."

Compared to many other post-reunion situations, this one is rather self-contained. No one else in Beverly's family has actually met Lil yet. They're scattered around the country and she's not that close to them anyway. Lil, however, is pregnant for the first time—a result, Beverly feels sure, of now knowing who her own mother is. The pregnancy, notes Beverly, creates a new and special bond between them. Besides, "our personalities are really quite similar."

Mothers who learn that their child had a "good" home, or were "better off" than they would have been without adoption, enjoy greater post-reunion equanimity than those who discover unhappy facts. The latter scenario means "feeling responsible when I was not responsible," which adds a new load of guilt to already overloaded circuits. Not infrequently, the guilt is turned into a moral imperative—to figure out what's necessary and provide it because "I owe her." It doesn't matter if the post-reunion going gets rough because "I couldn't live with myself by slamming the door again in her face."

Although a birthmother may want to come to the rescue and "fix it," the past is not easily rewritten. There is little a woman can do, for example, if she learns that her child was not adopted until age two; or that the adoptive father was an alcoholic, or mentally unstable, or prone to violence. There is nothing she can do when she's told that the adoptive mother favored another child and that hers got second-class treatment. The discovery that a daughter was raped by the adoptive father or brother, or that a son is bisexual, or that her own unwed pregnancy was re-enacted by her daughter, is difficult to accept. The discovery that well-to-do adoptive parents were unwilling to pay for college can make a birthmother furious, especially if she is able and willing to pay college costs herself. All these things happened.

Adoptees who reveal such unsettling and shocking accounts to their birthmothers are apt to choose their moment carefully. Demonstrating concern for each other's feelings in the early post-reunion period, they frequently delay distressing revelations until months or years into post-reunion, as this twenty-two-year old did:

> "When I first met them I thought, 'Oh my God, I'm going to have to tell them about my life,' and I didn't want to because I was concerned about how it would feel to hear these things. I started to tell them more when I knew that all the parents were going to meet, and I didn't want them to be surprised. What I thought at the time was, what they found was worse than what I found."

In our sample, there are more instances of birthmothers encountering unpleasant truths than of adoptees' encountering such material, but adoptees are often confronted with bitter realities also. They may find out that their birthfather is an alcoholic or drug abuser; or that he is in prison; or that they are the product of rape. They may be pained or disappointed by other kinds of discoveries: like the daughter who learned that the birthmother who surrendered her was in her twenties, not a teenager, as she had believed, or the son who was nonplussed to find out that his heritage was Latin American: "After all these years of saying Spic, now I *am* one." These things all happened.

From the birthmother's standpoint, the information-processing task means catching up on the child's life in the pre-reunion years. The operational question is, "Are you okay and what kind of life have you had?" Everyone in the adoption triad seems aware of the question intuitively, judging from the frequency with which post-reunion participants spend hour after hour going over "all the photographs" as though the succession of images will somehow fill up the vacuum and erase the time warp as well. (It won't, but it does seem to help.)

The adoptee in post-reunion also has a difficult assignment, because he is playing informational catch-up on several fronts at once: learning his adoption story; learning about his birthmother as a person, her current family connections, and the rest of the family tree; learning about the birthfather's side. What are the family "cultures" like? Who are all the relatives? What do they do? How do they spend their time? Celebrate holidays? What kinds of gifts do they give? The adoptee must integrate all this information and at the same time let go of the fantasies that have been his or her emotional mainstay for so long.

Occasionally, a piece of news can be so traumatic that the adoptee's interest in going further stops. It happened to Debora, the woman whose son was acquainted with his birthfather as a neighbor before he knew the man's identity as his birthfather. "Once he found out who his father was, it was like he didn't want to know anything about his history." In the case of Thelma's daughter, on the other hand, the girl's unwillingness to hear Thelma's story is part and parcel of her discomfort with the fundamental reality of being adopted; at the moment she's gone as far as she can go. Thus, while a few adoptees in the sample are refusing to hear more than they already have, they are the exceptions. More often, adoptees' desire for information is a hunger manifested as either a healthy appetite or an unlimited craving.

Faye recalls:

> *"I told her about my experiences with the agency for the two years before I gave her up. I told her about my life. She asked me hundreds and hundreds of questions about our family history, generations back on both sides of my family, and her father's family . . . and then there were more questions. Every time she comes, she asks more questions, and I'm glad to answer them."*

Acquiring their informational legacy produces various types of benefits for adoptees: the identity "clicks" ("so that's where my writing ability comes from"); the assuaged curiosities ("I always wondered where I got these funny toes"); the helpful hints ("now I know what to do about this unwanted facial hair"). There is a good deal to absorb, both intellectually and emotionally. Integrating it all into one's sense of self can take many years. When the discoveries are far afield from the adoptee's prior experience, integrating them may turn out to be more troublesome than otherwise, but correct information, however surprising or unpleasant, is almost always preferred to the amalgam of secrecy, half-truths, and guesses that was available before.

For birthmothers, an unanticipated result of post-reunion is that these women learn details about their *own* stories that they never knew. One woman discovered that her mother threatened her boyfriend and got rid of him years back—hardly an isolated occurrence in adoption annals. In another case, a grown adoptee met her birthfather, who passed along more information than the birthmother ever knew, including the fact that he had given money to her brother to help her out. Still another birthmother learned, twenty-nine years later, that her boyfriend's mother went along with his plan to marry her, but it was her own mother who "absolutely refused." (They married four years and two pregnancies later, at which point her mother "just threw up her hands and said, 'If this is what she wants, fine!'") Finding out such details often leaves a birthmother dazed and angry; she realizes that she was lied to and robbed of control. But the new information also enables her to possess her own history fully for the first time.

Mini-mysteries that existed for years are also suddenly solved when post-reunion lifts the veil of secrecy. In one family, a birthmother's brother and son felt intuitively that there might be a relative who was never spoken of, but were always told they were imagining things. They were relieved to find the rumor was true. In another household, family members understand now why a woman was always "sort of a Scrooge," around Christmas. More than one birthmother mentions that her teenage son understands now why she "pushed" birth control. Another cites her son's newfound understanding of why, when his girlfriend became pregnant, she and her husband provided money for an abortion, adamant that the girl not surrender a child. A few birthmothers tell us that their friends suddenly understood why they were always strongly involved with children. (Millie, a birthmother who adopted six children herself, in addition to her biological five, never "made the connection" until post-reunion.) Among Betty's friends, the mini-mystery of why Betty did not want children was solved: "some friends thought I was selfish not wanting children; now they understand."

The information exchanged between mother and child often turns up a host of uncanny coincidences of names, addresses, tastes and the like that people note with wonder and that introduce an aura of otherworldliness into the post-reunion space. A few refer to them as "synchronicities," the term Carl Jung used to describe events that were meaningfully related but could not be explained by the laws of cause and effect. Thus, we find that a birthfather's name was Silas and his daughter was living on Silas Drive. . . . Millie's son's name was Thomas and Millie's first adopted child had the name Thomas.

. . . an eighteen-year-old birthfather joined the Navy when he found out his girlfriend was pregnant, and his daughter was in the Navy when she was located twenty-two years later. Then there's the story of the birthmother and her daughter, each of whom behaved out of character in order to purchase the same corduroy jacket in 1976 (different color, different cities). How much of this kind of thing is genetic? How much is evidence of mother-to-child communications in the womb? How much strictly coincidence?

A related story concerns Nell, whose younger daughter (a daughter she raised) was told by a psychic that she had a sister. The conversation took place a few months before Nell had informed *her* about any such person, so the daughter told the psychic "you're wrong" and they dropped it. Some time later, she ran into the psychic and shared the truth, "You were right. I *do* have a big sister but I didn't know it," and the woman was not surprised. "I knew it. Even though you denied it, I knew it—but I don't argue with people in those circumstances." Prior to reunion, another birthmother was told by a psychic that her daughter could be found living in New Mexico. She wasn't then, but she is now.

Should I Call You Mother?

Outside adoption, and traditionally, the concept of mother usually means two things: the woman who gives birth *and* the child's primary caretaker. Inside adoption, the "nature" and the "nurture" aspects of mother are split between two different individuals. Who is the "real" mother?

Calling one woman the birthmother and the other the adoptive mother doesn't seem to answer the question for many people, possibly because it's cumbersome, more likely because the impulse to designate only one individual as mother is so deeply and strongly ingrained in all of us. The word conveys specialness, a privileged status. "Which one do you think of as your mother?" adoptees in post-reunion are often asked, which is another way of asking, to whom do you grant this prized title? Similarly, "What does he call you?" is one of the first things post-reunion birthmothers are asked, the inquirer's way of getting a quick sense of what their relationship is all about.

Birthmothers are acutely aware that the confusion about language is really a confusion about status. Phyllis, for example, explains her ambiguous position this way.

> *"Someone said to me, 'Oh, you're Sharon's real mother,' and I had to say, 'No, Harriet is her real mother. I'm her biological mother.' I couldn't let it slide. But Sharon always introduces me as her real mother. I always get a twinge of guilt when she says that. It still feels very uncomfortable to me when she refers to me as her Mom. I get this warm feeling rushing over me that maybe I'm okay, maybe she does love me, but yet I feel I don't deserve it."*

The problem of what to call whom also reflects the anomoly of the post-reunion relationship, which is often described as both a yes and no at the same time. "I'm his mother but not his mother," one says. "My daughter who's not my daughter," another puts it. "I won't be her Mom but she is forever my daughter," according to someone else. Strictly speaking, such sentences don't make any sense, but somehow because of the circumstances, they do.

Because thoughts and feelings often are out of sync with the labels, birthmothers try to find analogies to the post-reunion relationship ("well, it's sort of like a—") but mostly conclude that there's nothing else like it. It shares elements of other relationships—with other children, with friends, with a sister, or a mother, or a new love—but is not the same as any of them. Betty, who works as an actress, compares her relationship with her son to her relationship with the theater:

> *"It's being totally satisfied and being exactly where I want to be, and willing to go with the ups and downs. Like getting on stage in front of 8000 people and saying, 'What the hell am I*

doing? This is so scary!' and yet knowing that's exactly where I want to be, and getting out there and doing it anyway. That's what I liken the relationship to, because it's scary and yet I want to be there."

Looking for familiar roles that might serve as models, some people have suggested using step-relationships as a model, as we mentioned in Chapter 5. The role of godparent might be a useful comparison too; it avoids the unpleasant connotations of step, conveys the intergenerational feature, and suggests a responsible brand of caring that goes beyond friendship. In-law relationships are also analogous in some ways to post-reunion relationships. But such comparisons are of minimal help to birthmothers who are experiencing the tension and role ambiguity of "my child who's not my child." One suggests the analogy: "Think about a friend whom you nurture a lot."

Asked to identify other relationships with which to compare post-reunion, a few birthmothers to whom we spoke take the position that it *is* the same, now, as their relationship with their other children. A greater number, though, have found that trying to squeeze the adult adoptee into the familiar role of "my child" doesn't work.

A birthmother in a long-established reunion:

"I love her but I don't worry about her like I worry about my boys. And I didn't realize it until one time when she left here in the middle of a snow storm and I said, 'Make sure you call me when you get there.' Meantime, my son wanted to use the car and I said absolutely not. It wasn't the same feeling. And I felt guilty about that at first but it can't be the same feeling. It can't be."

A birthmother in a new reunion:

"I worry about her. I try not to think about it too much. I know she's got parents that can worry about her the way I worry about my other kids. I try not to give her advice, not to be too much

like a parent would be. In fact, one of the rea-
sons I don't do that is, I guess, I'm insecure
about our relationship, and I think maybe she'll
just thumb her nose at me and say, 'What are
you to me anyway, you're not my Mom, you
don't have any right to tell me that'. . . . I don't
treat her the same way I treat my other kids.
With them, if they get mad at me or if I do
something they think is mean, I know they're
going to be around tomorrow. I think she would
be too, but I don't know that for sure."

Despite the considerable difficulties of labeling one another, the majority of birthmothers we interviewed nevertheless report feeling parental towards their child. And, regardless of whether they feel obligated in the sense of "have to" or not obligated in the sense of "want to," just about all also have feelings of responsibility toward the adoptee. They qualify what they say, however. Feeling "parental" may mean feeling like a friend as well as like a parent; or like a parent "but without the parent-child history"; or like a parent only sometimes. Some disclaim feeling parental at all.

Assessing their children's motives, the majority also tell us that their sons and daughters were *not* seeking parental relationships at the outset. What these adult adoptees did want instead is variously described: being connected to blood relatives, being a member of a family; a sense of belonging; a sense of self, being loved unconditionally, relationships with brothers and sisters, new friendships, etc.[4] These are also the answers the mothers offer when asked about why their children are *continuing* in a post-reunion relationship now, as opposed to having their needs satisfied and leaving.

Ambiguities and all, reunioning pairs have to settle on an answer to "What shall we call each other?" the same way that newly married people have to work out what to call their in-laws. "Hey, you" won't do, and the situation can become difficult if the individuals have different ideas about what feels comfortable. A birthmother whose son or daughter wants to call her

Mother, but who prefers being called by her first name, is revealing not just a preference for language but her own discomfort with the maternal title. Then too, comfort can change with experience. Hattie's son, for example, started by calling her Ma, then changed to a first name basis. In another case, the mother wanted the adoptee to stop using her first name but was nervous about asking.

To defend themselves against feelings of disloyalty and betrayal, one approach adoptees use is to call their birthmother Mom if the adoptive mother has always been Mother, or some similar tactic to keep the differentiation clear. First names are also popular. And many adoptees who routinely address their birthmothers by their first names will break the pattern with a "hey, Ma," or Mom or Mother when they're feeling particularly venturesome or playful or secure.

The issue of "What shall we call each other?" symbolizes the essential ambiguity of the post-reunion relationship: indeterminate roles. The reason the ambiguity is so troublesome perhaps is that role identity *per se* so often defines things for us. We behave differently according to whether we are worker or boss, student or teacher, parent or child. The roles, and the labels that identify them, contain a multitude of information about what is and what is not appropriate, obviating the need we would otherwise have to make constant and innumerable decisions about each and every detail of daily living.

At the moment birthmothers and their children first meet, they meet as roles: abandoning birthmother (the woman who gave me up), rejected adoptee (the baby I gave away)—but these are roles for which no models or guidelines exist. More importantly, no one wants them anyway. Once post-reunion begins, these labels cease to fit in any case, and the individuals look to traditional roles (child, friend, aunt, sister, etc.) for guidance, but they have only limited appropriateness for these "funny mothers" of "funny children." Being unable to name the role, unfortunately, is a very real deterrent to feeling comfortable in the relationship. It's difficult to own an experience you can't name or to feel secure when the territory is limbo.[5]

Eventually, some reunioning pairs are able to transcend traditional role conceptions, becoming liberated from old labels instead of being confused or confined by them. Norma and her twin sons, for example, have a relationship which she describes as "a very complex friendship with an older woman who might be able to teach them some things." Nora anticipates something similar with her son, creating for herself a role we might call "accepting elder":

> *"I think he's going to come back and get in touch with me when he needs someone to hear what's happening with him. I'm not his parent but I can be that listening ear and that accepting person that a parent can't always be."*

What Norma and Nora have done is to tease out exactly which elements of other relationships apply and to recombine them into a new conception. What remains is for someone to give it a new name.

"Voluntary intimates," a term that's been used to describe friendship relationships,[6] would apply quite nicely to post-reunion too. Or, going a step further, we could also call the post-reunion relationship "voluntary family"—which differentiates it from the usual brand of family (the one you can't choose, according to the old joke) and which captures the essential contradiction that so many birthmothers feel.

Money Matters

An adoptee who grew up in lower middle class circumstances was reunited with a birthmother who lived in an affluent suburb, wore expensive clothes, and sent her other children to private schools. When people asked the daughter how she felt about finding her birth family so well off, her eyes filled with tears. It just didn't matter, she said; her feelings about them had nothing to do with money, and she was distressed that anyone would interpret her relationship with them in financial terms. Money isn't what she was looking for. On this, the birthmothers we interviewed would agree.

Despite the fact that money has the potential to strain interpersonal relationships of all kinds, in the post-reunion relationships we heard, it is one stress that is relatively lacking. Judging from these women's experiences, money isn't one of the "little minefields" for which reunioning pairs need to watch. But the subject does come up.

Money matters present themselves in two forms. The first issue is: do birthmothers feel a sense of financial responsibility to their adopted offspring and, if so, what do they decide to do about it? The second question is: how do birthmothers feel about these children in terms of inheritance; do they want them as heirs? (State laws generally provide that adoptees inherit from the adoptive parents, not the birthparents.)

As far as day-to-day living is concerned, the answer to whether birthmothers feel financially responsible, if our sample can be deemed representational, is somewhere between somewhat and not at all. Particularly when sons and daughters grew up in financially comfortable circumstances, these birthmothers don't feel that they have any financial responsibility, or that anyone would expect them to have it. It's not an issue that comes to the fore because "he's well taken care of."

If, on the other hand, adoptees grew up in needier circumstances, the mothers frequently want to do something, not because they feel obligated but because they're unhappy about how things worked out and want to help. They may be especially eager to give in this way if their son or daughter didn't have the kinds of material advantages that *they* would have provided (lessons or vacations or whatever). Still and all, many women who feel, "Sure I owe her some things" don't include money in the package, even if they hasten to add that "if she needs something, I hope I can be there to provide it." There is a willingness to give which signifies a special relationship, but the giving is not felt as a duty, even though it is often buttressed by guilt. Listen to these two birthmothers for instance:

"I don't feel I owe her anything, but I have feelings of responsibility in the sense of wanting to do things for her and be sure she's okay. I have

*a desire to help her financially, but I don't feel
any obligation."*

*"My son's quite in debt. I loaned him $3000 and
there doesn't seem to be any sign that I'm going
to get it back. It's going to take forever. But my
feeling is that it's a small gift; it isn't very much. I
have some feelings that I got away scot-free.
Scot-free, ha!"*

Many birthmothers use gifts or loans as expressions of their
desire to give and as symbols of the parent-child bond. Joan,
for example, wishes her daughter would ask *her* for the loan
she needs instead of asking her adoptive parents, because that
would signify Jenny's feeling that she can rely on Joan for help.
Willingness to accept gifts is often interpreted by birthmothers
as a sign of comfort with the relationship, as Betty's comment
also suggests.

*"When they needed a $300 new crib and I of-
fered to buy it, he said no. But now it's his birthday and he wanted this computer piece that
costs $125 and his wife told me, 'go ahead and
buy it,' so little by little we're getting there."*

Several birthmothers have volunteered help with college expenses. Several also pick up expenses that are specifically associated with the post-reunion relationship: air tickets to visit
one another, for example, or meal tabs when they go out. But
at least one woman makes a point of going Dutch because she
thinks it reinforces the idea that the relationship should be
adult-to-adult.

We also talked to birthmothers who would like to give
more than they're giving but who are limited by their own financial conditions:

*"My daughter's stressed financially. Unfortu-
nately I am too. She has a car that falls apart,
she has needs. She'd like to get divorced and*

can't afford it. I wish I could give her enough
money every month so she could live alone."

It's also possible that the adoptee is better off financially than
the birthmother and that the women may have to impose limits
on the kinds of things they can do together. For Nell, for example, a steady diet of get-away weekends is out of the question:

"Barb has inherited so much that there is abso-
lutely no need (from me). This trip we took, I
insisted on paying my half, and when it was all
finished I said to her, 'This is going to be the end
of this because I just don't have that kind of
money.' We needed the trip at that time, but I
don't need it every year or every five years."

Do birthmothers want these children to be their heirs? The
answer, in most cases we studied, is yes, but being an heir has
varying meanings, all the way from "equal with my other children" to simply receiving a meaningful keepsake. A key factor
that enters into these women's thinking about inheritance is
whether they are married and have other children, including
stepchildren, and the degree of financial need that each potential recipient is likely to have. Many also take into account how
much the adoptee is likely to inherit from the adoptive parents.
Some of the birthmothers haven't turned their attention to the
subject of legacies because their reunions are too new. Only a
few birthmothers have formalized their wishes in a will. Nonetheless, a good many have definite ideas about what they want
to leave to whom, and about the message these decisions are
meant to convey.

Carol, for instance, has decided that it's less important
to respond to the unequal financial circumstances in which her
children will eventually find themselves than to affirm the equality of their place in her heart:

"My husband and I have an estate that will be
divided between his three children and my
three. I thought about this quite a bit when I

realized that Joey's adoptive parents would leave him financially well off, while my girls can't really expect much from their father. For this reason I've thought about whether or not it would be fair to give the same amount to Joey . . . but I've decided that my initial instincts were correct, and that it's not the money but the thought. And the thought I want to leave with Joey is that he is equally one of my three children. So for that reason he will be one of my heirs, equally."

Marcie has taken the opposite approach, deciding to customize the amount to the individuals rather than giving the same to each:

"We have a mixed family here. I have two, he has one—a disabled son who lives in Arkansas. We've tried to do whatever we felt was appropriate for the child, rather than letting them share equally. She has her adoptive parents. My kids also have their father who's remarried. It's very complicated. So I didn't provide for her other than that I expect my other children to share personal items. But as far as sharing the real estate or financial stuff, no."

Marlene doesn't plan to evenly split her children's bequests. She is thinking about giving Paula a bequest of a stipulated amount:

"My boys have nobody else who will leave them anything, but she does have her adoptive parents and they're much better off financially than I am. She has given me my watch and some other jewelry and I would want her to have whatever she gave me, and some keepsake of mine. I don't think there'll be that much to share. But then I think, maybe I'll leave her a set amount of money. But I certainly don't think

that what we have should be split three ways evenly."

Ethel is thinking along the same lines as Marlene. She is concerned about how her other children would feel if Lucy's inheritance were identical to theirs:

"We are still in the process of deciding how our possessions and assets will be divided among the children. I feel that Lucy should receive a fair portion of my savings and an item or two from the household, but our other children might resent our leaving their father's estate equally to her, and I don't think she would expect that. . . . We'll need an attorney to help us determine a fair division of our assets among our five children, six grandchildren, and one great-grandchild so far."

Irene has "a lot of mixed emotions" about what Rita's share should be compared to Irene's two sons, her younger sister, and her husband's daughter by a previous marriage. Rita "will never lack for anything material," and "the boys are the ones that came up the hard way; they had the least and I owe it most to them." Still, "it's very confusing."

Some birthmothers have paid no attention to inheritance issues. One expressed her lack of decision this way: "I don't have much money and I don't have anything that's worth anything." Some can sidestep hard decisions about how to cut the pie because there are no other children to consider. (You may recall from Chapter 3 that Adrienne, for one, is leaving her twin sons everything, and is delighted to have someone to whom to leave it.) Another group aren't thinking about whether they'll bequeath money to these children because the adoptees are well off and/or will inherit money from their adoptive family. But many birthmothers spend time and energy turning the inheritance issue over in their minds because they see this kind of decision as symbolic of their feelings of maternal connection and responsibility.

We know of a birthmother who received a letter from her daughter's adoptive parents stating that, with reunion, the daughter now had somebody else she could turn to for financial assistance; they were adjusting their will accordingly. The couple sent a copy of the letter to the daughter as well. With this one stroke, the birthmother maintains, the adoptive parents "dumped" the daughter.

We stated earlier that money matters don't usually provoke problems in post-reunion relationships, but we won't know for some years how these sons and daughters will ultimately feel about, and interpret, the decisions their birthmothers are making about legacies. Inheritance symbolizes being part of a family. Inheritance can also mean being cared for. These birthmothers recognize that it can be used to affirm, even underline, an equality of family position or to imply (good intentions notwithstanding) that the adoptee is somehow different or apart.

9

About Birthfathers

He might have been an adolescent of sixteen or a man in his fifties. He might have been a thoughtless cad who abandoned a woman in trouble, or a frightened young innocent who did what he was told. It's possible that he never knew his girlfriend was pregnant. It's also possible that he was told and then consulted no further, stripped of influence by parents and social workers, and given his walking papers. In the unlikely event that he was not cast in the role of villain and banished, it's possible too that he stood by the birthmother during her pregnancy, lending whatever support he could, including the offer of marriage.

In short, although fathers have become more equal parenting partners with mothers in recent years, these adoptions took place when an unwanted pregnancy was mainly the woman's problem.[1] The unmarried fathers did not usually participate in the relinquishment decision and, if asked, generally agreed with it on practical grounds, seeing no other options. In the past, the general view was that the male had gotten the female "in trouble" (because men's sex drives were stronger, and women didn't know much about sex). All in all, a man's role in these events was not something he would be likely to look back upon today with pleasure or pride.[2]

Consequently, it's hard for birthmothers and adoptees to guess what they can expect of these men twenty or more years later. Where are these men now, and how are they likely to react to a phone call out of the past? What happened to

Victor, for example, the college junior whose parents didn't want him to marry his girlfriend because one was Jewish and the other wasn't, and besides, he was pre-med and couldn't be "encumbered"? What happened to Sean, the drama student who offered to marry Norma but was refused? (And how embarrassing for Norma to have to tell her son that she can't remember Sean's last name, even after hypnosis.) What about the man who dated Marlene for six months, but failed to mention that he was out on bail for one crime and that he had a wife and child in another state? And what about the birthfather of Ethel's daughter, her mother's boyfriend who was living in their house? What did all these men do with their lives? How did their stories turn out? Did they ever wonder what happened to the young women and the babies they fathered, or did they put the unhappy episodes out of their minds?

Birthfathers are in even deeper closets than birthmothers. Coming out of those closets to search for their children is comparatively rare, though the numbers have increased in the last few years as reunion generally has become more acceptable. At conferences and support group meetings where people gather to discuss reunion and post-reunion, the rooms are typically filled with women; men in these rooms are most likely to be adoptees. The few birthfathers who show up are conspicuous by their presence. Other attendees often hope that these brave men will illuminate "the birthfather perspective" and that they can help birthmothers and adoptees approach birthfathers who reside in *their* histories, or simply understand them better. As adoptees and birthmothers become less mysterious to each another, the enigmatic birthfather becomes a figure of increasing importance.

One man who has, Stan, laughingly admits, "We're coming out of the woodwork." Granted, a handful of individuals cannot be asked to represent the total population, but the men who are speaking up indicate that birthfatherhood has been just about as misunderstood as birthmotherhood. One birthfather to whom we've spoken, Stuart, never had children until twenty years after his first child was relinquished; he felt that it would be disloyal to that child—a rationale we've already discussed with respect to birthmothers. An ex-marine who lived by the marine code "never abandon a buddy," he's come to look upon his youthful history as a violation of that code. He's searching for his former girlfriend and his child now because he feels he abandoned them both. He wants to make amends.

Another birthfather, Marty, searched for his son with his wife's assistance when the boy's birthmother refused to participate. "Who gave you the right to corner pain?" Marty's wife asked the birthmother; "It's affected his life, his marriages, and his parenting." Marty adds, "There's this emptiness inside you. If a birthfather's in pain, the pain doesn't go away." When he found his son, the young man asked, "How long have you been looking for me?" Marty's answer: "Forever." A birthfather we'll call Bill tells us: "A birthfather's suffering is no different from any other person's. The quality of suffering is not differentiated by sex." Men have different barriers to overcome in having a reunion, he points out, but there *are* barriers.

In their roles of birthfathers, men have cultural and emotional biases with which to deal. For one thing, any father's attachment to his children in our society has always been considered less profound than a mother's and less central to his sense of self. Men have also been socialized to keep their emotions in check. Coming to grips with oneself as a birthfather involves dealing with issues which have nothing to do with adoption. A man who confronts his birthfatherhood must ask himself where fathering fits in his identity and what kind of emotions he has about these issues. Our cultural ideals of what's masculine and what's good parenting are out of sync. We've made it easy for men to back away from taking responsibility for unmarried parenting.

"How do I know the child is mine?" is the first thing some birthfathers say when they learn about a pregnancy—or a reunion. It may sound defensive, especially to a birthmother who feels abandoned, but the age-old truth is that he can never know with the same certainty that she can. (A reliable test of paternity is a recent development.) Bill is a birthfather who contends that we need mechanisms that will allow men like himself to come forward with impunity. Some are hiding because

BirthBond

they're scared away by birthmothers' anger. Some are afraid they'll be asked for financial support. Some are afraid of telling their present wives for the same reason that birthmothers are afraid of telling their present husbands. These are new issues for everybody.

Marty is in the minority of birthfathers-in-reunion, because he did the searching. Usually, adoptees initiate the search, even though it tends to be a secondary search for them —secondary in the sense that it takes place *after* the reunion with the birthmother, and secondary too in terms of its psychic importance. Indeed, a segment of adoptees who have been reunited with their birthmothers evince little or no interest in going further to meet their other birthparent; some point to close, loving relationships with their adoptive fathers as the reason. Sometimes, though, the opposite dynamic occurs and a relationship with a birthfather assumes especial significance, filling a "father void" and providing an adult adoptee with greater sustenance than the relationship with the birthmother does. It's possible for an adult adoptee to need "daddy" more than "mommy." It's also possible, regardless of which parent is needed more, for an adoptee to find that his or her birthfather is accepting of a post-reunion relationship when the birthmother is not. That's what happened when Audrey found Bill.

Bill's Story

Bill is a birthfather who feels a special obligation to the twenty-eight-year old daughter who showed up three years ago. The girl's birthmother, Hazel, will not establish a relationship with Audrey because she is fearful of her husband's wrath. (She watched him practically disown his own unmarried daughter when she became pregnant.) So Bill has committed himself to a post-reunion relationship which is painful, complicated, and a severe strain on his other family ties, but "the rest of the family will just have to deal with it as best they can." A soft-spoken, gentle man in his fifties, he seems slightly dazed by the endless reverberations which post-reunion is spewing forth. But, however confused and uncertain he feels, he is dogged in his inten-

tion to keep going. He sees it as a responsibility. He almost gave up at one point but he got a call from his daughter's friend: "Audrey needs to hear from you."

It was not the fact of a reunion which came as a shock to Bill. He knew about Hazel's pregnancy and participated in making the adoption arrangements shortly before he was sent overseas by the military. He remembers feeling angry and trapped, because he thought she might be trying to "hook" him into marriage, but she wasn't the person he wanted to marry. Being shipped overseas came something of a relief, but, as the years passed, he vaguely assumed that either Hazel or the child would seek the other out and that, somehow, he would become involved too. He wanted the contact. Even so, when the call came, he found himself wondering "what does she want?" "You go through a self-protective phase," he says.

The shock lay in Bill's discovery of how painful his daughter's adoption had been. "I don't feel guilty," he told her when they met. "Cheer up; you will," she countered. He proceeded to learn that she had been sexually abused as a child and had lived a "Cinderella, sweep-the-halls" kind of childhood. The young woman he met was "a devastated person." Like other birthparents who are confronted with these kinds of terrible revelations, Bill now believes that adoption is an evil institution. He had felt the loss of his child but had also believed the myths about perfect adoptive families. "My debt is to bring about change," he says, and he is trying to find ways to make amends, both to his daughter as an individual and in some broader way as well. These days, he also finds himself thinking about Hazel and re-evaluating their relationship. He's sad about her suffering.

Bill is hungry for advice about how to deal with Audrey. She's very angry—understandably so—and Bill describes himself as someone who doesn't deal very well with angry people. She is also tangled up in issues of loyalty and gratitude, not infrequent among adoptees, the results of which he first witnessed at what he ruefully calls "the six-hour lunch." He picked up the check he recalls, which is what he would have done with any of his other children, and the gesture provoked an agony of *examination, recrimination, and dialogue about Audrey's not wanting to be beholden to him.*

Sometimes his daughter lapses into long silences which she doesn't explain and he doesn't understand. Sometimes she disappears in the middle of occasions they had planned to share. Other times there are discomfiting sexual reverberations when Audrey, a grown woman, wants to be held like a child and the scene becomes reminiscent of "the way she was created." There is a pattern of attack and retreat, reach and reject, that's like a mating relationship, Bill observes.

It's possible that some of the issues between them will never be resolved. "It's a very uneasy relationship. I try to be available, but I'm not a psychiatrist." And in the absence of mutual history, every incident seems important and takes a long time to get over. Nothing gets sloughed off by either of them by virtue of familarity. Living on opposite sides of the country, as they do, adds to the difficulty of resolving conflicts.

Still, recovery and repair is only part of the story. Bill also speaks of his daughter with fatherly pride. She has taken his last name. She's "a very unusual person," a talented writer, to whom he's proud to be connected. Then too, their pain unites them. "We're the only people who really give a damn" about what happened.

Bill is the kind of man who was in the delivery room when his other children were born. He tries to give them everything. It's difficult for him to reconcile that kind of fathering, and that self-image, with Audrey's experience. She doesn't want him to meet her adoptive family because she says they're "weird," and they regard her as "the sick little weirdo". The guilt he feels is palpable when he looks you straight in the eye and asks, "Would you do that to a kid of yours?"

Bill is unusual among the birthfathers we studied in his willingness to be counted. For this reason, most of what is known about birthfathers comes via birthmothers. Similarly, when adoptees want to search for their birthfather, the best information about where to begin usually resides with the birthmother, but asking for her assistance can be a touchy matter, especially if she fails to volunteer it.[3] The feelings she has about the birthfather, good or bad, are destined to be strong, and probably include a mixture of hurt and anger that remains unresolved. He could have been her high school sweetheart—a boy she had been seeing for months or years—or he could have been a more casual affair, even a "one night stand." He could have been her first sexual partner, even her first sexual experience. He could have been someone she loved and wanted to marry, or someone she never would have considered for marriage. It's possible he was even her husband, maybe soon to be (or just recently) estranged.[4] And beyond what he meant to her in any of these ways, his attitude and behavior during her pregnancy, good or bad, is not something she is likely to forget. Birthmothers' feelings about birthfathers range from "I hate the bastard" to "I've always loved him; I'm a one-man woman."

Even when their feelings about the birthfather are confused, negative or frightened, reunioning birthmothers whose children want to find their birthfathers are unlikely to stand in the way. One hears about mothers who refuse to disclose the father's identity but, in our in-depth interviews, the birthmothers who were asked for information staunchly provided whatever identifying facts they could.[5] But, like Bonnie's, not every child has asked:

> *"I have his name and address but Jay says he has no desire to get hold of him. Jay feels that his birthfather, whose name is Howard, should make the first move, and Howard feels that Jay should make the first move. They're both pretty stubborn and neither has made contact."*

However, not every birthmother will volunteer information *without* being asked, sometimes because they are are worried about the man's character. Geraldine, for example, is fearful about telling her daughter that the birthfather was a rapist:

> *"She has not searched. I'm frightened about it. He would be fifty-six-years old now. The person I*

contacted didn't seem to think there was much possibility of his changing into a very good person. I've come to learn that a person who rapes one woman rapes others, and it would scare me if she should meet him."

Betty is another woman who characterizes her son's birthfather as, essentially, a no-good bum. The man was law-abiding at least, but reprehensible in other ways. He was twenty-one when she became pregnant, he was married, and he was "terrified they would press charges for statutory rape." He arranged for her "to run away and stay in a hotel where he would take care of me," and "when I got there, he had put me in a rat-infested hotel, and I sat there for two days and he didn't come." No wonder she's less than eager to have him materialize in person:

"I would almost rather have Skip not follow up with him, because he's such a cruel horrible person. I told Skip he looked just like James Dean and he had a motorcycle, and I'd rather leave him with that image."

A couple of birthmothers have a problem revealing who the birthfather is for different reasons. Until reunion, one of these birthmothers believed that her son's birthfather was the man she had been seeing around the time her husband left her. The son's strong resemblance to her ex-husband, however, which she couldn't see until the reunion, has cast considerable doubt in her mind and in the minds of their other children.

In a different vein entirely, a group of the birthmothers we interviewed went on to marry the man who fathered their child.[6] Like couples everywhere, some of them later divorced, but among those who remained married, the birthmothers' reunion with son or daughter amounted to a reconnection not just between mother and child but a reconnection also between the adoptee and his or her birthfather.

Marion's story illustrates the point with special poignance. Marion is one of the eight birthmothers who later married the father of her relinquished child. Her story is particularly dramatic because Dan, the birthfather, went to prison after they had married and had other children. They remain married to this day, a commitment Marion consciously renewed after he had been sentenced. He will not be released from prison for several more years. A very gratifying first meeting between Marion and Allen was immediately followed by a visit to the prison so that father and son could also meet. Allen continues to visit his father there, as does the rest of the family. This is how Marion recalls the beginning:

> *"It was time to leave. Dan kissed me and kissed the girls, and now it's Allen's turn. Well he grabbed him and kissed him, on the cheek, and held him. It was only about two minutes but it seemed like forever. And you could feel the emotion. And my husband just let him go, and turned his back and walked away and never looked back. He was crying. And he said he went in his cell and just lay there crying, he was so overwhelmed. And as time went on and we talked about it again and again and again, he said that when he saw Allen it was just like look-ing at himself."*

As one might expect, reunions between adoptees and birthfathers who are married to birthmothers are free from problems that the specter, then the presence, of a long-lost birthfather often introduces into post-reunion. But there's a strong chance that the appearance of the couple's mutual child, and the entry of that son or daughter into their ongoing marriage and family life, or their divorce arrangements, will bring its own brand of stress.

What happened to several of the (still married) birthmothers in this position is that reunion and post-reunion activated long-suppressed and unresolved anger at their husband about his role during the pregnancy and adoption proceedings. They had been, or felt, rejected and deserted, and even though the man was welcoming the child now, the echoes of having gone through their predicament alone resonated loud and clear.

BirthBond

A part of them couldn't help but feel hostile: Where were you when I *really* needed you?

Here is Marion again:

> *"I didn't realize until I found Allen that I had a lot of pent-up anger towards Dan, that he didn't rescue us. And I truly love this man but I felt, 'Why didn't you rescue us Dan? Why weren't you there for me?' And for the first time in twenty-six years we talked about what happened."*

And Jeanne:

> *"I discovered I had some unresolved anger toward him, stemming from the birth and relinquishment. Intellectually I couldn't blame him for any decisions that had been made, and yet I felt I had been abandoned."*

Both Marion and Jeanne feel their marriages have been strengthened as a result of these confrontations, but another couple with whom we spoke are still arguing and agitated, uncertain whether the resentment, anger and guilt which were released by reunion several years ago are leading them to a final crisis in what has been a periodically unsteady marriage, or to a new plateau of mutual acceptance and peace. How ironic it would be if their grown daughter, by finding her birthparents married to one another, turns out in the long run to be the precipitator of their divorce.

From the standpoint of an adult adoptee, discovering that your birthparents are husband and wife is an unexpected revelation, but not an unmixed blessing. On the positive side, there's the exhilaration of finding both parents at once, and the joyful knowledge that they must have loved one another. You're "a love child," as one daughter happily put it. Also, any siblings you meet are likely to be full-siblings, not half, making the genetic tie with these brothers and sisters complete. Then too, you don't have to worry about whether your birthmother is harboring hateful feelings toward a man who left her in the lurch, or whether her current husband will be threatened if she helps you search. On the negative side, though, you may feel especially betrayed to discover that their lives rejoined after the adoption and went forward without you. You may wonder, or wish sorrowfully, as Kate did, "If you went and got married, why couldn't you come and get me back?" "If only's" breed easily in these circumstances and feelings of "why me—why not one of the other children?" also seem more likely to surface when the adoptee finds the rest of the family intact. (Strong physical resemblances among all the children, as in Hattie's case, seem to exacerbate the adoptee's pain.)

Walking into a reunion after your birthparents have gotten a divorce produces a different kind of disappointment. Carol, for example, talks about Joey's reaction to this part of the story as both sad and resentful. He felt betrayed that the birthparents had married at all, then resentful yet again at not finding the family together. "He suffered grief over our divorce."

Charlene is another birthmother who married and divorced the birthfather, Ed. Their son, Rich, is caught in the divorce spin-off. Ed has remarried and acquired stepchildren but also remains father to the children he had with Charlene. Rich's siblings have welcomed Rich warmly, but Ed has been less than enthusiastic about Rich's appearance from the start. Charlene recalls:

> *"His reaction was not at all like mine. He was not very excited about it. He asked me three very specific questions that day: Was Rich going to be coming to his house every other Christmas; whether Rich was going to be changing his life-style; and whether I thought he should put Rich in his will. I didn't know how to answer them and suggested that he take one minute at a time. I stepped out at that point and let them create their own situation."*

Ed has continued to have "a hard time" and is "not welcoming Rich back into his life" for reasons Charlene does not understand. The two men have spent no time together alone. De-

BirthBond

spite Charlene's being disappointed about Ed's reaction (she doesn't want Ed hurting Rich by rejecting him), she's keeping her distance. "I'm not on terms with Ed where I can talk with him very much about this," she says. "As much as I'd like to go in there and shake him from head to toe and ask him what the hell's wrong with him, I can't do that." But since Rich spends time with his siblings and they all visit Ed, Charlene concludes that Ed will just have to work out his feelings about Rich and the two of them will have to "bang out a relationship." (At the time of our interview, the reunion was less than one year old.)

Virginia has the opposite problem with her ex-spouse. The relationship between daughter and birthfather has threatened to become too intense, overshadowing Virginia's own relationship with the girl. Virginia's view is that daughter Robin "had a great need for her father, maybe even more than for her mother." Robin "pumped" Virginia about Phil, and Virginia felt "a little used" and "kind of jealous." Robin and Phil felt a real kinship to one another as well: "His apartment was maroon and that's her favorite color, and she uses a scent that's his scent, and he's very intellectual and poetic, and that's not my thing." In the early days, there was also a problem of "sexual energy" between Robin and Phil, but that's passed. "Robin was so upset about it she could hardly tell me," Virginia remembers. Bill, the birthfather we met early in this chapter, spoke of the same problem. Sexual attraction between birthfathers and daughters seems no less common, or any less disturbing, than between birthmothers and sons.

In contrast to the situations we've just described, the search for a father does not usually result in finding a man who married the birthmother. More often, the adoptee will find a person whose life has moved along a different track from the birthmother's, with the two birthparents unlikely to have had any contact over the years.[7] Found birthfathers who have kept the secret are presented with the same dilemma that found birthmothers face: to tell or not to tell. The kinds of reunion and post-reunion relationships which ensue flow from this decision.[8]

A few adoptees in the sample presented themselves to birthfathers who proved unable or unwilling to tell their wives and families about the adoptee's existence. This usually is labeled "protecting his family" and amounts to a hello-goodbye contact which ceases after one or two meetings. Some reports of this type of reception are:

Irene, talking about Rita's experience:

> *"She walked in on him where he works. He said, 'Hi, can I help you?' and she said, 'I don't know.' He said, 'You look familiar,' and she said, 'I should.' (She looks just like him.) His face completely drained of color. He took her aside, and they talked for about an hour. He gave her a little family background, and said he would like to be friends with her but his wife and family couldn't know. . . .*
>
> *Later she decided she wanted to meet his daughters, her sisters. She went to sister number one, Evelyn, who was very nice to her. The youngest one, though, didn't want to meet her—wanted no part of it. Rita said to Evelyn at the time, 'Your father doesn't want your mother to know about this,' and Evelyn said, 'Well, I have to think about that; maybe she should.' But she never saw them again after that. She backed away, felt rejected. They live in a different state now. Every once in a while she talks about maybe getting in touch with Evelyn."*

Nell, talking about daughter Barb's experience:

> *"He was in his second marriage when they met. He had told his first wife but not the second one, I don't know why. (His first wife had three children by him. The second wife had two children by a previous marriage which he also raised; they were considerably younger, in grade school, when she was out there.) His wife works in his office as a receptionist and he didn't want to tell her. He asked Barb not to call him there*

*and give her name because his wife would go to
the files to look for it. So she really had no way
to contact him, and has had very little information since that first contact. She called once after that and got some information about her
health, but I don't know if she really needed it or
just wanted to have the contact."*

Other adoptees, in contrast, have established pleasing relationships with their birthfathers: close, caring, or loving interactions
that are satisfying to both. These are birthfathers who cared
and wondered about their children over the years, and for
whom reunion can be joyful and significant.

Emily Sue's daughter Pam, for example, was fortunate
in finding a birthfather like this. He had been a friend to Emily
Sue during the pregnancy and had helped her financially, even
though marriage was "the last thing" they wanted. Because
they had decided on adoption together and Emily Sue had
valued his friendship, support, and his sense of responsibility
back then, she expected that he would be happy to hear from
their child now—which he was. It's eighteen years later, and
he's married, but Pam is his only child. He had thought about
searching for her too, but was waiting until she reached her
twenties. He telephoned the day he received her letter; they
corresponded; he spoke to her adoptive parents on the phone
for three hours since "he didn't want them to feel threatened by
him"; and he met Pam at the earliest opportunity. She's a little
surprised that she actually likes him; he's not "the deserter" she
expected. He's offered to assist with college expenses, and he
wants to meet her adoptive parents.

Even when a birthfather is willing or eager to establish a
relationship with with the grown adoptee, the texture of these
relationships can be rough and unruly, as Bill's story illustrated.
A number of father-child unions are filled with all the uncertainties and confusions that occur in birthmothers' post-reunions,
including: his behavior long ago; and whether the birthmother
has come to terms with where he fits in the history. Millie's
son's birthfather, for example, is actively reaching out to

Thomas. He calls the son once a week, invites him to dinner regularly, and hands out presents to Thomas' children whenever he sees them. But Thomas has confided to Millie, "I don't know what to say to him," and Millie—who has her own bitterness to deal with—doesn't want to get in the middle.

Millie isn't the only birthmother we spoke to who finds herself anxious, displeased or disconcerted by the relationship her grown-up child is having with the birthfather—reactions which can complicate her own relationship with the adoptee. It happens quite often. Marlene is in the same position, and she is also one of the women who didn't want her child to search for the birthfather in the first place. (You may recall from the beginning of this chapter that he's the one who failed to mention he was out on bail and married.)

> *"I didn't want Paula to search for him because of his background. She expressed a desire to do it after a year or so. I called a friend who worked in the police department and was cautioned that he might use her and really hurt her emotionally. You don't know what kind of character he is now if he was in jail at the time. I discouraged her and it cooled for another year. Then she said she had to do it."*

Paula found her father, continues to be in touch with him, and is trying to convince Marlene to meet with them both, at least once. So far, Marlene "just can't handle this," but if a meeting ever *were* to take place, she would only have it in the presence of a counselor she's currently seeing. "What if he and I got into some argument and I walked out? What would *that* do?" she wonders.

Birthmother Joan has a different kind of trouble with her daughter's birthfather. He was "pleased and proud" of Jenny and tried to give her "all sorts of fatherly advice" (which she didn't want), but Jenny had become disenchanted with the man. She now describes him with a string of derogatory adjectives: domineering, chauvinistic, bigoted, sadistic, rude and cruel. Their personalities and values are "worlds apart," and she has decided, with much sorrow, that she will probably discontinue the relationship with this person she cannot respect. Joan is sad for Jenny but acknowledges that "I don't have to share her with him either"—a view raised by other birthmothers. Jealousy of the child's interest in the birthfather, including fears that a son or daughter will like the father better, or feel more connected to him or his family, are not uncommon. Worrying about what kind of influence a birthfather is having on the adoptee is another concern, as in Carol's case, where father and son have become drinking buddies.

In contrast to situations in which birthmothers consider the birthfather more or less the enemy, there are also situations in which renewed contact with the birthfather arouses feelings of revived romance. Beverly, for example, found that her ex-boyfriend was much more interested in talking to *her* than in meeting their daughter. Beverly spoke to the man a few times before she severed the connection and confided her "stirrings" to Lil. Thinking better of it— "she didn't need to hear that"— came later.

Vivien, as noted in Chapter 7, "fell in love all over again," and she and Roy "parented" Cindy as a couple for several months. (Cindy also went to live with Roy for a time but that wound up a "disaster.") Emily Sue suggests that her revived interest in the birthfather was connected to the bond they shared by virtue of having created this child. When she accompanied Pam to meet him . . .

> *"It was kind of a strange experience for me. I felt like I wanted to spend more time with him, and I wanted the three of us to spend time together. I wanted to share with him what he was feeling. I didn't really understand my feelings about that. Later when I looked back I thought, well maybe it's only natural because he and I share the same loss. We lost the same child. I wanted to know how he felt, and if he felt like I felt. My husband was so threatened that he didn't even want me to see him. He was very angry with me*

*when I said I was going anyway, so I only ended
up spending about five minutes."*

When Vivien declares that Cindy feels like a daughter of divorced parents now, it underscores the sense of connection
that these three people, and others in similar circumstances,
can feel for a period of time. This may be a key reason why the
birthfather's entrance into post-reunion can be troublesome.
The birthfather's entrance creates a new triangle—birthmother,
birthfather, and birthchild. The three participants constitute a
kind of "shadow family" that is rarely acknowledged, the family
that might have been if events had taken a different course.
When the players take their places side by side, in the flesh, it's
small wonder that they, or some of their respective families,
feel uncomfortable.

The fact that a man and woman *do* have a shared history can be obscured but not undone. The birthmother was not
the only birthparent of the child. The birthfather is a powerful
figure in the adoption-and-reunion saga, even if he never mate-
rializes in the post-reunion present. Several of the birthmothers
we interviewed felt that dealing with the birthfather and/or their
feelings about him, was the most difficult part of the post-
reunion experience. Nonetheless, the fact of their shared past
can also be helpful to birthmothers in post-reunion. It was Constance, whose story we told in Chapter 4, who needed to meet
and talk with the birthfather to "unclog" her own repressed
memories.

A few birthmothers to whom we spoke in depth expressed the wish that they could eliminate the birthfather from
the post-reunion picture altogether, simply because it would be
easier to manage their own feelings and relationships. Others
expressed wishes to move the birthfather into background positions. Meeting with birthfathers often produces the complications we've discussed: feeling caught in the middle and feeling
competitive about the child's affection, as well as the romantic
rekindlings which threaten present attachments. Many birthmothers keep stiff upper lips about their children's relationships
with their birthfathers because, for the sake of the son or

daughter who wants it, the women see the acceptance of such relationships as the "right" thing to do. On the other hand, it's also true that several women achieved more complete senses of resolution when their sons and daughters met their birthfathers: feelings that unfinished business had been taken care of and that the circle, finally, was closed.

There are also instances in our sample, as in the reunion culture we studied at large, where contact was not achieved until after the birthfather's death. At that point several adoptees went on to meet relatives from their birthfather's family, including half-siblings. As it is when the father is still alive, the personalities and circumstances of these individual family members become pivotal in determining whether the reception is warm or cool and whether continued affiliation lies ahead.

Major social changes in this country have sparked new concepts of fathering that did not exist when these adoptions took place and birthfathers were excluded from adoption decision-making. During the last twenty years, the women's movement and a high divorce rate have caused professionals and parents to reevaluate the role each parent should play and to reconsider what each parent contributes to a child's welfare. These changes have been felt in adoption thinking and practice too. In the 1970s, birthfathers' legal status in adoption started to change when court rulings began to affirm that unmarried birthfathers have a legal claim on their offspring. Practically speaking, however, birthmothers today retain their primacy in adoption decisions. Agencies continue to view the mother, not the father, as the primary client.

There is probably a connection between the claims that unmarried fathers are making on their infants these days and the cautious emergence of yesterday's birthfathers. A survey of birthfathers conducted in 1985 provided evidence that "even after extended periods of time, the surrender of a child for adoption remains a conflict-ridden issue." In the sample of 125 men, whose average age was forty, thoughts of searching for their child were practically universal and two-thirds had actually engaged in a search. Approximately half the sample had had some kind of participation in the adoption proceedings; over one-third cited external pressure as the primary reason for relinquishment. Some of the men also revealed that, like birthmothers, the adoption produced problems in terms of their marriages and parenting later.[9]

The fathers of children relinquished for adoption have been a silent, faceless group, but "the fleeting father" is on his way to becoming an outmoded stereotype. In circles where birthfathers feel more or less comfortable, one can hear men admit to feeling "guilty as hell" that they didn't come through for their kids or their girlfriends. Some state that they too were victims: of the girlfriends who failed to inform or consult them, of parents who told them what to do, of agencies that provided no alternatives, and of financial resources that just weren't there.

"It's an eerie feeling that you have a kid out there," one man says "You wonder about it all the time." If Reuben Pannor, one of adoption's most quoted experts, is right, most birthfathers have never forgotten about their children.[10]

10

About Siblings

An adoptee we know wrote the following poem.[1] As the poem tells us, when it comes to siblings, adoptees have a confused but full house. There can be brothers and sisters by birth (both full and half), and brothers and sisters by adoption (who may or may not be the biological offspring of one's adoptive parents).

Word Problem

If you are 26 years old
and had 1 mother who gave
birth to you but then
was taken away and
married someone else and had
1 daughter and 1 son
Plus you had 1 father who
married 1 woman who was
pregnant with 1 child that
was not his,
but then had 2
daughters after that
who were and then
married another
woman and had 1
son—
If all that happened,

plus, additionally
you had another
mother and father
who you knew and who
lived in a house that
you lived in also who
then had 2 sons;
How many mothers, fathers,
brothers, sisters, half
brothers, half sisters,
stepmothers, stepfathers,
aunts and uncles do you
have including the ones
you haven't met yet?

Sudden Siblings (Siblings by Nature)

Finding a brother or sister you never knew can be as significant as finding a parent. Especially in cases where the birthmother is deceased, reunions between adoptees and their birth siblings become paramount. Sibling reunions can also be a substitute for meetings between adoptees and birthmothers if the birthmother is alive but refuses to meet. Why should she have the right, adoptees ask, to prevent me from knowing her other children, my own brothers and sisters?

There are situations in which the desire to discover and connect with siblings is what initiates the search. One woman, thirty-two, started to search after watching her own children play together and wondering if she too had any such connections. Adoptees who know about siblings they've never met often have compelling desires to meet them. Many of those who lack the knowledge ponder the possibility. Connecting with a birthparent means filling a void, but connecting with a brother or sister is a bonus. If the adoptee grew up as an only child, finding a sibling can be especially meaningful.

It sometimes happens that reunions take place between siblings who actually spent a few months or years growing up together. It's possible that the older child remembers when they were separated; or, if not that, remembers when the mother was pregnant with the baby who was subsequently adopted. In our sample, the latter happened in Hattie's family. Her eldest son remembers Hattie's going to the hospital "with a tumor." He never knew that a baby brother was being born and relinquished. It is probably just as well. That particular memory could easily have left him anxious about whether the same thing was ever going to happen to him.[2]

A case like this, though, is an exception. The preponderance of sibling reunions that result from adoption are not really *re*-unions at all. Because relinquishments generally result from unwed mothers giving up infants (the pattern both in our sample and in the country overall), brothers and sisters in reunion are usually meeting one another for the very first time.

The absence of a shared upbringing does not preclude the possibility of strong, even instantaneous, kindred feelings. Shared heredity often creates felt ties of its own, and sudden siblings can feel connected to one another from the outset. "They were immediately all pals," Charlene says. Indeed, we have heard stories about birth siblings raised apart who, on meeting as young adults, felt closer to one another than they ever did to their adoptive siblings.

With twins, in whom the genetic tie is most complete, research currently underway is revealing unexpected similarities between identical twins reared apart—more so than among fraternal twins reared apart or reared together.[3] One set of brothers, united at age twenty-five, were amazed to discover that their bathroom medicine cabinets were stocked with the same items, product after product—from their hair lotion (Vitalis), to their cologne (Canoe) to the same exotic Swedish toothpaste. (They were both smoking Lucky Strikes when they met, but they've both since quit.) Researchers from the University of Minnesota's Center for Twin and Adoption Research have observed separated twins who knew about one another and experienced feelings of loss and inner emptiness for years. With reunion, they frequently become very enmeshed with one another, even moving to the same town and developing close relationships. Fortunately adoption agencies these days are more cognizant of trying not to separate twins.

Among the birthmothers we interviewed, eight were otherwise childless. The other twenty-two had become mothers to a total of seventy-three other children (sixty-eight biological and five adopted).[4] Sooner or later, introductions had to be made. Compared to the first encounters between adoptees and their birthparents, siblings seemed to greet one another with a cleaner slate, less encumbered by the sticky issues of a complicated past.[5]

Siblings who meet appear to have an easier time than their elders for several reasons. First, the relationship is less likely to be derailed by unresolved issues. Second, the individuals are closer in age (the same generation anyway) and grew up in an era when the prevailing attitudes about sex were more relaxed and accepting than in the birthmother's era. Third, family size and composition can work in their favor. If the birth family is large, for example, one more brother or sister can be accommodated with relatively little fanfare: "With five kids already, one more was okay." Or, if the family is small, the adoptee may encounter an only child who always wanted a brother or sister, or one who always wanted an additional sibling of whichever gender was lacking; young children may even make the adoptee into an object of hero-worship. Listen to Joan talking about her ten-year old, for example:

> "I remember driving in the car the first week we were together and Melanie asked, 'Mom, is Jenny really my half-sister?' and I said yes she was, and Jenny said, 'As far as I'm concerned you're my sister'; and Melanie just grinned, she was so pleased. So pleased to have this big sister that she can talk to. As she's grown older and gotten into her teen years she emphasizes that. What you can talk about with a big sister and with a mother is just different."

At the outset, though, the birthmothers shared a common dread about telling their other children about the adoptee's existence. For some, it was the most agonizing aspect of the reunion and post-reunion experience. For the reasons we've indicated, however, the other children frequently failed to be as horror-struck, or as devastated, or as shocked, or as judgmental and unforgiving as the mothers feared. The women typically began these conversations in the most somber tones. Some of their listeners responded with relief: "Is that all? I thought somebody died." "So what? These things happen."

Birthmothers never anticipate a "no big deal" quality to their children's reactions, because they are anxious, embarrassed, and concerned that they will lose their children's respect. Even under the best of circumstances, displaying one's sexuality to one's children is something most parents would rather avoid, and these confessions are all the more uncomfortable because the mothers are worried about what kind of message or model they're presenting. As it turns out, sons and daughters occasionally express anger or disappointment, not for the deed, but because it was kept a secret. They thought their mother never lied to them; they thought they knew "everything" about her. "If I could tell them *that,* I could tell them anything," one birthmother learned, and the women often discover that there is value in their children's coming to understand them better and see them as "a real person."

Occasionally children had "heard talk" over the years, but, even if they were shocked to learn their mother's story, the usual response in these families was to rally round and extend support. "That must have been hard for you Mom," they recognized. The women are grateful.

> *"I was so taken aback, I couldn't believe that the two of them took it the way they did and were so good. From there on, whenever I told anybody about the reunion, I told them about my kids too and how wonderfully they were accepting it."*

> *"My son was surprised and excited. He viewed it as a very positive thing and he wanted to meet her. He said he changed his opinion about me*

> *after I told him—he thought I was a lot more*
> *human. A lot of children put their parents up on*
> *a pedestal, as though they're perfect, and he*
> *was glad to know I was a human being, and he*
> *didn't come from a perfect person factory."*

As things progressed in these sibling relationships, the birth-mothers, because of their own anxiety and confusion about whether and how to incorporate the adoptee into the family structure, generally stayed on the sidelines. From that vantage point, the associations between the adoptee and their other children can look relatively serene. If a problem doesn't force its way to their attention, they don't go looking for it.

Hardly any of the women indicate that siblings' relationships are a problematic part of post-reunion as far as *they're* concerned. They want all their children to love each other or, if that's not possible, at least to like one another or, if that's not possible, to be polite. They may suggest from time to time that the children they raised "be nice" to the adoptee in various ways—call, write, send a birthday card, invite him to your house —but they avoid pushing too hard because of their own discomfort. Several have specifically told either the adoptee or one of the others, "Don't ask (or complain or tell) me. Ask him. I don't want to be in the middle."

Other children, for their part, are sensitive to the awkwardness of post-reunion. Some protect their mother by putting on company manners or by not telling her their complete feelings about having a new person in the family's midst. As Millie, mother of eleven, says, "Because of me, they wouldn't directly insult him." The pattern some birthmothers witness after a while is that their other sons and daughters will be friendly to the adoptee when he or she visits, but they don't seek the new person out.

Many birthsiblings don't understand the adoptee. They need to be educated about the loss issues which are the adoptee's lot, and the adoptee's position (versus theirs) as the one who was given up. Many siblings, however, sympathize with the adoptee immediately and some are deeply empathic. "I'm glad it's not me" or "My God, it could have been me" are commonly voiced thoughts. One son said that he owed his life to the adoption, reasoning that his mother would not have had a second child (him) if she had kept the first. Others have the same thought but do not tell their mothers. One birthmother's grown children were so sad, angry, and guilt-ridden upon learning the details of their sister's childhood (which was far less loving than their own) that their loyalty and affection shifted *away* from their mother *to* the adoptee. More than ten years into post-reunion, this birthmother was suffering anew, punished yet again because her other children had "turned against her." The interaction between the siblings was driving the post-reunion dynamics and making *her* the outsider.

More generally, though, when birth siblings are in their twenties or thirties, an older stage of life helps them to the perception that something has been gained, not lost, when an adopted brother or sister appears. When Faye's son was reunited with his fifty-ish sister, for example, he was delighted. His only other sister had died in an auto accident years before, contributing to his pleasure in suddenly having another one. But even without having suffered such a loss, grown-ups can be more magnanimous than children. They are occupied with lives and families of their own. Some live far away from both the birthmother and/or the adoptee, which makes it unlikely that a newly arrived sibling will affect their lives in any negative way. It's very different, and usually far less threatening, than stepfamilies in which a new kid comes visiting on a regular basis, or moves in, while you're a pre-teen or teenager still living under your parents' roof.

Young or old, the birthmothers' other children bring with them into these new sibling relationships their own histories, personalities, and insecurities—and they greet the adoptee in character. Even in the same family, two brothers had quite different reactions upon hearing about their adopted sister. One immediately accepted her as his long-lost sister, the other contended that her position in the family was more like a cousin. Several years into post-reunion, these initial reactions continue to hold, though the one who says "cousin" is relenting a bit. But the boys' mother is aware that her sons' different attitudes affect her own behavior. She feels freer to include the young woman in family events, and to talk about the daughter, in the presence of the son who thinks "sister" than with the one who does not want her in the family's inner circle.

Even with Jeanne, whose reunion terminated after three years, each of her three daughters took a different view of their brother Steve. The fifteen-year old made an effort to get to know him and treat him as a brother, "but she was too young to completely absorb the information and fit it into her life." The nineteen-year old was "thrilled to have a brother and the most willing to develop a relationship." The twenty-two-year old, who had been away for a year, "expected to come home and tell us about her year in France and instead was hit with the news of a new brother. She was immediately jealous," and told Steve he didn't belong in the family. "Her status as the oldest child meant a great deal to her, and she never did come to terms with her feelings."

When Jeanne and her husband severed contact with Steve, none of the daughters continued to be in touch with him. Interestingly, though, Jeanne has come to the conclusion that Steve's appearance may have actually strengthened the family and brought them closer together. "I now feel that I'm a good mother," she says, "and I'm pleased with the way the girls have turned out."

Regardless of what the adoptee symbolizes to his new-found relatives, the siblings he encounters are not just responding to some cardboard figure labeled brother or sister. They are responding to an individual. Carol's children, for example, had a particularly rough time when Joey entered their lives, less because of rivalry, or because they wanted to make him an outsider, than because he was a genuinely difficult person:

> "*Joey is a very strong personality, and especially because he was very confused at the time we first met him. It created some hardships in the relationship with his sisters. There was hostility between them, but yet they still ended up with*

*a good, sound, brother-sister relationship. My
youngest daughter doesn't approve of his drug
use and his immaturity, and Joey, being the big
brother, felt he had to tell the girls what was
right and wrong and how to behave, and they
resented that. It was a little sad because Joey
wanted to be the big brother right away, and
they weren't about to have anyone telling them
what to do with their lives. I let the relationship
take its own course and tried not to interfere."*

Carol's household is not alone in having domestic tranquility
challenged while siblings work through their own feelings and
relationships. Resistance to welcoming the new person is not
uncommon, but it can also dissipate after the initial shock. Several birthmothers were aware that their eldest child had "some
problems" moving down a notch in birth order ("being gypped
out of first place in line") or that a child who was accustomed to
being the only son or daughter in the family didn't want to lose
that distinction. Nora handled the problem this way:

*"My boys were eleven and six when I told them
about Colin. Adam, the older boy, thought for a
minute and said, 'You mean I'm not the first?'
And I said, 'Adam you will always be my first
child, your Dad's and my first child. There's
nothing that can ever change that.' And he
thought for a minute and said, 'You mean we're
both firsts?'"*

Several birthmothers saw their children vying for their attention, "evaluating their position" or asking for reassurance of
their love. The women's calming response was to "try, somehow to make them understand that I love them all," regardless
of whether pre-teens or grown-ups were at issue. Some are
hopeful that the siblings will "work it out" if they have not already done so. One says, optimistically: "It takes a little time to
assure them that in a family there's love to spare."

Listen to Ethel, whose children were in their twenties:

"When Lucy first came on the scene, I was almost obsessed with her. I not only told the others about her, but I kept talking about her and
things that had happened to her. I showed each
new picture with excitement. Gradually, after a
few expressions of non-verbal 'so what's?' I fig-
ured it wasn't the best way for her to gain acceptance with her sisters and brother. Now I tell
them the good and the bad so that they know
she's no more perfect than they are."

Marcie's children were teenagers when Lee appeared:

"There's a certain amount of sibling rivalry at
times. My daughter Sally said to me, 'Lee looks
more like you, Lee's personality is more like
you.' And Lee is saying, 'Sally looks more like
you.' Both girls have dark hair, dark eyes; they
both look like me, but in different ways. They're
five years apart in age. They're very close. They
both play musical instruments. Lee went to live
with Sally. But yet I think they're just trying to
find their position in the family, with me. I don't
see any great amount of jealousy—just a little
bit."

Nora expects that several years will go by before her older son,
Adam, will be mature enough to reach out to Colin, his older
brother:

"Jeremy's seven. He's still the young child. He
and Colin connected immediately. Jeremy was
in his lap at every turn. We went out to eat one
evening and he even crawled up in his lap in the
restaurant and just folded into him. It was lovely
to see. But with Adam, the thirteen-year-old,
that's the age when you're starting your own
separation process anyway. Adam had said to
me at one point, 'I wish Colin hadn't even been
born.' Now he wasn't saying that because of

Colin personally. He really likes him. He's in-
trigued with the idea of having an older brother.
But he resents the discomfort I'm feeling. What
he was really saying was, 'I wish he wasn't pull-
ing you away from us the way he is.' And since
Adam is just entering his teen years now, I don't
see that they're going to come together any
time soon. The ages are just working against
them. Also, Adam's at the age where he wants
to protect his mother, and how could he possi-
bly be warm to someone who he knows is the
instrument of a lot a pain for his Mom?"

The kinds of sibling relationships that presented themselves in
our sample ranged from extremely close to guarded and per-
functory. Some are of the take-it-or-leave-it variety, and some
run "hot and cold," but there is only one case where the
younger siblings' disinclination to accept the adoptee is proving
to be a crisis for the birthmother. That is Debora, whose story
we told in Chapter 3. Her younger teenager has made it clear
that he doesn't want another older brother; he doesn't get
along that well with the one he has. He's angry and feels abandoned. Her other son "totally denies" the reunion, despite her
attempts to win him over. "I said to him, 'If I remarried and had
a child, that would be the relationship you have with Teddy,' but
he refuses to see it."

At the opposite end of the spectrum, Emily Sue's children were immediately receptive to their eighteen-year old sister, including the eleven-year old girl who had felt "very threatened" at first "but as soon as they met it was like instant love."
Her fourteen-year old boy also experienced an immediate rapport, making this a case where the sibling relationship helps the
post-reunion between birthmother and adoptee flourish.

"Here we are, walking in the airport and the two
of them are poking one another, hitting one an-
other, and insulting one another just like broth-
ers and sisters who have been separated for
maybe a week or two. It was just like they had

always known one another. I laughed at them in the airport saying 'I can't believe you two just met.'

"One thing we have going for us is that Pam really loves her brother and sisters a lot and wants a relationship with them. Not just a friendship but a brother-sister or a sister-sister relationship. I'm not saying that if I didn't have other children she wouldn't be interested in just me, but I think she's more interested in a relationship with me because she does have the brother and sisters. My son and Pam have wonderful rapport. And she understands him better than she understands the brother she grew up with, because they're a lot alike temperamentally. When he does something, she says, 'I know why he did that.' Part of the reason we have such a good relationship is that she feels real connected to these other kids too."

Suzanne is another birthmother whose children have reached out to their new sister in kinship and love. They see each other several times a week.[6]

"They've become extremely close. The boys help her do things because she's single. She just moved here this week, bought a house, and the boys and my husband moved her, and one of her brothers has been over there rebuilding her cupboards and putting in a new countertop and sink, and we've been painting and plumbing. They have a very close relationship now. They're very much alike. It worked out fine. After they met Kim, the kids would invite friends home for dinner to meet their sister. Their attitude was if their friends didn't like it, then they weren't their friends anymore."

About Siblings

In the middle ground, between the rejection represented by Debora's sons and the acceptance represented by Suzanne's, stand a number of sibling relationships that are friendly but not close, cordial but not warm: uncertain and polite. Some of them have met only briefly, often at large family gatherings where the opportunities for dialogue are constrained by the occasion. Most birthmothers feel they need to get to know each other better. But some have spent time trying to develop relationships and have discovered incompatibilities and irritants of various kinds, including unequal interest in maintaining a relationship.

Irene's sons, for example, continue to have an uneasy association with Rita:

> *"A few years ago Larry was going through a very bad time with medical problems and Rita was living here and she got a babysitter and ran to the emergency room to help him, and yet they may not even talk to each other two days later. And George, I think, loves Rita a lot. He's gone out of his way to buy her an antique phone, and she didn't even send him a Christmas card. She said 'I don't have any money but I'll give you an IOU' and he waited for three years. I think what he wanted is for her to be more reliable, and she isn't. He bitches and complains before she comes—'your daughter who can do no wrong'—and then she gets here and they're as happy as can be, and then she leaves and he's mad at her."*

Hattie's children have extended themselves to Roger. They're waiting now for Roger to take some initiative. Marlene's children are disenchanted with Paula, and Paula thinks they resent her. Marlene says:

> *"The first Mother's Day, Paula gave me a rosebush. The next year my son was working in a garden shop and he bought me three rose-*

*bushes over the summer. She resented that.
And of course they denied everything she said
and looked at her like, 'Hey lady, where are you
coming from?' Now the relationship mostly consists of family get-togethers and the boys have
a take-it-or-leave-it attitude."*

Eventually, some of these "middle-ground" relationships will
find the adoptee relegated to the category of distant relative—
a person you almost never see or think about—but they
haven't reached a final disposition yet.

The bottom line question that most adoptees and their
birth siblings pose for one another is: "Do I love you like a
sister," *or* "Do I like you like a friend," *or* "Do I have to put up
with you because we're related?" Whether the adoptee is a full-
sibling or half-sibling does not seem to be a determinant of how
warm or cool feelings will be; we hear of warm acceptance of
both kinds and we also hear of cool resistance to both. However it turns out, birthmothers are glad they've met and that
their biological kinship has, at least, been acknowledged. Beyond that, the mothers seem unlikely to interfere. But as one of
them muses: "I'd like to think that someday, when I'm gone,
they'd be there for each other."

Adoptive Siblings (Siblings by Nurture)

Birthmother Phyllis compares an adoptive family to a
group of people thrown together in a college dormitory:

*"An adoptive family with two adopted kids and
parents, it's like roommates: two people that
got married and then two people from totally
different backgrounds. It's worse even than a
roommate situation because in a roommate situation you screen people first. Here, you throw
these four people together and you expect
them to get along."*

A bleak analysis to be sure. Adoptive siblings get along the
same way that birth siblings do and don't. Still, the fact is that

brothers and sisters in adoption start out without the genetic connections that link biological brothers and sisters together. Endowments as basic as racial, religious, and national origins could be the same or different, not to mention interests, talents, character traits and the like.

Like many adopted siblings, Kate and her brother Warren didn't talk much about being adopted while they were growing up. Kate calls it a "dynamite" subject that some adoptive siblings never discuss until *after* a reunion, if then. But whenever Kate announced to the world "We're adopted," people would ask if she and Warren had the same parents. Her answer: "We don't know."

Adopted siblings display their individuality in the different feelings they express about searching for birthparents. One may think about it a lot; the other not at all. It's possible they split roles on the issue while growing up, with one becoming the "good adoptee" and other becoming the "bad adoptee"[7] in the family. The "good adoptee" was the one who was well-behaved, didn't give the adoptive parents any trouble, and acted as though being adopted was of little or no import. The "bad adoptee" was the rebellious troublemaker.

Once adopted siblings become teenagers or adults and one of them initiates a search, the other may become angry that his counterpart is being disloyal to their parents. The angry one may actually want to search too, but be reluctant or scared about "putting them through that" again. Then again, he or she may have decidedly different views on the matter, which can put a thorn in the sibling alliance. In birthmother Ethel's case, for example, daughter Lucy's adoptive brother (age forty) maintained that he didn't want to know his biological parents if they didn't want him (an oft-heard refrain), and Lucy's relationship with her brother went downhill after her own successful reunion. The brother knows about Ethel but has expressed no curiosity about meeting her or about the reunion's progress, which leaves Lucy isolated from anyone in her adoptive family.

When adoptive siblings are in their teens or twenties, a few months or years can elapse between the first sibling's search or reunion and the second's (or third's or fourth's), partly because the brothers and sisters are different ages but also because the one who is not actively engaged in search and/or reunion is sitting back and observing: perhaps becoming stimulated and intrigued himself; perhaps just lying low examining his own feelings; or perhaps becoming frightened when a brother's or sister's experience turns out to be too difficult or disappointing. When birthmother Phyllis searched for daughter Sharon, but Sharon's adoptive brother's birthmother did not search for him, Sharon worried about the effect of *her* reunion on her brother. Was he thinking that *his* birthmother didn't care enough to find him?

Hundreds of miles away, Warren told Kate that he didn't want to search for his birthmother but "it would be nice to be found." Kate set the wheels in motion. Both consider themselves "survivors" of the same unhappy household, and she is hoping that her action will effect a kind of closure between them. Because Kate feels a more primal connection to her birth family (which includes two full brothers), she can anticipate having some kind of link with Warren long-term, but only a peripheral one. He's like someone she went to grade school with years ago. If they had been closer growing up, she might be more inclined to bring him into her post-reunion family now, but they weren't. It's possible the whole association will trail off as the years go by.

Another risk that faces siblings in adoption is the chance that the parties will encounter sexual issues that biological brothers and sisters do not. One of the adoptees in our sample, for example, told her birthmother that she had been raped by her adopted brother. When siblings are connected only by environment and not by blood, surely the incest taboo is weaker, this mother argues. It also seems to be weaker among reunited siblings, some of whom experience strong feelings of physical attraction to one another.

Sibling issues have yet another complexion in adoptive households where one child is biological and one is adopted. The question for the adopted child is: are they treating me equally? am I just as important? Both negative and affirmative answers show up in our sample.[8] Emily Sue reports that her daughter, for example, is an affirmative example:

> *"They've given her a lot. She always felt loved. She told me she didn't feel like she was adopted; she didn't feel like they treated her any differently than they treated their two other biological kids. When I've been there she's just like anybody else; she gets yelled at and she gets loved just as though she weren't adopted."*

Suzanne's Kim was less lucky:

> *"The adoptive mom was very much into the son she had at home. Everything was Tony, Tony, Tony. Tony is thirty-two years old, never had a job, went to college for ten years, never graduated. As soon as he got close to graduation he changed his major. He told the adoptive mother and Kim in the last year that they should be supporting him, and that's brought a further distance between Tony and Kim."*

In mixed families like these, the adult biological child has to contend with another kind of question—namely, if my (adopted) sibling searches, who is his birthmother to *me?* And who are all those *other* birth relatives to me?

Reunion and post-reunion change the boundaries of the family, as we will continue to see in the next chapter.

11

Post-Reunion and the Birthmothers' Network

Reunion is not a private event. The number of people whom it touches includes birthmothers' husbands, their own parents and siblings, and their friends. In this chapter, these individuals become our main focus, and we'll explore what happens between the adoptee and these people.

During reunion, people with the same label assume different identities in different cases. A birthmother's mother, for example, can either assume the role of grandma ("birth grandmother" is the term that's used) or she can be cast in a more tangential role, according to how everyone feels. Some adoptees are more interested than others in claiming the birth family as their own. Birthmothers like Joan, have a different view:

> *"I somewhat regret the fact that she doesn't feel very much a part of my family. I think perhaps I should have stressed more, 'your grandmother' instead of saying 'my mother,' or 'your uncle' instead of saying 'my brother.' But I don't know whether that would have influenced her feelings about my family much. I think that what she wanted was to know her birthmother and birthfather, and their children, but she wasn't looking for a whole bunch of cousins, aunts and*

*uncles and grandparents, simply because she
felt she already had them."*

Like the sibling influences we saw in Chapter 10, the birthmother's family can cast a positive, negative, or neutral hue on post-reunion proceedings. When the hue is positive, the family members act to bolster the relationship between the two principals, helping it root in greater depth than it would without their presence. When the influence is negative, these interactions account for many of the "little minefields" that the reunioning pair must negotiate.

Husbands

When the husband is the birthfather, as discussed in Chapter 9, reunion and post-reunion present an opportunity for the couple to scrutinize and thresh out their shared past. When the women are married to other people, which is more frequently the case, post-reunion puts a premium on husbands' understanding and patience. Fortunately, most of the women had told their spouses about the adoption before they married, but there was often a post-reunion period of upset or adjustment anyway due to the wife's preoccupied state of mind, her overt attraction to a male child, or the fact that another man (the birthfather) suddenly became prominent, either in memory, conversation, or in person. The reader has only to recall the possibility that birthmothers can "fall in love all over again" to imagine how very threatening post-reunion can be to husbands and to understand why they so often feel excluded.

Nora's description of her husband's feelings going into the second year of her reunion, stands for many:

"I know he's disturbed with my not being present. Even when I'm with the family, my mind is somewhere else. But he trusts that. I spoke to him about it one time and he made reference to the sexual attraction I'd had with Colin and he said, 'You came back to me, and I know the rest of it is going to get resolved too.' He's felt a lot

*of pain with this. He hasn't enjoyed watching me
spend so much time with it. I think it would be
very naive of me to say there hasn't been jealousy, but not of Colin as an individual, of the
time I spend with the process."*

Marlene's account illustrates that husbands can be excluded
from post-reunion by virtue of what the adoptee does or does
not want, not just because their wives' attention is elsewhere:

*"My husband was very happy about reunion and
wanted to be a part of it. He thought everybody
was going to be one big happy family, and that
wasn't at all what Paula wanted. He went
through feeling rejected and feeling jealous at
times. He'd say, 'You sit and talk to her for hours
and you don't have anything to say to me.' He
wanted to know everything we did and everything we said; he wanted so much to be a part
of this. It's been a strain."*

When a reunioning birthmother is in a second marriage, as
some were, the stress of post-reunion is superimposed on what
can already be a stressed household. Carol explains: "We already had a lot to cope with, with a new blended family and ex-
spouses, and that made our marital relationship difficult from
the beginning as far as time alone together was concerned." If
her husband had given her an ultimatum about the time she
was spending with her son (which, wisely, he did not) she's not
sure that the marriage would have survived.

The consequences of reunion were almost ruinous in at
least three of the marriages represented in our interviews. More
commonly, though, the birthmothers indicate that their husbands or men-friends have been supportive to them in post-
reunion and kind and gracious to their son or daughter in spite
of any initial difficulties. The men usually understand how important these relationships are for these mothers. Many have
grown fond of the adoptee and have evolved pleasing, friendly
connections of their own, with a dash of parental pride or con-

cern occasionally thrown in. Some were "ready" for these relationships, because they knew their wives were searching. One welcomed his wife's daughter with special warmth because his own daughter from an earlier marriage had been lost to him decades before as a result of divorce. Ready or not, though, tension between a birthmother and an adoptee in the household can affect everyone. According to one perturbed and long-suffering husband, "you can feel it in the air."

In addition to bringing another person into the couple's domain, the birthmothers also point to other ways in which reunion and post-reunion have affected their marriages. Geraldine, for example, says that reunion has produced new insight about the nature of her own role as a marriage partner.

> *"It brought up the feelings that I'd always had of being a victim of a system, and of my parents, and of the guy who raped me, and I realized that I still fell into a victim role in my marriage. I'm trying to undo that, which has caused a lot of problems."*

Reunion has also been ameliorative for Ethel, who made her husband promise before they married that he would never speak of the baby she gave up; though she wasn't aware of it before Lucy's call, "there was always an invisible barrier between us, a subject we didn't discuss." Her husband honored his promise for forty years, "but there was an unhealthy bond based on deception" and he is "almost as happy as I am that we can level with each other and face the situation more openly."

For Betty and others, a husband's love and support through the trying post-reunion times have reinforced the good, solid marriage that was already there: "I appreciate my husband like I never, never appreciated him. There's nothing that could wreck our marriage now." For Joan, whose husband had children by a prior marriage (she did not), the appearance of Jenny in their life acts to "even out" their positions.

Sometimes reunion produces no discernible effect on a marriage. A few birthmothers who were in what they considered bad marriages anyway, tell us that reunion-related events made no difference one way or the other.

The one striking exception among our sample's husbands is Fred, who discovered for himself that wife Emily Sue had a baby before she knew him. He found out well into their marriage when he was "snooping around" and came upon a journal she had kept the year she was pregnant. Ironically, it was the fact of his uncovering the secret that loosed her bonds of silence and enabled her to begin the long climb toward becoming comfortable at acknowledging her first child's existence. Fred's reaction was unkind and unforgiving. He viewed her as "used material"; he told her it ruined their marriage; and he has held it against her for the eight years he has known. It would have been better to tell him before they married, she now thinks, and it remains to be seen whether the marriage will survive the tension, heartache and recriminations that ensued from his discovery. Still, he has met Pam and he was pleasant to her, "until the very end, when her birthfather showed up."

Emily Sue has changed a good deal since the day Fred found her journal. "I've done a lot of work on myself," she says, and finding Pam (including the process of searching) has changed her life. "My feelings about my marriage are confused right now," she admits, "but I can't say I regret anything that's happened."

Birth Grandparents

In many of the cases we studied in depth, today's senior citizens were yesterday's decision-makers. Their responsibility in the original decision inevitably colors the way they view reunion.

For some, the materialized adoptee represents the problem they thought they solved, newly arisen. Others find that the passage of time means they can now accept what was once unacceptable because society has changed, they have grown old, and it can be wonderful to have a grandchild. Birthmothers can't know which of these positions their parents will take until they reveal the reunion event. When parents are elderly or sick, the women frequently choose not to, thinking it better to let them live out their days without disturbance. But it's a judgment call and a piece of unfinished business a woman may later regret. This is the position in which Joan now finds herself:

> *"I had made the decision to search for Jenny two years before my father died. He was sick with cancer and he lived far away. I had a good relationship with him prior to his death, better than during my childhood and the difficult years after surrendering Jenny. I did consciously decide not to tell him I was searching and I've somewhat regretted that. I was too afraid to bring up all those difficult emotional things with him, and I decided not to risk it. I sometimes wish now that I had because I think he would have been glad."*

The vicissitudes of parents' health and aging sometimes takes the choice out of birthmothers' hands entirely, which is what happened to Marlene:

> *"My mother was senile and in a nursing home when Paula came back. I tried to talk to her about it, but I didn't get anywhere at all. Paula saw her there once, and went to her funeral, but she never knew her. But if she had been of sound mind when Paula came back, I can imagine what her reactions would have been: 'What does she want? What is she doing here? Now everybody's going to know.' My mother didn't even tell her sister who she was very close to back then. She didn't tell anybody."*

Some of these grandparents, however, didn't know about their daughters' pregnancies in the first place,[1] which means that reunion produces a grandchild they never knew they had. They are spared being defensive or feeling guilty about any role they might have played in the original separation, but they're likely to have decidedly mixed feelings about their daughter's failure to inform them at the time of her dilemma. Such was the case with Bonnie's parents. Bonnie's Jay was their only grandchild. Her mother was shocked to learn about Jay, but "I think she was sort of happy that she had a grandson that old." Her father's reaction was "not negative" but their ensuing interaction has shifted:

> *"It caused some problems with my father and I. He doesn't come right out and say it's a problem but I believe it is. It seems as though we argue more than we used to. I really think he feels bad that I kept it a secret. I think he almost resents me for not telling him of my problem, of my pregnancy, and I think he's having a harder time dealing with it than anyone else."*

Bonnie's parents are pleased by the idea of becoming real grandparents to Jay and complain that they don't see him enough. All that concerns Jay right now is his relationship with Bonnie. The reunion is quite young, so some patience on their part is going to be necessary before Jay is ready to turn to the grandparent aspect of his post-reunion agenda.

In contrast to Bonnie's parents, parents who participated in (or insisted on) the adoption decision are more typical in our sample. With that history as backdrop, reunion revives the old resentment the birthmother often felt about *her* mother, and the two begin to settle old accounts. It's analogous to what we saw among birthmothers who married birthfathers and then, with reunion, finally confronted their angry feelings about the young men's failure to rescue them. So too, with their mothers, airing old grievances is potentially mending and truth can become a lubricant to better relationships. But not always. Some birth grandmothers are disinclined to *mea culpas,* and some birthmothers persist in blaming them.

At the time of our interview with Geraldine, the birthmother whose rape set off feelings of victimization for years to follow, she was grappling with intense anger at her parents.

One year into post-reunion, everyone's emotions and under-standings are being reassembled.

> *"I've been angry with my parents. My father has avoided the fact that she was born for twenty years. My mother made references to her, inqui-ries over the past twenty years, but I didn't want to respond; I didn't want to talk to her about it. So after finding Wendy I started thinking about how controlling they were. I started remember-ing my mother's manipulation and screaming and my father's rather passive behavior. Al-though he said that he would keep her if I wanted to, my mother ruled the roost and felt she would have to be Wendy's mother. I've talked and cried with each of them about these things since Wendy surfaced. They're still saying they did the right thing. They both believe they had the right to make the decision. At least I've gotten a few things off my chest.*
>
> *I'm starting to feel somewhat more forgiving, not because I think they were right but because I think my mother was in an extremely stressed-out situation at that time. She had five kids, she had a baby, and she didn't want that baby, let alone my baby. And my father was working fourteen hours a day and she was alone with five kids. And the more time I spend alone with my kids with little support, the more I can un-derstand her stress."*

Another birthmother who was in the midst of processing her feelings about her parents' past role is Vivien. Vivien has had marital troubles as a result of her reunion too (we spoke of them in Chapter 7), but, while the marriage seems to be in repair, the rift with her parents continues to be severe. Like Geraldine's, hers is a young reunion which makes it possible, but hardly certain, that matters will improve.

> *"My mother's first comment was, 'What does she want?' Was she looking for money, my mother wanted to know. One night when they were nearby I took her over to meet them. They were polite but that was it. They didn't say anything like 'I'm glad we're finally meeting you' or 'hope to see you again'—nothing. They haven't accepted her. I've never been very close to my family—I live an hour away and use that as an excuse—but this is the last straw. The way they treated her really hurt Cindy. Now there's very little involvement with my family on my part."*

Fortunately for Cindy, Vivien's in-laws have accepted Cindy more than Vivien's parents have. The birthfather's family has been welcoming. In most cases, the bigger the network of family relationships, the more chances there are that warm, affectionate greetings will occur. Grandparents can refuse or be reluctant to meet their grandchildren. They can still be concerned, as they were years before, about what to tell the neighbors and what people will think of them. They can be struggling with a view of themselves as villains in the piece. Or they can embrace their grandchildren as pieces of eternity, claims to their own immortality.

Extended Family

If the essence of grandparents' reactions to reunioning adoptees tends to lie in whatever meanings lurk in past events, the reactions of extended family members—by which we include birth aunts, uncles and cousins—are less colored by this particular strand of determinism. These relatives range from "not interested" or embarrassed to warm and welcoming, and their stance affects the birthmother's view of her relations. What frequently happens is that reunion produces a greater emotional charge between the birthmother and *her* brothers or sisters than between the adoptee and his aunts or uncles, perhaps because sibling relationships are closer and more charged to begin with.

Families who are far-flung geographically may get the news of a reunion by letter or Christmas announcement. In the absence of personal contact, they can be left uncertain about how the birthmother *really* feels. They may be less than comfortable themselves with "airing the dirty linen in public." Large family occasions often turn out to be the time when the extended family meets the adoptee, preventing them from going beyond casual conversation to find out who the adoptee really is or what his motives are (assuming they want to). People who have adoption connections in their own lives, as adoptive parents say, bring personal predispositions about reunion to the news.

In Thelma's family, for example, a cousin's teenager, adopted, started asking Thelma about her reunion, and the cousin "almost sees me as a threat now because I'm somebody her daughter can go to and circumvent her." Thelma is educating the mother about search and reunion and has promised she will not interfere. In Irene's case, another birthmother in Irene's extended family did not reveal herself as such until five years into Irene's reunion when the woman embarked on a reunion of her own. Irene marvels now, "When I think of all the times I was going through things with Rita and I would tell them, and she was there, and she never opened her mouth."

Anxious or uncomfortable family members show their distress in different ways. One of the birthmothers recalls her brother being "terrified" and "white as a ghost" when he walked in to meet her daughter; he kept saying "Isn't this weird? Don't you feel weird?" Nell's brother, who was instrumental in helping arrange the adoption, was furious at her for writing to the rest of the family about her reunion with Barb:

> " 'I asked you to respect my rights,' he said, 'and then you send a letter like that.' He was so angry that when we finished our conversation I made up my mind that I wouldn't call him or write him. But I told Barb and she felt terrible. She thought

it was terrible that I would be that way with him because she knew how fond I was of him. And she said, 'I just feel that I've done something very harmful and I do wish you'd resume the relationship you had before because otherwise it's going to make me feel guilty for the rest of my life.' And I could see her reasoning. So I started calling again, on his birthday and things like that, but I didn't do a whole lot of writing."

Hattie guesses that a lot of people in her family "probably talk their mouths off" about her reunion, but she doesn't care. Joan, as mentioned earlier, is disappointed and resentful that her family ignores Jenny; "It's like she doesn't exist; they don't ask questions." In a few cases, including Nell's, the birthmothers' siblings are unwilling to meet the adoptee at all.[2]

But then there are the counter-examples. Many family members are loving, understanding, supportive, thrilled—including the occasional person who "always knew" but had been told never to say anything. Some make welcoming gestures to adoptees (writing letters, sending family pictures), and gratifying relationships take hold between adoptees and their aunts, uncles, and cousins, similar to or "just the same as" the other children's relationships with these people.

Others take more neutral positions. Beverly's family has been "positive" about her finding Lil, for instance, but their involvement stops there. "I'm not that close to my family and I don't feel any particular urge to have everybody meet, but if they do that's okay." Taking noninvolvement a step further, Bonnie sees no reason to share the news of her reunion with relatives she's barely in touch with anyway.

"They live four hours away from here and they're all in their sixties and seventies and I'm lucky if I see them once every three years. It has no effect on them. By not seeing them a lot there's really no reason to tell them."

If Bonnie changes her mind, her extended family might when confronted with the relative they never knew respond to his role (i.e., Bonnie's son), not to Jay as an individual. Many families behave more or less along these lines. They honor the role with appropriate gestures, they act in a friendly manner when holidays or other circumstances bring them together, but they don't develop close relationships. A number of these birthmothers are uncertain about whether the new relationships between the adoptees and these other family members will continue (though they're certain that their *own* future with the adoptee is assured). Still, birthmothers and adoptees agree that whether some of the extended family relationships fade out is less important than the fact that they were instigated.

Friends

Friends are an important part of our lives, especially at times of crisis, so it comes as no surprise that these "voluntary intimates" play a role in birthmothers' reunion and post-reunion experiences. Mainly, we find them displaying, by offering support and encouragement, the loyalty that most of us want from our friends. Their focus is on helping their friend, rather than befriending the new son or daughter, and so, like many in the extended family, they respond to the adoptee more in role-related terms than as an individual.

Some birthmothers say that their friends were "surprisingly positive" or happy and excited for them when they learned about the reunion. The friends made their good wishes clear, sent flowers or did other "wonderful" things like entertaining the adoptee when he came to town or going out of their way to be hospitable. Betty says of her friends, "Nothing but positive beauty has come out of this. It's actually changed people's lives."

Other friends' reactions are harder to read. "Nobody shunned me," or "If anyone had anything negative to say about it, they never said it to my face," or "Not everyone was too enthusiastic but no one was nasty." When friends have this type of superficial reaction—comments like, "I'm glad you're happy about it" or "That's great for you," or "I wish you a lot of luck"—it leaves the women wondering what they *really* think.

Being a friend to a birthmother who's had a reunion often becomes an education in psychology or social policy. One explains: "Many know little or nothing about adoption and reunion." What do you say after you find out how the reunion happened and how your friend feels about it? Which questions will come across as expressions of interest and which are intrusive? The vast majority of these birthmothers to whom we spoke were more willing to talk about the details of their experience than anyone ever imagined, but a respect for privacy is never inappropriate as Thelma reminds us:

> *"They wanted to know the details of my preg-*
> *nancy—the gory little gossip, the sex and scan-*
> *dal. Once I wouldn't discuss that, they didn't ask*
> *me anything, not even about my daughter."*

To avoid this kind of offense, friends told us they tend to restrict themselves to the here and now, shying away from questions that might appear unseemly about circumstances years ago. Some friends assume the woman is trying to forget all that so certainly *they* won't mention it. In the effort to be tactful, they squelch their natural curiosity, leaving questions to hover unanswered. Ironically, the birthmothers sometimes feel that they had their chance and can't keep talking about adoption and reunion *ad infinitum.* Despite the fact that many find it therapeutic to return to these events over and over, they're concerned about seeming obsessed and driving their friends away. Still, it's usually possible to find new people to talk to, as Norma does:

> *"I tell just about everybody, especially now that*
> *Peter's a part of my life. If someone comes in I*
> *say, 'This is my son,' and if the circumstances*
> *are propitious I tell them how he's my son.*
> *Sometimes people say, 'I thought you and Cy*
> *had no children.' Then I have a few sentences:*
> *'When I was very young I had twins, and they*

*came back' and everybody always says, 'Oh,
what a wonderful story.' I think that the repeating of the story is quite healing."*

Being judgmental of a birthmother who's happy to have a reunion can threaten or ruin a friendship. Jeanne reports that of
the handful of friends she informed, one was particularly judgmental and they are no longer friends. Jeanne is not the only
birthmother to whom we spoke who terminated a friendship for
this reason. Although most would concur with one who said,
"the more I tell, the better I feel," the birthmothers' self-esteem
is often shaky, and they are not eager to be challenged or to
take on new assaults. Marion recalls that, before her reunion,
she found it easier to tell people that her husband was in prison
than to let them know she was a birthmother. It is an indication
of just how much shame she felt about the illegitimate birth of
her child, and just how much courage it takes for some women
to speak out.

　　As reunion and post-reunion unfold, it's natural for
friends to wonder about and express concern about the adoptive parents. Many don't realize that this can be a touchy area
for birthmothers to discuss. A few of Vivien's friends "had the
sense not to bring it up," and in retrospect, "I realize how sensitive they were." Friends who are adoptive parents themselves,
or who have adoption in the family, can be discomfited by
these events, "and it was obvious to me," a few birthmothers
tell us. Being able to report that one has spoken to or met the
adoptive parents is one way of assuaging their fears. Making
contact signifies acceptance, approval or acquiescence from
the adoptive family—which, in fact, it often does. Geraldine's
anecdote points up that even the closest of friends sometimes
need to be assured that the adoptive family is giving its permission for reunion to occur.

*"My best friend, who's listened to me sob about
this for fifteen years, caught me by surprise.
She thought that now that I found her that
would be simply enough. That's what my father
thought too. She was delighted that I could fi-*

nally be at peace, but she thought that just knowing Wendy was alive and well would give me that peace. When she found out I wanted a relationship for the rest of my life, she was very defensive for the adoptive parents. Now that she knows how the adoptive parents feel, she's eager to meet Wendy."

Once birthmothers have gained confidence, they venture beyond the protection of close friends into the ranks of not-so-close friends and acquaintances—the array of neighbors, co-workers, tradespeople, etc. —and tell them about the adoptee. Birthmothers say they appreciate whatever kind of support is proffered. Millie remembers:

"I took the article about my reunion and put it on the wall in back of me at work. I was so grateful to the people in the office—four out of nine—who actually spoke to me about it. What galled me were the ones who never said a word to me. I didn't talk to them about it unless they mentioned it to me."

Public disclosures like this often cause the other person to communicate information that has not been shared before about adoption in his or her family.

Some birthmothers reach a point where they can finally tell anyone and everyone about their reunion without worrying about being judged. Lila introduced her daughter to the butcher one day and realized that somehow, without knowing when, she had stopped caring whether he or anyone else would condemn her for what she had done twenty-five years ago or, indeed, for the relationship she was having today. She told us that on the day she told the butcher, she felt as though she had been released from prison. On that day, she felt finally and completely free.

As we have seen, reunion becomes a community event and the reactions of people in the birthmother's network can either undercut her post-reunion pleasure or reinforce and expand it. None may be more significant in this regard than the adoptive parents. We give them our complete attention in the next chapter.

12

Post-Reunion and the Adoptive Parents

We've written throughout this book about the adoption triad or triangle because the parties to adoption create a threesome. But a triangle isn't necessarily a good image for adoption participants to internalize because the idea of a triangle almost automatically conveys overtones of rivalry and competition which are better left outside adoption proceedings.

Like it or not, though, the tension and conflict inherent in any triangle situation appears in adoption and reunion also because the nature of threes is to shift into various two-against-one configurations. One of these configurations consists of the birthmother and adoptee as a pair and the adoptive parents as the odd one out; the second consists of the adoptive parents and the adoptee as pair, with the birthmother in the outside position; in the third, the two sets of parents are paired and their mutual child stands alone. Somewhere along the way in post-reunion, everyone gets a turn at being the outsider.

Some people suggest that it would be better to discuss the parties to adoption as forming a circle. The idea of a circle reflects a modern spirit in adoption thinking. As we've discussed in preceding chapters, in earlier decades the two families in adoption proceedings were advised that they had no need to know each other, advice which left an adversarial feeling in its wake. Adopters were told to proceed with only minimal information about the biological family. No one entertained the possibility of a cooperative spirit, much less a cooperative arrangement, to benefit the child.

Some adoptive parents' adversarial thoughts about the birthmother stopped while their children were growing up. These parents came to believe that it would be in their child's best interest to know his origins, even if it entailed search and reunion. They were supportive of a child's expressed desire to search, even willing to help if they could, but the impetus had to come from the child. Many held back information and support until they were certain it was being sought. Since children often think about their adoption without verbalizing their thoughts, the consequences of such restraint can be ironic. An adoptee in her forties, for example, found out that her eighty-year old adoptive mother had been burdened for years with information she was eager to hand over:

> *"My adoptive mother became aware that I was searching when I went to her. I thought she was going to drop dead for sure when I asked her what she knew about my natural parents, but it was I who almost dropped dead because of how much she knew. I was amazed at how much she had known and kept to herself all this time, wanting to tell me, and I had been blaming her all these years for not being willing to tell me. I realized that I hadn't been open, or at least hadn't given the vibes that would free her to tell me. She said, 'I've been wondering why you never asked; I thought you didn't want to know,' and here I was absolutely aching for the information."*

Adoptive parents' reluctance to broach the subject of search and reunion may also be a result of disagreement about how the issue should be handled, with one parent being supportive of search and the other opposed. Adoptees often report that one of their parents is significantly more comfortable or understanding than the other.

> *"When I finally got the courage to tell her I had already found my birthmother and father, she said, 'That's wonderful; that's your right to know; that's why I kept the records. I didn't tell you before because of your father, and I obeyed his wishes.'"*

As a group, adoptive parents are generally on the sidelines of search, but it's not unheard of for them to take the lead, which is how one of the reunions in our sample came about. In another unusual twist, the two mothers, Hattie (birth) and Anita (adoptive), have become close friends and enjoy a warmer relationship with one another than Hattie does with son Roger, a turn of events with which Roger is less than comfortable and an example of the kind of triangle where the two mothers feel themselves somehow paired and the child is odd one out. These two women are "very protective" of each other; Anita sympathizes with Hattie when Roger backs away. From the vantagepoint of friendship, she is also in a position to understand the dynamics of Hattie's post-reunion relationship. She concurs with Hattie that Roger is "stuck" in unexpressed anger about being given up, but she also points out that Hattie and Roger deal with hurt feelings like two peas in a pod: they both clam up: "I think they have to sit down and talk really honestly and I don't think they can."

The bond between Hattie and Anita began the first time they met, seven years ago. Anita recalls that they were having lunch and Hattie was telling her what it had been like to be a welfare patient in the hospital, in labor, out in a hall somewhere, surrounded by hospital staff who were unsympathetic and unkind.

> *"And then she looked at me and said, 'Wow, it must have hurt like hell not to ever have had kids,' and I cried and cried. I thought to myself, 'My God, of all the people who never said that to me, never gave me that moment.'"*

In another sense, of course, their bond was established years earlier, when Anita became the mother to Hattie's relinquished child. Hattie was a blank to Anita—Anita only knew her by the label birthmother—but the invisible cord of fate had bound them together regardless. Furthermore, as a woman, Anita could empathize with how the other woman must have felt when she was confronted with an unwanted pregnancy in the 1960s. She could imagine the distress that an untimely pregnancy would have caused in her own younger life, even though her own eventual heartache was of a different kind.

Gina, another adoptive mother, describes awakening to the birthmother's position just after her son Cal made contact with his birthmother, a search in which she had been happy to assist. Although Gina is also a biological mother of two children, her understanding of the other woman's position was not instinctual, but she quickly learned about, and could empathize with, a birthmother's pain:[1]

> *"I tried to walk a mile in her shoes. When Cal first found Beth, he went to two libraries and got out as many books as he could. He came home with about twelve books. He read some and I read them all. I sat and cried for days. It gave me a keen awareness and a sensitivity to what it was like to give up a child. That's a painful thing. So I tried to do some things that were thoughtful that would be meaningful to her."*

Gina is exemplary in the degree to which she has extended herself to make Beth feel accepted and to help the reunion take root. Hattie and Anita are unusual in the degree to which their post-reunion relationship has flourished. More commonly in our interviews, adoptive parents are aware that a reunion has occurred (the majority), have spoken to the birthmother, and have met face-to-face,[2] but they don't necessarily develop a warm future union.

The first in-person meeting between birth and adoptive parents is not easy, but those who confront their counterpart can achieve insights, and resolution, that were before inaccessible. Writing to reassure her son's adoptive mother, one birth-mother put it this way: "Birthmothers are a bit like shadows. But take them out into the daylight and they're just another woman in the supermarket wondering what's for supper." Lila talks about being "extraordinarily curious about the strangers to whom I had given this child. I wanted to meet them face to face, not just to have Kate's description of them. Meeting them fit in another piece of the puzzle of this enormous void." According to another: "It's hard to be angry or accepting of something you don't know; you need to know."

Sometimes, as with Thelma, these initial contacts prove surprising because the women sense a connective cord they didn't expect:

> *"I dialed her number and spoke to her mother and asked for Sara. She said, 'Sara isn't here, she's in college,' and her next statement was, 'Are you her birthmother?' A split second hesitation and I said 'yes' and we talked for forty-five minutes. We had this wonderful conversation and I felt very close to her."*

Some adoptive mothers go through the child-rearing years giving little conscious thought to the woman who bore their child. But once they admit to themselves that they are curious about the original mother, it's no better for them to be weaving fantasies about her than it was for the adoptee to have been doing the same.

Anita's fantasy, for example, was put together to suit her own needs. She imagined Hattie as a schoolteacher in a tweed suit who had only had sex once, the time she conceived Roger; then, according to the fantasy, the relationship broke up and the poor woman lost both the man and the baby and never got over it for the rest of her life. What Anita wanted, she realized, was for Roger's conception to be meaningful to someone, and though her fantasy was harmless enough, it was a distortion of reality. She had to let go of it when Hattie and her real story (three "mouths to feed" and a disappearing husband) came along.

When the birthmother presents herself in the flesh, not every adoptive mother is as ready or able to greet her as Anita was. Nora, for example, is in the second year of post-reunion, and senses that despite a professed acceptance from her son's adoptive mother, the woman is not really ready to deal with her:

> "She's setting the pace for the letters between us. Months go by without hearing from her. I have the sense that she wants to know *of* me rather than know *me* right now. I'm still pretty powerful, and I'm only powerful because there's a reluctance to know me. She gives me the power."

Their son, Colin, in contrast to a segment of adoptees who very much want the two mothers to meet, takes the position, "if it happens, it happens." He knows the two women are curious about each other, but "if they could watch the other through a two-way mirror that's how they'd want to do it." If they do meet, it will be out of his hands. He doesn't want to be "a third party" in such a meeting because "it's just between them." What he's saying, in effect, is, no triangles, thank you.

Judging from most of the accounts we heard, the first meeting between the two mothers has little reunion magic. The occasion is marked by discomfort and nervousness, and birthmothers often feel they have been jettisoned back to a sorry past. Even when the adoptive parents are gracious and welcoming, birthmothers tend to feel inferior, because these are the people who "took care" of their "mistake." Consider Joan:

> "I was having quite a hard time with the idea of meeting them. They turned out to be fine; they did everything to put me at ease, and I felt terribly, terribly uncomfortable. Somehow I managed to let myself feel as though I were that terribly inadequate screwed-up teenager who couldn't manage to do anything right. Everyone was doing their best to make me feel comfort-

> *able, but I couldn't wait to get out of there. I felt*
> *so out of place, and it made me feel so much an*
> *outsider."*

Carol describes Joey's adoptive parents as "helpful but cautious" when she first approached them in her search for Joey. Indeed, caution is the watchword on everyone's part, even if adoptees and birthmothers are well-known to one another by the time the parents are introduced. These early meetings often have a superficial or formal quality. Mutual expressions of appreciation, gratitude, admiration and respect are predictable, along with symbolic gestures meant to convey a similar generosity of spirit. Adoptive parents frequently offer the birthmother pictures of the child growing up, a sign of goodwill and a way of assuring the birthmother she has a rightful interest. Adoptive parents may even take photographs of the birthmother or make a videotape of the gathering. Throughout, people are studying one another's looks and forming impressions about what kinds of individuals they are.

Marlene recalls the mutual discomfort under the polite exterior:

> *"I met the adoptive parents a few months after I*
> *met Paula. Paula called and warned me that her*
> *adoptive mother was going to invite me to*
> *lunch. I went to their house, and I don't know*
> *who felt worse. Paula wasn't there. Her mother*
> *was saying, 'If there's anything you want to ask*
> *me . . .' And she said, 'I thought we owed this*
> *to Paula,' and I thought, 'You're not doing this*
> *for yourself.' We made a lot of small talk conver-*
> *sation. I didn't want to give her a cross-examina-*
> *tion."*

Irene recounts how she and the adoptive father staked out their positions:

> *"Before Rita came to live here, her father called*
> *one night and said he was going to be in the*
> *area on business, could he stop over. I thought*

he was coming to kill me. This delightful man appeared with more pictures than you can imagine, movie projector, and all the movies of her growing up. He told me she was the joy of his life and that when they adopted her he made a commitment that this child would grow up to be a healthy, happy human being. I assured him that was my aim too, and from my knowledge of children who had been adopted (from the groups I belonged to) I was very much aware she would never be a full person until she had knowledge. Not that I wanted to be her mother. That wasn't my need; I have children. Yes, I had to know she was okay, but I also had to give her what I had taken away. No one else could give that back to her."

Thelma recalls feeling both pressured and mystified:

"I was in the area and they picked me up and took me to this restaurant. They wanted to go at 5 o'clock and nobody eats dinner at 5 o'clock so the restaurant was empty. They had all these photo albums but they wanted me to take them into the restaurant and look at them in the restaurant. I tried but I couldn't do it. I had to excuse myself and go into the bathroom at one point and cry. It wasn't something I could deal with. Then they invited me to their house, so we drove all the way and they called their son up, who was also adopted, to come meet me, like it was some big event. I thought it was really odd."

Norma laughingly remembers a kind of female rivalry:

"I had heard a lot about her—the boys always spoke well of her—but this was the real lady. I found her to be much prettier and younger than expected. I guess I had wanted her to be, maybe, older, so that I would be the beautiful

mother, which is sort of silly; we're so different. But I like her. And I'm very grateful for her. She's had a hard, hard life and did a good job, considering."

Geraldine remembers an overflow of mutual feeling:

"Within the first month her mother wanted to meet me. We went out to dinner. It was incredibly emotional. We hugged and cried for a couple of hours. She told me about Wendy growing up. Her first words were 'thank you.' She didn't know how she could have gotten through the last few years without Wendy in her life."

But what about the adoptive mothers sitting on the other side of these tables—what were *they* thinking and feeling? If Anita and Hattie are in the category of more than usually receptive, what are their counterparts like? What challenges do reunion and post-reunion thrust upon them? What ghosts begin to stir and stalk?

Faced with an enduring post-reunion, many parents in traditional closed adoptions have feelings of fear, worry, or anger. While it's true that some grew into accepting the desirability of their children's reconnecting with birth origins, the possibility of a *post*-reunion between birthmother and child is something on which they didn't dwell. When the prospect of an "ever after" relationship with the birthmother rears its head, it's not unusual for adoptive parents who have been supportive of search to withhold their blessing. They become threatened, at least temporarily.

It's not just that their adoption procedure was guaranteed "search-proof" and that they may regard reunion as legally wrong and morally unjust from the perspective of contracts or what is "fair."[3] Less obvious is that many of the feelings that come forth hark back to the time they decided to adopt, usually because they were unable to have biological children.[4] According to the well-respected Sorosky research team, "The key issue to understanding the psychology of the adoptive parents is the effect infertility has on every aspect of their lives, though it has been denied and repressed from consciousness."[5]

Infertility is a loss and should be mourned, but many adopters in these reunions were not encouraged to mourn the child they would never have. In such cases feelings of loss tend to remain unresolved, and reunion revives them. One adoptive mother countered her son's announcement that he had found his birthmother by responding in kind: "Don't you think I wanted to have my own kids?" she challenged. When he got over the shock of her words, the son reflected that it was the best reply she could have given; it put them on an equal footing and forced him to see adoption, for the first time, from her eyes.

In addition to reviving the loss of biological parenthood ("I'm suddenly very aware that I end right here," says one adoptive mother), reunion also threatens to be the actualization of a lifelong fear: the fear that the adopted child will someday return to, or be taken back by, the birthparents. Related to this, reunion can also stimulate adoptive parents' doubts about their legitimacy as parents, a concern that some harbored all along. Not having been biological parents, some feel themselves imposters, mistrusting that their parenting experience has been just as real and just as valid. Adoptive parents are typically referred to as "the psychological parents" in the adoption literature, but reunion undermines their security.[6]

Anita, for example, talks about not knowing if there would be a bond between a birthmother and child that would be different from the bond she had. Would they have "some incredible recognition for one another" she wondered? Would blood be thicker than water? Less fundamental but also upsetting to contemplate, she worried about whether her son would simply *like* the birthfamily better. After all, it was she, the adoptive parent, who had been the disciplinarian all these years.

Beyond issues of loss and legitimacy, reunion and post-reunion can stir up other powerful feelings and fears.[7] Adoptive parents may be either consciously or subconsciously angry at the adoptee for being interested in the birthmother at all. They may worry that they've failed the child—otherwise why would he or she need to search. They may be afraid of admitting that they too are curious about the birthmother, lest their interest be interpreted as lack of love. They may worry that the adoptee will be rejected by the birthmother, or hurt by what is learned; or that the adoptee will disturb the birthmother's life. They may fret about whether the birthmother will be more attractive than they (she's likely to be ten or fifteen years younger). They don't know if a post-reunion relationship will be brief or prolonged, loving or fitful. Some worry about whether they'll lose the grandchildren they've got or the ones yet to come. Post-reunion is a frightening unknown.

An adoptee who reassures his adoptive parents about the strength of his attachment and love can reduce the risk quotient considerably. "I've been here with you for twenty-five years; do you think that's going to go out the window?" one challenged, and his adoptive father was instantly relieved. Available research confirms the young man's point, indicating that the effect of reunion on the relationship between adoptees and their adoptive parents is, almost always, either to improve it or to have no effect; only rarely does it becomes worse.[8] The way Anita thinks of it, post-reunion adds "another dimension."

Many adoptive parents bolster their own security by staying informed and involved in reunion and post-reunion, which is why one search consultant advises her clients to include the adoptive parents in any search activity, especially if the son or daughter is still living at home.[9] Some adoptive parents also try to include themselves in post-reunion interactions between the adoptee and the birthmother because they feel pushed aside or shut out when the pair spend time alone. But other adoptive parents encounter the opposite dilemma: they become aware that the adoptee is shutting out the birthmother when good manners (the manners *they* have tried to instill) dictate treating her with greater kindness or consideration.

Learning about or being reminded of a birthmother's pain in giving up a baby isn't easy or pleasant. Some adoptive parents will tune it out. Some get angry, retroactively, when they realize that there can be pain for everyone in the adoption process and that their child may feel rejected no matter how loving they've been. Some have problems dealing with the reality that their good fortune came via another's distress. Not being willing to have a relationship with the birthmother is sometimes a way of avoiding these difficult truths.

H. David Kirk, a sociologist who first published his theory of adoptive relationships in the early 1960s, describes three possible modes of coping with the uniqueness of adoptive parenting: "acknowledgement of differences" (today's wisdom), "rejection of differences" (yesterday's approach), and "insistence on differences" (also an unfortunate approach of yesterday). Here is a son whose adoptive parents illustrate what is meant by the third:

> *"When they moved into a new house, they told the neighbors he was adopted. He said they'd always do that with whomever they'd meet. So what are you really saying? You're saying that he's ours but he's not really ours, and he picked that up all these years. His self-esteem is really low but he's doing much better now."*

Another example of insistence on differences is the family who each year celebrated both their son's birthday *and* the day of his adoption, a practice which his birthmother was distressed to learn about.

Kirk's writings were among the first to call attention to the fact that the adoptive family is different from the biological family in important ways, whether or not the differences are talked about. To acknowledge difference is to acknowledge what's true. "Perhaps the most important outcome of the search and reunion process," according to current clinicians "is that it can enable the entire adoptive family to 'let go of denial.' "[10]

Being adopted, or becoming parents through adoption, is not necessarily better or worse, but it is different, says Carol Gustavson, adoptive mother of three and president of Adoptive Parents for Open Records. Many adoptive parents turn away from adoption issues, she says, and don't want to believe that adoption is related to their children's problems. They think they can "love away" the feelings of rejection or the questions with which their children live. But "we do not replace one another," she maintains. "Life does not begin when a child is placed in our arms through adoption." Birthparents are "extensions of our children" says Gustavson, and she personally has always felt a "shadow mother bond" with the birthmothers of her own, all of whom have had reunions.[11]

Another spokesperson on the adoptive mothering experience is psychologist Patricia Baasel, mother of two by adoption when her birth child came along, and a woman whose experience with the three has changed her views about adoptive parenting. Adoptive parents have a more difficult task than biological parents, she feels, for two reasons. First, because it's harder for the adoptive parent to understand the child (to get on the child's wavelength, as she puts it); second, because the child has "additional burdens" himself by virtue of the adoption. "I still see adoption as a desirable procedure that brings together parents and children into a loving family. But I no longer see it as the same as rearing a birth child," she concludes. She believes that other individuals who are parents by both adoption and birth also see differences in the two experiences but have been reluctant to say so for fear that different will be taken to mean less.[12]

Some outsiders presume that the adoptive family is less strong than the non-adoptive family, and, for this reason, disapprove when their friends' adopted children become involved in search and reunion. Adoptive parents also occasionally find that in helping their children search, some of their personal friendships are threatened, as if the neighbors fear that a blow is being struck against the foundations of the family unit generally. Anita gets angry at people who ask her if she worries about losing her kids. "My God," she exclaims, "you lose them to an in-law; you lose them to a lot of people as they grow older. They're not possessions." Gina echoes the sentiment:

> "It all depends on your attitude. You can think of it as losing someone or as gaining another person in the family. . . . I don't think children are

> *possessions. I think they're only lent to us for a
> time, whether they be natural, adopted, foster,
> or whatever."*

Fortunately, people are capable of transcending the kind of thinking which makes children into possessions or which pits one triad member against the others. Adoptive parents who sometimes think of the child as having been a gift, a gift from God some say, avoid these traps. They see themselves as players in a trio, not a triangle, like the adoptive mother who wrote these cherished words to her son's birthmother:

> *"You gave life to Howard, he gave love and fulfill-
> ment to me, and God designed that many influ-
> ences should make him the person he is."*

Birthmothers' Assessments of the Adoptive Home

Integral to most decisions to relinquish their babies for adoption was the expectation by birthmothers that they would be raised by two loving parents, in a stable and fortunate environment that would surpass what the birthmother could provide—the fairy tale about the perfect family, several birthmothers point out. Now that they can judge for themselves (based on what they've been told and had augmented in some cases by personal meetings), these birthmothers have found that fantasies and reality sometimes do not mesh.

The lucky ones feel very positive about the homes their children had, marveling sometimes at how good the match was, and praising the adoptive parents for being loving, understanding, and providing psychological and material advantages, "like God hand-picked them." A few don't think they could have done as well.

There's Beverly, for instance, whose story we told in Chapter 8. Her satisfaction with the adoptive family is central to her being at peace with the adoption decision:

> *"Everything I've learned about the home sounds
> very, very good. Demographically, they resem-
> ble me. They exposed her to the culture of a*

> *huge city; she had the best education; she had a loving family; she has a loving grandmother who's still alive and means a great deal to her. She was very welcome in their home. They went out of their way to get this baby and they did everything they could to do a good job with her, and they did."*

Thelma, whose decision to relinquish was freely made and who also does not regret it, has a similarly positive assessment:

> *"Overall, I'm very pleased. I think she got good parents. I think they raised her very well. Considering how much she's like me, I think she was very lucky; she could have ended up a problem child if she had had parents like I had. She had very good, understanding people, and I think it worked out very well for her. I certainly don't fault them at all. I think she's a wonderful person. I don't think I could have done half the job that they did."*

Emily Sue likes the adoptive parents so well that "if I could have picked parents for Pam I probably would have picked them." Charlene also likes what she's learned from her son and is eager to meet the couple herself:

> *"It was a very secure homelife, very consistent. He calls it dull, vanilla, around his house. He's the type of person who wants excitement in his life, a fast pace, and his family doesn't seem to be like him that way at all. But I think when it comes to basics that his parents have done a great job raising him. He's got his feet on the ground and knows where he's going, and he can only thank his parents for that. He loves them very much."*

Nora believes that her son is a fortunate beneficiary of his double heritage:

> *"I think he got the balance from the family he grew up with. I gave him the intuitive and the creative. But what's beautiful is that his family knows how to make power work; they understand power. I've never understood power. They understand the social system, and they've given him that gift."*

Other birthmothers are fainter in their praise. Like this one:

> *"They were good people. Very devoted to her despite their hang-ups. Even with all their quirks and their own problems I think they've done well by her, the father especially. They could have been a lot worse; let's put it that way."*

And this one:

> *"It's not the perfect family; it's an average family. Because of my work in the adoption movement and all the families I see, I'd have to say that they're better than average. They don't have the education, they don't have a lot of money, but they're a warm, loving family."*

Another group of birthmothers express feelings about the adoptive parents in which the ambivalence is less muffled, a result of disappointments about the kind of childhood their son or daughter experienced or how he or she turned out. When the adoptee did not bond to the adoptive family, birthmothers feel particularly disenchanted with this decision to relinquish. Suzanne is one:

> *"Her adoptive parents were forty-three and forty-six when they adopted her, which I think is terribly old to be adopting an infant, and she was always around older people. They had one biological child older than Kim and they had lost a couple of children after that . . . Kim was always a replacement child for a child who had died, which I think was unfair to her."*

Post-Reunion and the Adoptive Parents

The problem in the case of Joan's daughter was not a failure to bond, but Joan has become aware of "some things that weren't quite as rosy as they first appeared." She wasn't pleased to learn that the adoptive mother had "some emotional problems"; on the other hand, "it wasn't as bad as it is for many, many people."

When a birthmother and an adoptive family live by different values or subscribe to different religious beliefs, the birthmother can feel unhappy about the environment into which her child was thrust. Constance for example:

> *"There was a time during the 60s when Peg was getting a little rebellious, but they were rather restrictive. She went to Catholic school up until she graduated from high school and they said they would pay for her college education if she'd continue to go to Catholic college. She said she wouldn't be willing to do that, so she went out on her own. I've always had difficulty with the restrictions that the Catholic religion puts on people. Not being Catholic myself, it would be easy to feel that way I guess."*

Carol, in contrast, has no complaints about the people who raised her son but faults the adoption system that separated them in the first place. The other mother's behavior has been "so accepting" that "it's been hard to have resentment toward her, which I would have liked to have had, because I was feeling that she got what was stolen from me." But Joey was "the bundle of genes," the child on such a different wavelength from his adoptive family that he represented a puzzle from early childhood, and Carol gauges that reunion and post-reunion have been less traumatic for them than for either Joey or herself:

> *"They're good people and intellectual people, moral and kind, and they're very good to Joey. However Joey was quite a handful for them, and I feel that because of the genetic differences*

*they were really unable to relate to Joey the
way I do, and he was able to pull the wool over
their eyes and get away with murder so to
speak, without them ever realizing, and this got
him quite off the track. I don't blame them for it,
though, as they just didn't know."*

Granting their disillusionments, the birthmothers often take so-
lace from the fact that their children's upbringings were not as
dreadful as stories they've heard about. The idea that it could
have been worse—that the child was not abused or deprived in
some serious way—is reassuring but cold comfort. Reflecting
on an adoptive mother's possessiveness, "I'd rather have killed
with love," says one. "I guess they did the best job they could,"
says another. "I think they made a lot of mistakes but nothing
intentional," says a third. "I'd like them to be a little warmer—
more perfect!" laughs a fourth.

We also talked to birthmothers who are angry and filled
with sorrow about what their children experienced. They are
reluctant to label the home bad, but they are clearly displeased
nonetheless. Jeanne, the birthmother who terminated her relationship with her mentally disturbed son, is one of these. Her
counterparts, with children whose histories were less destructive, express their dissatisfaction by saying something to the
effect of, this is not what I would have chosen.

Lila's daughter Kate, for example, grew up in a rural,
blue-collar neighborhood with a father who hit and frightened
the children time after time. Kate was cast in the role of caretaker to a deaf sister who was born a few years after the adoption, and she accompanied the younger girl to a camp for the
deaf for numerous summers. Every once in a while, the parents
would acknowledge to Kate how difficult her life was, but they
also presupposed that she would be "in the street" if they
hadn't adopted her. Even knowing that the home was chaotic
and dysfunctional at times, it took a while before Lila would
admit to herself, let alone anyone else, that she was critical of
people in a lower socioeconomic position than hers, but the

details of Kate's upbringing have been a bitter pill to swallow: "I realized the adoption was all for nothing."

Birthmothers who report that their children had rough lives often speak about conditions and events which everyone would agree are injurious: an alcoholic father married to a "long-suffering mother who hung in there"; a teenager raped by an adoptive brother; an adopted child being treated like Cinderella; a child's being raised by a dutiful relative after both parents died. Sometimes, though, the evils which the birthmothers point to are more subtle or subject to opinion, amounting to differences in temperament, style, or values between the other parents and themselves. For instance:

> "They gave him what they could; it's not what I wanted for him. I certainly wanted them to be more open, more flexible, more caring. I don't think they're very physically loving and that bothers me a lot."

Years back, of course, the pregnant young woman wasn't focussing on personality types or styles of parenting. The idea that her values or standards as a mother wouldn't be the ones the child would grow up with was not her foremost concern. But it is often the case in post-reunion that birthmothers must come to grips with the realization that they would have done some of the parenting, perhaps a good deal of it, differently. They try to stifle the very human thought that their style, whatever it is, would have been a better way.

The Two Mothers: Rights and Rituals

Most of the mothers in our sample who have met one another maintain some kind of continuing contact, but, unlike Hattie and Anita, the style tends to be closer to tolerant acceptance or necessary civility than warm friendliness. Caught between being allies and competitors, they invent a relationship of sorts, but neither is quite sure what to do with the other. The birthmothers in these relationships feel that the adoptive parents' goodwill is an asset to be prized ("I felt I was in their life by invitation only" says one) so they take great pains to maintain it. The adoptive parents take pride and satisfaction from the knowledge that they're aiding their child, but if they had their choice, many would prefer that none of this had ever happened. The relationship is like an uneasy alliance, remaining in effect until someone upsets the delicate balance.

Adrienne, you may remember from Chapter 3, characterized her relationship with her sons' adoptive parents as "a pact," by which she meant that each of them expressed gratitude to the other and that neither was trying to go much beyond that. The tone is proper and stiff, like a ritual dance. In a variation of this same propriety, another adoptive mother said to a birthmother:

> *"I'm sorry this whole thing had to happen, but I'm glad we were the ones who got him."*

The birthmother responded:

> *"Knowing where he was is part of my healing."*

The etiquette requires that each give the other her due, and the two women make various gestures to signal their desire for peaceful coexistence. "I have a great need for her to think I'm okay, that I'm not the bastard mother," one birthmother confides. Often, each is seeking affirmation from the other.

Phyllis is an astute observer of the ways in which the two mothers in post-reunion tread with caution, each attuned to the rights she perceives the other to have and each trying "not to tread on turf that doesn't belong to me." Phyllis speaks about the hurt she thinks Sharon's adoptive parents live with "in the gut," even though they accept, intellectually, all the reasons that Phyllis and Sharon should continue to have a relationship. Trying to deal with the adoptive mother's insecurity one day, Phyllis remembers telling her, "You're her mother in ways that I can never be and I'm her mother in ways that you can never be," one of the essential truths of adoption and reunion. But she feels competitive nonetheless, and she knows that the adoptive mother, Harriet, feels competitive with her. More than once, Phyllis and Sharon planned an excursion together, but when Harriet answered the door she was dressed for the outing, asking if she might come too.

Feelings of competition can be aroused over the most trivial things. Phyllis doesn't pride herself on being a particularly savvy shopper, for example, but when Sharon mentioned during a shopping expedition that Harriet had taught her to bargain hunt, a pang went through Phyllis's heart. Did Sharon like Harriet better than her? Was Harriet a better mother? If Sharon says something like, "My mom makes this killer potato salad," Phyllis thinks, "Oh yeah? Well I make killer potato salad too." Lila has had the same experience. Ordinarily, she doesn't care whether people think she's a good cook or not, but when Kate was eating a meatloaf she'd made and remarked that her adoptive mother made "a mean meatloaf," the same pang went through Lila. She feels like a fool when she catches herself, caring about such comparisons, but it happens anyway.

Phyllis remembers the feelings of inadequacy she had vis-a-vis the other mother when the reunion started. "How can I hold a candle to this woman who raised my child?" she wondered then. Three years later, she is tuned in to all the ways in which they are different from one another, and she is sure that each of them is making judgments about the other. She is not asking herself "Who is the 'real' mother?" but in countless ways what she seems to be asking instead is, "Who is the better mother?" Lila also feels the need for differentiation. The question she finds herself pondering is which mother is primary and which is secondary. Her answer keeps fluctuating.

Difficult as it is for everyone to accept the fact that adoptees have two mothers, the irony is that they sometimes seem to have none. Marlene tells the story of an important occasion in her daughter's life at which neither mother felt she could claim title; each was being scrupulous about deferring to the other:

> *"At her graduation, we were in one section and her adoptive parents and her children were in a different section. They asked for the parents of the graduates to stand up so the graduates*

> *could applaud them and neither her adoptive
> mother nor I stood up! Paula said later, 'I'm
> thirty-five and still nobody will acknowledge me!'
> And I said to her, 'Well you know I didn't do
> anything to help you get that degree; at my
> son's graduation I'll stand up.' And she said to
> me, 'That's not true. If it wasn't for the feeling
> you gave me, for the security you gave me, I
> couldn't have gone back to school and worked
> as hard as I did to get that degree.' "*

Considering the parent rivalry that can develop, it wouldn't be surprising if one mother secretly wished that the other was inadequate or unlikeable in some important way. Vivien's husband said as much when he suggested to Vivien that maybe she was happy that her daughter didn't get along with her adoptive parents. But Vivien was amazed he could think such a thing; her daughter's well-being depends on having good relationships with everyone, she says. Emily Sue addresses the same point, also indicating that concern for her child's welfare overrides her own dormant rivalries:

> *"It bothered me a little bit when she'd say 'Mom
> this' and 'Mom that' to her adoptive mother, but
> I wouldn't want her to have a bad relationship
> with them either. She had a pretty good grow-
> ing up and I'm glad for that. In a way, I thought
> 'Gee, it would be nice if she had rotten parents
> and she really needed me' but I'm glad that her
> parents are the way they are because she feels
> free to have a relationship with me. She doesn't
> feel threatened by them, like they're going to
> lose their love for her."*

Even with time and education, some adoptive parents will remain staunchly opposed to search and reunion. Our interviews present several illustrations of parents for whom this may be so, as well as adoptees who are convinced that they must not inform their adoptive parents about the reunion. One of these cases is Debora's, whose story we told in Chapter 3 and who regrets ever having spoken to the adoptive father on the phone; he called her a slut, asked her how she dared find them, and seems unlikely to change. Another is Marion, who almost destroyed her relationship with her son by insisting he tell his adoptive parents about it. She wanted the announcement as "a validation that he accepted me as his mother," but she withdrew, finally, when she saw he might end their association, because he was afraid his adoptive parents would "haunt" him from the moment they found out.

Still, as a general rule, adoptees and birthparents should not presume to know what the adoptive parents think or feel. We have only to remember the adopted woman who spent a lifetime operating under a wrong certainty about her adoptive mother's point of view, and who concludes that search and reunion frees the adoptive parent as much as it frees the other parties in the triad:

> *"My adoptive mother looks so much better, she acts so much better, she's so much more casual with me. Don't let anybody insist that an adoptive mother is going to be hurt by such a reunion."*

Even Helaine, whose daughter's adoptive parents have refused for five years to meet her, does not dismiss the possibility that things may change.

> *"I used to say, 'If ever they want to meet me, forget it after what they put me through' but I don't feel that way anymore. If it were for the sake of making her happy. . . . I used to hate them so much and now I don't. I can empathize with them and understand where they're coming from. They couldn't have children."*

13

Some Conclusions

There's no such thing as a perfect reunion. Every reunion is built on the foundation of closed adoption, and the closed adoptions from which these reunions sprang were permeated with secrecy, guilt, shame, and loss. It's a wonder that anything good and healthy could spring from such a soil, but it has.

There's no such thing as an easy post-reunion, because too many people are involved, each with his own personality, history, conflicts and uncertainties. Having a reunion and building a post-reunion is like erecting the Tower of Babel: a precarious balance must be achieved in a scene of noise and confusion, a discordant mixture of needs, desires and personal styles. It's a marvel that people connect at all. Yet fantasies are put aside, reality is acknowledged, jealousies are soothed, insecurities fade, feelings of loss and threat are resolved, issues of all kinds get dealt with, and relationships endure.

The pangs of reunion and post-reunion are no less real than the pangs of birth, but the rewards are great. It wasn't true that these birthmothers would forget their children, put the pregnancy and adoption behind them, and get on with their lives after the surrender. It begins to be true after reunion, when birthmothers can derive peace of mind, enhanced self-esteem, and feelings of liberation. Post-reunion can produce some measure of closure.

Just as impressive is what post-reunion can accomplish for adoptees. We see men and women taking on the sense of being real, normal adults, just like everyone else. We see self-esteem strengthening after adoptees learn the circumstances of their birth and find out they weren't "dumped." We see an ending to the paralysis of the unknown, the flow of unleashed potential. Adoptees get rid of "the adoption difference" and move on.

There are physical changes as well. Adoptees wear them visibly: a straighter carriage, a less deviant style of dress. "The celebration starts happening around the body" a birthmother says. It doesn't happen all at once. It takes time for adoptees to unify their doubleness, redefine who are they, and re-think their view of where they fit in the world. But the changes can be profound, as they have been for twenty-one-year-old Colin:

> *"I've made a lot of changes in my life as a result of the reunion. I feel a lot stronger now, a lot more complete. I know who I am. I know what my potential is now. I know what to expect from myself. I didn't before. It's been 'go out and get 'em' since the reunion, nonstop. I've been involved with all sorts of organizations. I'm pushing myself very hard now. It's just a feeling I can't explain: knowing who you are after not knowing who you are. You just feel so ready to get up and go. I've redone my entire art portfolio, I'm thinking more about a career, I'm having a relationship after a year and a half of not seeing anyone. A lot of things have changed for me. I'm much happier. The depression is gone. I've decided to stop drinking and partying, because I feel I have a lot more important things to do now. I'm much more receptive to my adoptive parents. There have been a lot of changes. Too many to list."*

Personal Strategies

We do not wish to leave the impression that reunion or post-reunion will solve all the personal problems that birthmothers and adoptees bring into them. Reunion and post-reunion are not the magical cure for all life's problems, despite the parties' understandable inclination to present them that way and to minimize the disappointments and difficulties. Until society favors reunion with approval and with social amnesty, reunion advocates can be expected to accentuate the positives and play down the negatives when they are explaining their experiences to everyone else.

Post-reunion unfolds like a marriage: you have to work at it. Basic survival training in "birthmotherhood" should include the following pieces of advice, according to the women in this book, women who've been on the front lines:

• *Get help:* join a support group; see a professional who's versed in adoption/reunion issues; find a "buddy" who's been through it. Read whatever books and newsletters you can find. You'll discover you're not alone and you're not crazy. Don't wait until your reunion hits a snag; do it right away. And consider the possibility that your spouse might benefit from counseling too (especially if the birthfather re-enters your life).

• *Expect an emotional roller coaster ride,* from depression to ecstasy. Try to be in touch with all the contradictory feelings. Try to express them. It's okay to feel whatever you feel. It's okay to be angry.

• *It's not unusual to feel guilty* about relinquishment, or about what the adoptee didn't get, but try to avoid self-flagellation. You can be sad without being guilty. You have it within your power to interpret the past in a way that will make you feel better or in a way that makes you feel worse.

• *Take it slow,* one day at a time. Don't try to make up for years of separation (or guilt, or deprivation or whatever) all at once. Try not to overwhelm the other person. Take your fears one at a time too.

• *Give the relationship time,* be patient. Even outside adoption, feelings of connection between parents and children need time to develop. *Any* relationship takes years to build.

• *Be honest.* Adoption has been full of secrets. Be open

and truthful. If you can't deal with something, say so. Don't lie about your feelings to please, or to avoid hurting him or her, either. Those lies will just cause trouble later.

• *Give a lot, but set limits* if you must. You don't owe the adoptee everything he or she ever missed. Resist the impulse to spoil. Don't take on an uncalled-for role, i.e., mothering—if mothering is not what the adoptee wants.

• *Be cautious,* think before you act. These are complicated relationships and powerful emotions. Behave with an eye toward continuing the relationship. Try not to be judgmental.

• *Appreciate* whatever you have in reunion. Try to be content; don't push for more.

According to many birthmothers, a religious outlook or a philosophy of life is also beneficial in dealing with post-reunion issues and stresses. Some women take great strength and comfort from such beliefs. Betty, for example, believes that her lesson is to "go with the flow." She is trying to do so and not demand more of her son than he is willing to give. Nora believes that the meaning of reunion and post-reunion is to teach birthmothers a lesson about love:

> *"If a birthmother were with me now and about to go into reunion I would say to her, 'Your primary goal is to learn and understand unconditional love. That's what we're going through this for; this is the lesson. We're talking about a love that's not human. Humans don't know about that, humans always have conditions. Here is a situation where we cannot have the luxury of conditions if we really want the relationship.'"*

Tough going or not, just about all the birthmothers we interviewed expect that they and their children will be part of each other's future forever.[1] Mainly, their vision of the future is "more of the same" which means, for most, that the bond will grow stronger as time passes and as mutual history accumulates. Birthmothers in rockier relationships hope that the future

. will get easier. Women whose relationships are calmer anticipate "being a family for the rest of our lives," or, simply, "sharing our lives." No one takes these relationships for granted.
They are precious, handle-with-care miracles, and they will be
cultivated with resolve, even in the face of difficulties.

Nonetheless, the history from which these relationships
spring can not be eradicated. It is not possible to make up for
all the lost years, no matter how long-lasting or how lovely post-
reunion becomes. With their bolstered self-esteem, the women
generally take pride in how well they've handled reunion and
post-reunion events and challenges. It feels like a major accom-
plishment. Like burn victims, though, many expect that they
will bear the scars of their "birthmotherhood" forever.

Public Policy Implications

The individuals we have highlighted in this book are a
particular group of women who have developed a particular
point of view about closed adoptions, but the issues they raise
concern tens of millions of Americans today. These birthmothers feel strongly that men, women, and children who live with
adoption now, those who will join the ranks soon, and the agencies and lawmakers who participate in adoption law and policy
need to understand that the closed adoption system is neither
healthy nor humane for large numbers of people. Despite good
intentions, all segments of the triad are its victims.

The most innocent victims, of course, are the adoptees,
who never asked to be born or adopted, and who, today, are
bound by rules they had no part in making and by agreements
they did not sign. They become legal adults at the age of majority, but the adoption system continues to treat them as children and gives them no rights. Prohibited from obtaining their
adoption records legally, on demand, many contend that their
constitutional rights are being denied and that they are being
treated like slaves. They are making a crucial distinction between their legal rights, on the one hand, and their emotional
relationships, on the other. Some are working on bills to bring
the issue to the attention of the Supreme Court.

BirthBond

Given sealed records and people's continuing reticence to come forward to announce their adoption connections, it is not possible to identify random populations of triad members. Researchers are unable to undertake the kind of studies that have "representative samples" or that produce results of the "statistically significant" variety. If the criteria for decision-making are the statistical and experimental criteria associated with most kinds of science, the truth of the matter is that the adoption knowledge base is still shaky. But the information being heard from triad members who present themselves is that something went wrong. Almost none of the women we spoke to would choose to have their children's adoptions proceed the same way. The system produced too much hurt, vulnerability, damage, and disorder. There was too much wasted time, energy, and potential. One expert speaks of reunion as a "correction" and proposes that perpetuating closed adoption be looked upon as a kind of "malpractice."[2]

If public policy about adoption is going to be formulated on the basis of scientific data, we need to undertake the kinds of longitudinal studies which will show the impact of closed adoption on all segments of the triad. Surveying the attitudes of existing (and potential) triad members about alternative adoption policies would also be in order, especially in a public which should be educated about adoption issues.[3] So far, these kinds of studies are in short supply, and the self-selected nature of the voices we're hearing is a weakness from the scientific standpoint. It leaves us wondering about the groups who are *not* represented: the adoptees who are not searching, the birthmothers still in hiding, the adoptive parents who are silent about what adoption has meant in their households. Some percentage of them, presumably, came through it all just fine. But we do not know how high or low this percentage is. Adoption, unfortunately, is still a subject where we don't really know what's majority or minority experience.[4]

Still and all, not being able to see the whole picture doesn't invalidate that portion of it which has, finally, come into focus. And what many spokespersons as well as birthmothers are saying is that American adoption is an institution in ill-repair. It flies in the face of common sense by denying that the adoptee has two sets of parents. It appeals to the worst in people by encouraging adoptive parents to think of the child as a possession, whom they own. It presumes that adoptive and birth parents will be ruled by base motives and will make decisions in which their interests take precedence over the child's. It values exclusion over inclusion. It ignores the primal call of roots. It honors one set of parents and dishonors the other.

Some reforms in adoption procedures have already become common practice, like collecting better medical information about birth families, for example, and giving it to the adoptive parents. But the question of how open or closed adoption should be is the central issue in adoption today. Over the years, great disagreement has existed about how much information should be given to adoptive parents about the child's birth history, and about how much should eventually be shared with the child. Now the debate has a new complexion: what role should the birthmother have as the child grows up? What kind of information should she get? What kind of contact? And where does the birthfather fit in?

The answers are not self-evident. Adoption is an institution that varies from country to country and century to century, taking its shape from the society in which it operates. In the historical scheme of things, it took its present shape in the United States quite recently. The first sealed records law was passed in 1917[5] but sealed records did not become routine until the late 1940s. There are several foreign countries in which records are not sealed and never have been. There are countries, Great Britain for example, where sealed records have given way to open records and adoptees can request their birth information when they reach adult age. The concept of retaining one's birthright even though a person is legally adopted exists in Judaic law, among Hawaiians and Eskimos, and also in Thailand, to name a few. As we write this today, new adoption concepts are being explored in countries such as New Zealand, where practitioners are wondering whether the idea of ownership, so ingrained in adoption thinking, can be replaced by concepts more like stewardship or guardianship. In America, concepts like legal guardianship and long-term foster care are being re-examined.

In 1987, the Child Welfare League of America issued a statement expressing an "increasing concern with the lifelong implications of adoption." With respect to new adoptions, it urged agencies to advise prospective adopters that confidentiality could not be guaranteed in their futures. It also asked agencies to assist, "within relevant statutes," all adult triad members in existing adoptions who wish to establish contact with one another.[6]

If and when a particular adoption search comes to court, the courts require that "good cause" be shown why an adoptee's sealed adoption record should be opened, and, as noted in Chapter 2, judges have been reluctant to accept most arguments. Ruling that adoptees' "good cause" violates birthparents' right to privacy, they have refused to compromise the confidentiality which was part and parcel of yesterday's adoption process, even though many participants never asked for, or depended upon, such "protection." Ironically, approaching someone to ascertain their feelings today can itself be construed as a violation of privacy. Also ironic is that many birthmothers never signed papers promising they would never reveal themselves to their child or see the child again. What they signed was a waiver of parental rights. They expected confidentiality because it was assured, but it was a verbal promise from the agency, not a written contract.

But what about birthmothers who *do* want privacy because they fear their lives will be ruined if a child appears? Shouldn't their identity be protected? No, say open records advocates. A woman who brings a child into the world has a responsibility to that child. Only she can give him his story and explain why the adoption took place. Only she can deliver to the child his biological and historical identity. She can always refuse the petitioner, they say, but society should not guard her with the protective cover of anonymity. If someone has to be favored, they argue, let it be the innocent party, the adopted adult, who maintains that his rights are being denied and his best interests not being served by yesterday's arrangements. If psychological or biological imperatives are at work, shouldn't these supersede expectations that were planted in another era and agreements that were made before any of this was understood? If adoptees need to be reconnected to their origins, why should separation be judged the higher good?

If adoption records were officially opened, some kind of search would still be required in most cases anyway, because people move and names change. Also, safeguards could be put in place. First, contact could be made through a third party, for example, to give the birthmother an opportunity to prepare herself and state any wishes she may have about meeting arrangements. Perhaps she would agree to one meeting only, in a private place where no one would recognize her. Perhaps birthmothers who do not wish to meet adoptees in person would be willing to answer questions in writing and offer photographs instead. The point is: removing the legal prohibitions on the road to reunion is not the same as forcing a meeting against people's will. Society can open records, but it can't legislate whether a door gets slammed or a welcome mat goes out.

Rather than opening records, several states have initiated registries to help people reconnect. Relatively few matches have been accomplished this way, though, for several reasons. First, people don't know about the registries because they're not widely advertised. Second, some charge a fee, which not everyone can afford to pay. Third, some require that individuals get "counseling" before any meeting takes place, a provision that birthmothers and adult adoptees consider demeaning. In the so-called passive type registry, both parties need to register before a match can be made. In the active type, an intermediary is supposed to notify the second party after the first has registered. But ours is a mobile society and unless names and addresses have been updated periodically, it's no easy task for an intermediary to track someone down, especially if they've left the state. How much perserverance can an uninterested state government worker be expected to muster on a stranger's behalf?

The registries are an attempt by the establishment to respond to people's desire for reunion, but there are important practical problems. Some kind of national registry system would be preferable; a bill to create such a mechanism has languished in Congress for several years. But some triad members contend that *any* registry system is less desirable than just opening records. The state registries currently in place, they feel, are simply being used as an excuse for avoiding a more profound kind of legislative change.

Regardless of who wins the battle over yesterday's records, the forces working for open records have already had an important impact on the shape of new adoptions. Happily, open adoptions are gaining favor, but the term covers a wide range of possibilities, including the possibility that birthparents could meet prospective adopters without identifying information being exchanged. What is meant by open adoption can run the gamut from using the agency as an intermediary that gives the birthmother annual reports about the child, to agreements about frequency of visitation and the role of each parent in the child's upbringing.[7] The specifics of how open adoptions work are evolving differently from case to case. It is a body of experience whose record is just beginning. (Already, there are reports about one parent or the other wanting to change the terms.)

Every birthmother we interviewed favors open adoption as an improvement over what she experienced, but they differ in the details with which they, personally, would feel comfortable. Immature and frightened teenagers negotiating the details with prospective adoptive parents would find such negotiations even harder. But these women, now, would insist upon some mechanism to insure their peace of mind, and many would want periodic, two-way communication to accommodate their continued sense of attachment.

The crusading spirit of reunion pioneers—the triad members who are attempting to rewrite their own pasts—is being felt wherever adoption is being discussed, and the debate is healthy. Open adoption did not exist as a choice years ago. But liberalizing the laws is a slow, painful process in which the courts are the field of battle. Individuals who have yet to achieve reunion contact would be foolish to hope that the right to meet one another will be granted by the legal system or by the adoption establishment easily or without a fight. People who have succeeded in having reunions had to fight city hall, literally, to do so. The walls are more easily scaled by today's searchers than they were five or ten years ago, but the walls are there still.

Compared to other reform movements—the civil rights movement or the feminist movement, for example—adoption reformers feel they are moving slowly.

One problem they cite is that adoption, and adoption reform especially, is most often considered a women's issue, meaning the subject has aroused more intense feelings from birthmothers than from birthfathers, and that adopted women are more outspoken than adopted men. As we noted in Chapter 9, however, the courts have given the birthfather greater rights to his child since the 1970s, and birthfathers play a greater role in adoption matters than they did a generation ago. To the extent that yesterday's birthfathers become more visible as well, the male voice can be expected to lend new power to the reform movement.

Another inhibitor to reform is the fact that the people who generally care most about it—namely, adoptees and birthparents—often lack the wherewithal for effective action because they are not strong, confident, or assertive initially. Their adoption connections have made them troubled and insecure in the ways we've seen throughout this book—the "walking wounded," as one of the birthmothers calls them.

Next, the weight of professional expertise has for years come down on the side of closed adoption, even though the stance was more a reflection of social attitudes than the product of defensible scientific knowledge. Adoption workers and people in the other helping professions were inclined to drag unwed mothers and their illegitimate babies out of sight.

Finally, the reform movement faces powerful resistance in legislative chambers, not just in the form of respect for contracts but also from the law's representatives, and from everyone who benefits, or perceives they benefit, from a closed system.[8]

However, the reunion and post-reunion experiences reported in this book make a powerful statement that closed adoptions should be ended, and that those who were caught in the web of the closed system should be granted some reprieve. Adoption is a lifelong process, but it does not have to be a lifetime sentence. There is no reason why adoption cannot be more humane.

In rethinking adoption, we ought to give greater respect to the feminine "voice," the ways in which women's psychology is different from men's. As discussed in Chapter 3, caring, responsibility, and relationship occupy the highest positions in women's morality, more honored than abstract concepts of right and wrong. According to this body of thinking, women operate according to the morality of connection, and will try to adjust the rules to accommodate the relationship. Men, who operate with the morality of justice, are more likely to accept the rules and let the relationship take care of itself. The biblical story of Abraham is the story of a father willing to sacrifice a child to prove his faith in God. Elsewhere in the Bible, two women each claim the same child and King Solomon identifies the real mother as the one who calls out to spare his life even if that means losing him to the other.[9]

These are wrenching images: the child caught between two mothers; the biblical threat of a child being cut in half to satisfy warring grown-ups. But the wrenching image of traditional closed adoption is no more pleasing. The future of adoption must lie elsewhere. We must neither deny that adoption involves two families nor make them competitors. Birthmothers need to know that their children are alive and well. Adoptees need to know where they come from. Adoptive parents need to know that acknowledging their child's heritage does not detract from the relationship they build and share.

What Post-Reunion Means for the Rest of Us

In studying the dynamics of reunion and post-reunion, we have come to appreciate some basic truths.

First, reunion teaches respect for biological continuity. Knowing our place in the biological and historical chain of life is something that non-adopted people take for granted, an inattention to matters of lineage that fits with the ideal of American society that the individual can create his or her own destiny. Indeed, the American dream tells us that we can escape our origins and be anything we want, not that we should worship our ancestors. What reunioning adoptees are teaching us, though, is that the knowledge of roots is somehow basic to emotional well-being. Without knowing where we come from and who preceded us, we are somehow impoverished. Without being able to see our personal characteristics mirrored in others, we grow up somehow disadvantaged, lacking validation. Being denied a connection with one's origins is a handicap. It amounts to setting out in life without the identity that everyone else has.

Reunion and post-reunion also teach respect for the family as a social unit at the same time that they change our definitions of who's included. Divorce and remarriage have changed the shape of the American family. Biological ties are not the only connectors that join people to one another in family groupings. Now, with reunion and post-reunion, the definition of family is further changing definitions of family because, instead of one family, adoption has two, each of whom counts the child its member. Possessiveness or ownership or exclusive claims by either family are ill-suited to the reality of the adoptee's double membership. The dynamics of adoption challenges all the players to make the family circle larger, and to include in definitions and affections individuals who are tied to the participants either by heredity *or* by environment, without demanding or pretending that it be both.

Reunion and post-reunion also have something to teach us about privacy, on the one hand, and secrecy, on the other. The way ethicist Sissela Bok explains it, privacy is the condition of being protected from unwanted access by others. It becomes secrecy when hiding is introduced. "But privacy," Bok points out, "need not hide and secrecy hides far more than what is private. A private garden need not be a secret garden; a private life is rarely a secret life."[10] What happened in closed adoption is that secrecy was substituted for privacy. In today's world especially, as one of the birthmothers exclaimed, "All this secrecy is ridiculous!"

It's appropriate to end our work by returning to Betty. Her reunion, like most, has been a blend of bitter and sweet, because her son is one of the ones who will not tell his adoptive parents about their relationship. He insists he never will. That the deceit is being perpetuated casts a shadow of sadness over Betty's delight in their reunion.

Three years into post-reunion, her son's children are reaching an age when a casual reference about her to their other grandparents could reveal their secret—something as innocuous as "Betty gave me the new sweater" ("Oh? Who's Betty?"). If that doesn't happen, the fact that her identity remains hidden means that adoption-related deceit is being carried into the next generation. Post-reunion is easier for Betty than reunion was because today her son accepts her and she's more relaxed about the relationship; but it's harder in another way because his attempt to keep her presence secretive weighs more heavily.

Continuing to live a lie isn't healthy, and Betty knows it. She also suspects that, because of her loving relationship with the grandchildren, her true identity cannot remain hidden. But fundamentally, she feels that whatever happens in post-reunion, the reunion was worth it:

> *"If the worst possible thing could happen and I never saw my son again, still, I met him and I told my son, right to his face, that I loved him, and he knows who I am."*

Notes

Introduction

1. In half the sample, the interviews were administered in person; the other half tape-recorded their responses to the same interview questions.

2. Only one reunion represented in our sample has terminated (after three years). The termination occurred because of the adoptee's mental illness, a condition which finally resulted in the birthmother's decision to sever the relationship, but she did not negate the possibility that the relationship could resume in the future if her son becomes sufficiently stable.

3. This would be the case, of course, regardless of which part of the adoption triad we selected as our main focus.

4. We have chosen to keep all names in the text fictional, nonetheless, for purposes of consistency and for legal considerations.

5. These tapes, generally prepared by people in the search and support movement for educational purposes, usually include both general commentary and individual accounts of specific reunions.

6. Naming and possessing may be applicable to the world of adoption for two reasons. First, adoptive parents are free to change whatever first name their baby has already been given. (Not all of them choose to do so.) The discovery by a birthparent-in-search that the adoptee's given name was not changed by the adoptive parents is often taken as a sign that they may not stand in the way of reunion. Second, adoptees' birth certificates routinely substitute—not add—adoptive par-

ents' names for birthparent names, obliterating any trace of birthparent identity.

7. Rillera, *Adoption Encounter,* p. 64.

Prologue

1. In his chapter "Unwed Mothers in America," Aigner, *Adoption in America,* details the changing social and professional views of unwed mothers since the early part of the century, demonstrating that the unwed mother was considered either "very deprived, very immoral, very stupid, very deviant, or perhaps very exploited," until, after World War II, she began "to make brief appearances in the behavioral science literature as Everywoman, a figure who represented a cross-section of society as a whole."

2. This proportion is higher than the figures we've seen in other studies, suggesting that the fact that the birthparents marry one another augurs well for birthmothers' openness to reunion contact and/or post-reunion relationships.

Chapter One

1. See Aigner's *Adoption in America* for a detailed treatment of social attitudes toward unmarried mothers and illegitimate babies during this century.

2. Theoretical understanding of attachment, including the work of psychoanalyst D.W. Winnicott in particular, holds that a bonding process between mother and child begins in the womb and is not completed until months after birth. Winnicott calls this the period of Primary Maternal Preoccupation.

3. More than half the adoptees in our sample were placed in foster homes before reaching their adoptive homes. There are also instances in the sample of birthmothers refusing to relinquish their babies for six months or more after birth, hoping to

find a way to keep them or seeking reassurance that a good home had indeed been identified.

4. Betty Jean Lifton's *Lost and Found: The Adoption Experience* details "the adopted self" from a number of different perspectives. One of these is "the adoptee as survivor," about which she writes: "Since most adoptive parents are unable to see the child's loss of the birth parents as a psychic trauma, but rather as a felicitous event that had enriched their own lives, it is hard for the adoptee to deal with his survivor role. Although he perceives that a piece of his world has been swept away, he also perceives that he must not attempt to retrieve it."

5. Erik Erikson, a psychologist who is best known for his thinking on identity issues, never knew his own birthfather.

6. Rillera, *Adoption Encounter,* p. 42.

7. *The New York Times,* Thanksgiving 1987, dateline Fremont, California.

8. Lord, Lewis J. *U.S.News & World Report,* October 5, 1987 pp. 59–65.

9. Janis, Chris, *New Haven Register,* "Mom hunts for the son she gave up" (1987). The newspaper also reported that a committee of state legislators formed to study the state's adoption laws had proposed a change in the law pertaining to the transmittal of medical information.

10. Glenn, M.D., "The Adoption Theme in Edward Albee's 'Tiny Alice' and 'The American Dream,' " *Psychoanalytic Study of the Child,* Vol. 29, pp. 413–429.

11. Four women in our sample surrendered before that, in the 1930s and 1940s.

12. Donahue (1986). Transcript 04046.

13. Deykin, Campbell and Patti, "Postadoption Experience," *American Journal of Orthopsychiatry,* 54 (2), 1984

14. "Adoption Dilemma," *New Haven Register,* April 12, 1987.

15. Bok, *Secrets.*

16. See Aigner, *Adoption in America,* and Riben, *Shedding*

Light on the Dark Side of Adoption for extended discussion of this point.

17. Watson, "Birth Families: Living with the Adoption Decision," *Public Welfare.*

18. Klaus and Kennell, *Parent-Infant Bonding* p. 268, mention this same question as being a painful one for the parents of a stillborn child or an infant who died. After a few months, those parents usually decided to give an answer that mentioned the baby.

19. Ganson and Cook, "The Open Records Controversy in Adoption: A Woman's Issue?"

Chapter Two

1. United States Children's Bureau Research Division, as quoted in Rillera, *Adoption Encounter,* op. cit.

2. "Child Adoptions by Type," 1952–71, Statistical Abstract of the United States. 1973; No. 508. As quoted in Rillera, *Adoption Encounter.*

3. Close to one million unmarried women have abortions each year, according to statistics of the Centers for Disease Control. Prior to 1973, some percentage of these unwanted, unplanned children would have been carried to term and placed for adoption.

4. According to a national survey conducted by the National Committee for Adoption and reported in the Committee's publication, *Adoption Factbook.* Of the estimated 141,861 adoptions, 50,720 were adoptions by non-relatives and 91,141 were adoptions by relatives. The 50,720 unrelated adoptions include adoptions of children from other countries, adoptions of children with special needs, and adoptions by foster parents. Adoptions of healthy infants account for a minority of the total: 17,602.

5. *Ibid.* Adoptions of foreign-born children have increased in recent years as the availability for adoption of American-born

children has declined. In 1984, over 8,000 foreign adoptions took place.

6. By 1978, five years after the Supreme Court decision legalizing abortion, only three percent of middle and upper income women gave birth to unplanned babies, according to McKaugham, *The Biological Clock.*

7. Figures from the Alan Guttmacher Institute; Stanley K. Henshaw. *U.S. Teenage Pregnancies Statistics,* March, 1987. Of the one million teen pregnancies each year, 400,000 end in abortion, 470,000 give birth, and the remainder miscarry. Literature from Planned Parenthood indicates that three-quarters of American teens have sex by age nineteen and that only one-third of teens use birth control every time.

8. See Aigner, *Adoption in America,* p. 52. Regarding birthmothers' ages. Aigner quotes a 1963 source saying that increases in illegitimacy since 1940 have been greater among twenty to twenty-four-year-olds than among teens.

9. Data from the National Center for Health Statistics, reported in the *Boston Globe,* "Long Waits. High Costs in Baby Market" by Jerry Ackerman, March 20, 1988.

10. National Center for Health Statistics, *Monthly Vital Statistics Report,* vol. 36, No. 4; July 17, 1987.

11. Anderson, Campbell and Cohen, "Eternal Punishment of Women: Adoption Abuse." In the Spring, 1989 publication of the American Adoption Congress, *Decree,* Carole Anderson, past president of CUB, noted that United States policies and attitudes often encourage the separation of families, rather than keeping them together. She also reported that other nations "were shocked to learn that adoptions (in the United States) can be arranged by non-social workers, that independent adoptions are often a big money business and that people can advertise for babies in the newspapers."

12. According to the *Adoption Factbook* of the National Committee for Adoption, the 1982 National Survey for Family Growth found that about 6 percent of premarital births were placed for adoption—12.1 percent of births to white mothers,

but only 0.4 percent of births to black mothers. The Factbook also states that black children constitute fourteen percent of the child population, thirty-four percent of foster care, and forty-one percent of children free for adoption. State laws on color-matching in adoptive placement vary, and transracial adoption is a controversial issue.

13. See Hocksbergen, ed., *Adoption in Worldwide Perspective,* for a discussion of worldwide adoption practices.

14. A study by Triadoption Library in California found that over a quarter of a million people were contacting search and support groups in a year's time. (Reported in *Adoption Encounter,* op. cit., p. 116.) *People Searching News* reported that "more than two million adoptees and a near equal of birthparents are searching." (September/October 1987.)

15. Pavao, Joyce, Program Director, Post-Adoption Consulting Team, the Family Center, Cambridge, Massachusetts, Personal Interview.

16. Interview with Florence Fisher, May 2, 1988, Channel 9 (New York), Chris O'Donohugh reporting. Ms. Fisher estimates that three to four million are searching.

17. Sorosky, Baran, and Pannor, *The Adoption Triangle.*

18. States that give adult adoptees some access to their birth information are: Minnesota (birth certificate with birthparents' consent, also the right to contact birthparents so long as they do not refuse the request); Alabama (excluding birthparents' names); Alaska and Kansas.

19. Aigner, *Adoption in America,* p.42, who writes that "a substantial body of evidence can be compiled identifying the influence traditionally exerted upon child relinquishment by such forces as punishment, coercion, harassment, biased counseling, legal disenfranchisement of parents from their offspring and numerous other forms of manipulation and pressure."

20. Klaus and Kennell, *Parent-Infant Bonding,* describe the need for structures to facilitate mourning in order to eventually free parents from loss.

21. Lifton, *Lost and Found,* discusses "I Never Was Born," pp. 20–21, as a feeling common to adoptees. She also claims that life begins for the adoptee at the moment he gains consciousness that he is adopted and thus different.

22. The National Committee for Adoption estimates that of the more than 51,000 adoptions to non-relatives in one year (1982), around 19,000 were arranged by public agencies, around 15,000 by private agencies, and around 17,000 by private individuals. *(Adoption Factbook,* 1985.)

23. In contrast, in the 1800s, the father was the parent viewed as having primary rights. (Donald Humphrey, attorney and legal counsel for AAC. Personal Interview.)

24. The umbrella organization for the movement is The American Adoption Congress (AAC). It was founded in 1978 and describes itself as an international network dedicated to promoting openness in adoption through education. As of early 1988, there were ninety adoption organizations and over nine hundred individuals in the membership.

25. Concerned United Birthparents (CUB), one of the AAC member organizations, addresses the birthparent position most directly. Adoptive Parents for Open Records, another member group, takes the adoptive parent as its primary focus.

26. A few groups have arisen in the past year or so dedicated specifically to post-reunion issues.

27. This is not surprising, since we located them through the support group networks.

28. One birthmother in Virginia publishes a newsletter for birthmothers with recent relinquishments, planning a pen pal column, matching birthmothers with similar yearly relinquishments—in effect, a support group by mail.

Chapter Three

1. Winkler and Keppel, *Relinquishing Mothers in Adoption,* asked 213 Australian birthmothers to rate the severity of stress

resulting from placing their children for adoption. Between "not at all stressful" and "the most stressful thing I have ever experienced," the majority considered it "the most stressful thing," as did three-quarters of the women we interviewed with a similar question.

2. These studies include the work of Sorosky and the works of Winkler and van Keppel. The Sorosky group refers to a study of thirty-six birthmothers, half of whom continued to have feelings of loss and mourning.

3. Ibid. The authors also found that relinquishing mothers had significantly more problems of psychological adjustment than a matched control group. See, too, Millen and Roll, "Solomon's Mothers: A Special Case of Pathological Bereavement," a paper based on twenty-two mothers seen in psychotherapy, which described ways in which the bereavement process was distorted or delayed in these women, stating "Mourning reaction can be inhibited and prolonged—i.e., that grief . . . can often be pathological." Millen and Roll also note that "the women we have worked with have struggled to understand the intense bond they feel for a child whom they know only as a memory or a fantasy."

4. Pavao, Joyce, Program Director, Post-Adoption Consulting Team, The Family Center, Cambridge, Massachusetts. Personal Interview.

5. Winkler and van Keppel, *Relinquishing Mothers.* The mothers they studied felt that their sense of loss and problems of adjustment would be eased by knowledge about what had happened to the child. Similarly, Sorosky, Baran and Pannor, *The Adoption Triangle,* pp. 38–40, note that, in their study, over eighty percent were interested in a reunion when the child reached adulthood, provided the child wished it. The majority also wished the agency to keep updated information for the child.

6. Deykin, Campbell and Patti, "The Postadoption Experience of Surrendering Parents," state "Nearly eighty percent of the 219 subjects stated that their earlier surrender of a child had

exerted a powerful impact on their subsequent parenting attitudes. Overprotectiveness, compulsive worry about the children's health, and difficulty in accepting children's independence were the most frequent negative features cited."

7. Silverman, *Helping Women Cope with Grief,* Chapter 4,
"The Grief of the Birthmother."

8. Lifton, *Lost and Found,* "The Adoptee as Double," pp. 34–
38, suggests that the adoptee is "haunted by a series of
doubles" which include, among others, the other possible self
one might have been had one been kept by one's birthparents,
and the self one might have been had one been chosen by a
different couple.

9. Klaus and Kennell, *Parent-Infant Bonding,* p.53.

10. Viorst, *Necessary Losses,* p. 21, synthesizes what the medical experts say and discusses the "high cost of separation"
noting that "when the separation imperils that early attachment, it is difficult to build confidence, to build trust, to acquire
the conviction that throughout the course of our life we will—
and deserve to—find others to meet our needs. When our first
connections are unreliable or broken or impaired, we may trans-
fer that experience and responses to that experience, onto
what we expect from our children, our friends, our marriage
partner, even our business partner."

11. Two of these eight were adopted at six months or older.

12. In a content analysis of letters written by adoptees to federal government officials commenting on proposed legislation
regarding the opening of adoption records, the investigators
noted that a majority of adoptees focused on the issue of identity development and that the common theme underlying the
comments was a sense of incompleteness: the adoptee is not
whole, a part of him/her is missing. Ganson and Cook, "The
Open Records Controversy in Adoption: A Woman's Issue?."

13. See Lifton, *Lost and Found* (Chapter 8: "Adolescent Baggage") for an exploration of whether and how adoptees are
prone to emotional maladjustment. The chapter includes a review of some of the key researchers in the field, presenting

such concepts as "genealogical bewilderment," "adoption stress," and "hereditary ghosts." According to Lifton, adoptees account for up to one-third of the population in certain adolescent inpatient psychiatric facilities.

14. As reported to us by Donna Cullum, President of Yesterday's Children, an active search and support group based in Chicago.

15. Sorosky, Baran and Pannor, *The Adoption Triangle,* pp. 115–25, regarding adult adoptee dynamics. Also, see Lifton, *Lost and Found,* on the subject of adult adoptee characteristics, referred to as "the adopted self."

16. Florence Fisher, the founder of ALMA, engaged in a search that extended over twenty years.

17. Anderson, "Why Adoptees Search: Motives and More." pp. 15–19.

18. Rillera, *Adoption Encounter,* p. 64.

19. Sobol and Cardiff, *Family Relations,* pp. 477–483.

20. Women searchers predominate in our sample by a ratio of about 2 to 1.

21. Miller, Jean. *Toward a New Psychology of Women.* Miller illustrates the difference between men and women, "Men are encouraged from early life to be active and rational; women are trained to be involved with emotions and with the feelings occurring in the course of all activity."

22. Ganson and Cook, "The Open Records Controversy in Adoption: A Woman's Issue?" addressed the question of whether adoption is experienced and interpreted differently by male and female participants. They concluded that gender is a major determinant of the degree to which adoption is a salient status for the individual, with women more likely to view adoption as a primary influence on their identities and life experiences. Challenging this view are Sobol and Cardiff, *Family Relations,* who conclude that sex bears no relationship to the degree of searching and that it may be wrong to believe that women have a greater proclivity to search than men. They sug-

gest that women may be more prone to volunteer information about search.

23. Emma Vilardi, International Soundex Reunion Registry. Personal Conversation.

24. Sobol and Cardiff, *Family Relations,* listed the following reasons for not searching: fear of hurting adoptive parents; sense of identity with adoptive parents; lack of interest/need; fear of hurting or disrupting birthparents; fear of undesirable or unknown consequences; lack of time or money; feeling search would be useless; lack of knowledge or emotional support; fear of rejection.

Chapter Four

1. Susan Darke of The Adoption Connection (Peabody, Massachusetts). Personal Interview.

2. Lifton, *Lost and Found,* Chapter 15, "Varieties of Reunion Experience."

3. Numerical conclusions such as these should be viewed with great caution, not just because they tend to be made by the same groups who are doing the searching, but also because they obscure the nature of whatever events and interactions lie behind a loaded label like "rejection." A similar caution extends to studies which attempt to judge reunion and post-reunion experiences as successful or unsuccessful, or favorable or unfavorable, unless the terms are clearly defined.

4. The assumption that one person or the other is mentally ill is a reason for post-reunion termination that appears with some frequency in our survey. Other reasons include: birthmothers' unwillingness to disclose pregnancy/adoption to immediate family/friends; adoptees' guilt vis-a-vis the adoptive parents; not liking each other and/or having incompatible values.

5. Carl and Lois Melina contrast the attitudes of yesterday's generation with today's, "Care of the birthmother years ago was predicted on the belief that placing a child for adoption was

an experience that could be permanently denied or forgotten. It is now acknowledged that placing a child for adoption is a difficult decision that a birthmother will live with for the rest of her life . . . Success in adjusting to the decision to place a child for adoption is connected to the opportunity the birthmother has to discuss her feelings about adoption, receive support during her grief period, and resolve her feelings of loss."

6. Transactional Analysis is a school of psychology which describes personality as comprised of three states: Parent, Adult and Child. Although these terms are given quite specific meanings within the TA system, the lay understanding of what they mean suffices for our purpose. That is, when adoptees function in their Child, smooth transactions with birthmothers will occur so long as the birthmothers are functioning in *their* Parent.

7. In our sample, under half were in long-distance relationships, and more than half were within driving distance, a few with drives two hours or more.

Chapter Five

1. Twelve birthmothers met teenage children: four sons and eight daughters.

2. The special stresses which adoption puts on adolescence are discussed in Lifton, *Lost and Found,* and Sorosky, Baran and Pannor, *The Adoption Triangle.*

3. Eight of the twelve teen reunions in our sample resulted from the birthmother's finding the adoptee.

4. Twelve birthmothers in our sample had reunions with children in their twenties. In eight of the twelve, the adoptee took the active search initiative. In three of the four cases in which the birthmother was the active searcher, the women were looking for sons; and, post-reunion, all three sons are maintaining a separation between the birth and adoptive components (either not telling the adoptive parents about the reunion or keeping the birthmother away from them.

Notes

5. Six reunions in our sample involve adoptees age thirty or older. Four came about as a result of the adoptee's searching and two from registry matches.

6. In our interviews, more of the reunions involve daughters than sons (eighteen versus twelve). Similarly, in our interviews, when the adoptee took the active role, that adoptee was more likely to be a daughter—the pattern seen in the search movement generally.

7. Genevie and Margolies, *The Motherhood Report,* pp. 288–9. Almost 9 in 10 reported that there was a difference between mother-son and mother-daughter relationships. Of these, only one in five said that they felt closer to their sons than their daughters. "For the overwhelming majority, four out of five, it was mothers and daughters who were closer, a bond that for many women was due to their closer identification with their girls. A son, as wonderful as he may be, is very different from mom. A daughter is mother in miniature—physically, psychologically, emotionally—and her likeness creates a strong connection."

8. Jung and Kerenyi, *Essays on a Science of Mythology.*

9. "Genealogical bewilderment" is a term introduced in the 1950s by H.J. Sants, a British psychologist, to describe adoptees' condition of being cut off from their natural parents.

10. In the five cases of our sample in which adoptees have not informed their adoptive parents about the reunion, four are with sons.

11. Davenport, Gail, M.S.W. (Psychotherapist and Director of Birthparent Support Network.) Personal interview. She feels that a son's first frame of reference vis-a-vis his birthmother is likely to be a sexual one because, very often, all he knows about her is that she was a "loose woman." If he comes into reunion with this image, she will have to undo that image.

12. Jeanne, the birthmother who terminated her reunion with her son, experienced this attraction and views it as one of the complicating factors that made it difficult for her to sort out

what was happening during the first year, but it was not the reason the relationship terminated.

13. These terms are used in their popular sense. "Delayed bonding" or "re-bonding" might be better labels.

14. Rillera, *Adoption Encounter.* "The adoptee who does not feel able to have a relationship with both the adoptive and birth families may have feelings of disloyalty, entrapment, inadequacy, or unstable identity."

15. Baran and Pannor, *Open Adoption as Standard Practice,* suggest that step relationships may be a useful model for the adoptive family. "Many of the problems faced by adoptive families have much in common with patterns evolving in so-called mainstream families, resulting from divorces and remarriages that create numerous stepparent households. These families deal with complex and overlapping loyalty demands, putting a special emphasis on acceptance of differences, good communication, trust and integration—needs similar to those we are attempting to deal with in adoption."

16. None of the adoptees in our reunion interviews was a teenager at the outset, and all but one of them did the active searching.

Chapter Six

1. About half the mothers in our sample met their children alone, without others being present.

2. TRY Newsletter, January/February 1989. Notes taken at a workshop "Adoptees' Sense of Self: Identity Issues in Adoption" were converted into a newsletter article, "As anyone reading this newsletter probably knows, so intimately, perhaps the most profound issue in identity for adoptees is how we look. For many of us, the bottom line in a search is, 'I just want to see her face!' We need to know we look like someone else on the planet; it is a physical, fundamental sense of belonging and relatedness . . . Statistically, more adoptees are likely to go into the performing arts than non-adoptees, or, at least, profes-

sions or avocations in which they are in the public eye. Those who talk about this in relation to their adoption say it is the yearning to be recognized."

3. The term "post-reunion" is not defined in the professional literature. The definition we suggest is that post-reunion begins at that point in time when the reunioning parties agree that they will have some sort of future together. Eventually, reunion and post-reunion will be defined in professional literature, but we are not aware of any work along those lines to date.

Chapter Seven

1. Eight birthmothers we interviewed in depth believe that their sons or daughters never bonded with the adoptive parents.

2. Vivien is the youngest birthmother we interviewed, and also one of the few whose reunion and post-reunion took place without search or support assistance from a group.

3. Rillera, *Adoption Encounter,* p.108. "Triad members make a lot of statements that are founded in caution and self-protection, but are not entirely true. An example is a birthmother's saying, 'I don't want to be your mother. You have a mother' or an adoptee's 'I don't want anything from you.' Probably the most honest statement we can make is 'I don't know what I want, but I would like to get to know you and find out.'"

4. Penny Partridge, "The Social Worker As Her Own Client." An unpublished paper presented at the Smith College School for Social Work, July, 1988. Partridge, a social worker, adoptee, and founder of a fifteen-year old search and support group, suggests that there are four stages that adult adoptees must move through in the development of a solid adult identity: acknowledging earliest separations, moving toward some kind of reconnectedness, integrating the pre-adoptive background with the post-adoptive experience (incorporating both into one identity) and effecting a new (adult) kind of separation from both sets of parents. Partridge sees these as developmental tasks

which adoptees have in addition to those which all adults face, and she believes that only the luckiest are able to move through the complete cycle.

5. Lenz, *Once My Child, Now My Friend.* Author of one of the few books that treat the relationship between parent and adult child, Lenz suggests that, ideally, the parent should become an ex-parent, phasing out as a parent and phasing in as a friend.

Chapter Eight

1. "All About Twins," *Newsweek,* November 23, 1987. Discussing the results of research by Thomas Bouchard, University of Minnesota, among a sample of 350 pairs of identical twins reared apart, the article reports that "the Minnesota team found striking similarities between the pairs in several major personality traits, suggesting a strong role for genetics." Holden, *"The Genetics of Personality,"* states, "As enumerated by J. Philippe Rushton of the University of Western Ontario, traits and conditions for which substantial heritabilities have been detected include activity level, alcoholism, anxiety, criminality, dominance, extraversion, intelligence, locus of control (personal autonomy), manic-depressive psychosis, political attitudes, schizophrenia, sexuality, sociability, values and vocational interests."

2. Plonim, Robert, as quoted in "The Genetics of Personality," *Psychiatric Times.* The Colorado Adoption Project, started in 1975, has a sample of 245 adoptees and their families. Project co-founder Plonim reports that it is increasingly clear "that the impacts of many environmental influences are genetically mediated . . . for a number of measures used in the study, the correlations between infant environment and development—that is, "good" environments correlating with "good" developmental outcomes—were higher in the biological than the adoptive families."

3. Twenty-five of the interviewed birthmothers cite resemblances between themselves and their child; among the five

who do not, each mentions resemblances between the child and another birth relative.

4. As noted in Chapter Seven, eight of the birthmothers believe that their child did not bond to the adoptive family and *did* need a maternal relationship—a "mommy." In contrast to the majority, these women *do* feel that their children were seeking a parental relationship.

5. Hyatt and Gottlieb, *When Smart People Fail,* provide a particularly cogent discussion about the power of labels.

6. Pogrebin, *Among Friends: Who We Like, Why We Like Them, and What We Do With Them.*

Chapter Nine

1. Most often, the birthfathers in our sample were in their teens and twenties, but six were age thirty or over. Nineteen were single, six were married, and five were separated or divorced when the adoptee was conceived.

2. Four of the birthfathers in our sample offered marriage and another three were considered supportive. In the rest of the cases, the women (and their families) dealt with the adoption.

3. In the past, birthmothers were commonly advised to list the birthfather's identity as "unknown" on the birth certificate. Similarly, for many adoptions, agency information about the paternal side of the family (including medical) was sketchy at best.

4. This was the case of one of our interviewed birthmothers. Also, Deykin, Patti and Ryan, *Fathers of Adopted Children: A Study of the Impact of Child Surrender of Birthfathers* disclosed ten percent of birthfathers were married at the time of surrender.

5. In seventeen of our cases, the adult adoptee has had a reunion with the birthfather. In six of the remaining cases, the man's whereabouts are not known.

6. Eight of our sample married the birthfather. Four of the couples later divorced. Also, in their independent study of

birthfathers, Deykin, Patti and Ryan note the large percentage of birthfathers (44%) who at some time were married to the birthmother. Twenty-five percent were married to the birthmother at the time of the survey and ten percent had been married at the time of surrender.

7. Eighteen of our interviewees had had no contact. Among the rest, only three had had some kind of contact (other than marriage).

8. None of our survey had birthfathers who denied paternity.

9. Deykin, Patti and Ryan, *Fathers of Adopted Children.* made no claims to being a representative study. The fact that almost all of the men had either considered searching, or had actually done so, is a function of the way in which the respondents were located.

10. Until Deykin, Patti and Ryan's *Fathers of Adopted Children,* the only major look at birthfathers was Pannor, Massarik and Evans, *The Unmarried Father,* whose focus was on helping the teenage father at the time of relinquishment. Co-author Pannor believes that the image of birthfathers as uncaring, uninterested and irresponsible is unfair and inaccurate. He urges adoption workers to revise their thinking, provide counseling to unmarried birthfathers, and involve them in adoption decisions. He also suggests that birthfathers having been insufficiently involved is one of the reasons that birthmothers feel abandoned (Cf. *Adopted Child* newsletter, June, 1988.)

Chapter Ten

1. We wish to thank AmyJane Cheney for permission to use this poem.

2. *New York Times,* March 1, 1987. In the dispute over Baby M, one of the arguments advanced on behalf of granting custody to "surrogate" mother Mary Beth Whitehead-Gould was that her other children had become attached to the baby, and that removing the child would be painful not only to her, but to them as well.

3. Donahue, 1988, regarding twins and other adopted siblings, by Cf. Dr. Nancy Segal, Assistant Director, University of Minnesota Center for Twin and Adoption Research.

4. The five adopted children were all in one family.

5. The idea of protecting brothers and sisters from one another has been sanctioned by the positions of courts and agencies, even when they know the older generation is deceased.

6. On the high side compared to the rest of the sample. In long-distance situations, siblings may not see each other more than once every few months, or once or twice a year.

7. In Lifton's *Lost and Found,* "Good Adoptee-Bad Adoptee" suggests that taking on the role of one or the other is almost inherent in the condition of being adopted and adoptees, in recollection, are easily able to place themselves in one or the other of these identities.

8. Biological children were present in seven of the sample cases.

Chapter Eleven

1. In our sample, four of the birthmothers did not tell their parents they were pregnant. One of these four has not told her mother about her reunion because of the mother's age.

2. Only three of our birthmothers reported their family members unwilling to meet the adoptee: in two cases, it was an unwilling sibling; in the third, the birthmother's mother.

Chapter Twelve

1. It's frequently suggested by search advisors that adoptive parents who also have biological children tend to be more sympathetic to a birthmother's desires for reunion than those who do not.

2. In the cases in our sample, adoptive parents are aware of the reunion in twenty-three cases, and there have been meet-

ings between the birthmother and the adoptive parent(s) in eighteen.

3. In the Ganson paper, op. cit., describing responses from triad members to proposed legislation to open adoption records, the author notes that with respect to the justice theme, the adoptive parent sample approaches the issue of justice from a morality stance, "but there is also a focus on the legality of the dilemma of open records. Adoptive parents are more likely to argue that the status quo, i.e., sealed records, is legally right, therefore, it is morally right . . . They appear more concerned with protecting the rights of adoption participants as set forth in the original adoption contract, focusing less on 'who is hurt' and more on 'what is fair.' "

4. As noted previously (in connection with siblings), seven of the adoptive families did have biological children either before or after the adoption; in three cases, the natural child died before or shortly after the adoptee came into the family.

5. Sorosky, Banan and Pannor, *The Adoption Triangle*, p.74.

6. Genevie and Margolies, in *The Motherhood Report*, pp. 280–81, a quantitative study of women's attitudes to mothering generally, noted a difference between biological and adoptive mothers in "The Adoptive Mother's Insecurity," in which they wrote, "Although there seemed to be no difference in the overall quality of the mother-child relationship between mothers and adoptive children, those women who also had biological children seemed to have a psychological edge over mothers who had only adopted children. With firsthand experience of having both adoptive and biological children, there seemed to come a feeling of security and confidence that they were as real a mother to their adoptive children as to their natural children. Women who only had adopted children, on the other hand, often expressed a subtle feeling of insecurity that their children did not view them as their "real" mothers." The adoption literature (Sorosky, Baran and Pannor, and others) frequently makes the same point. See, for example, Winkler, Brown, van Keppel and Blanchard, *Clinical Practices in Adoption*.

7. See materials produced by Carol Gustavson, president of Adoptive Parents for Open Records, for elaborations on these points.

8. In 1975, Sorosky, Baran and Pannor, *The Adoption Triangle,* reassured adoptive parents, "One feeling (about reunion) . . . was shared in some measure by all adoptive parents: they feared losing the love of their adopted child to the birth parents. Not only was this fear unfounded, but if one statement can be made unequivocally, it is that a primary benefit of the reunion experience is the strengthening of the adoptive family relationship." By 1988, reunion researchers and participants were talking in terms of "no impact" on the adoptive relationship, as well as about its strengthening or damaging effects. In a study presented by Phyllis Silverman and Trish Patti (AAC Conference Workshop: "The Impact of Reunions," April, 1989), representing fifty-three cases, 42% reported positive impact of reunion on adoptive family; 30% neutral, and 28% negative.

9. Susan Darke of The Adoption Connection (Peabody, Massachusetts) suggests that searching birthmothers write one letter to the adoptive parents, enclosing one for the adoptee. Requesting that the adoptive parents give the letter to the adoptee returns control to them. She credits the practice with her organization's high success rate in achieving reunion meetings.

10. Winkler et al., *Clinical Practice in Adoption,* p. 82.

11. Cf. "Exploring the Myths in the Adoption Experience: An Educational Outreach" (unpublished paper); and "Myths and Adoptee Fears" (audiotape), Adoptive Parents for Open Records, Hackettstown, New Jersey.

12. Baasel, "Genetics and Your Child."

Chapter Thirteen

1. Since our sample group consisted of people in reunion for a minimum of six months, the probability of enduring relationships was already built into the sample.

2. Reuben Pannor. Personal Interview.

3. The Census could supply figures regarding the number of birthmothers and their feelings about reunion, as well as being the obvious vehicle by which to gather accurate statistics on numbers of adoptees and adoptive parents.

4. Aigner, *Adoption in America,* Chapter 2, presents a critical review of behavioral science and its impact on adoption practice, tracing the way conventional wisdom has changed over time and concluding that, "the absence of reliable data can be shown to be characteristic of this institution, which in more than a century has yet to find firm scientific or experiential ground on which to stand.

5. By Minnesota, one of the first states to later repeal the practice and allow adoptees access to their original birth records.

6. The League is the largest private child welfare organization in the country, representing both placement agencies and other children's services groups. See also Report of the Child Welfare League of America: National Adoption Task Force, Washington, D.C., 1987.

7. See Demick and Wapner, "Open and Closed Adoption: A Developmental Conceptualization," for a discussion of emergent types of open adoptions.

8. The black market, for example.

9. See Gilligan, *In A Different Voice,* for a full development of these ideas. Among a group of psychologists who have written about the differences between male and female identity (notably, the primacy that attachment, and relationship, holds for women) Gilligan points out that women "not only define themselves in a context of human relationship, but also judge themselves in terms of their ability to care." The construct that women would try to change the rules to preserve a relationship, whereas men would abide by the rules and count on replacing the relationship, is hers. These ideas have become widely accepted.

10. Bok, *Secrets,* pp. 10–11.

Bibliography

This list includes a selection of current research and thought on adoption, reunion, and post-reunion. It also includes some sources of a more general nature which we found useful.

Adoption Factbook: United States Data, Issues, Regulations, and Resources. Washington, D.C.: National Committee for Adoption, 1985.

Aigner, Hal. *Adoption in America, Coming of Age.* Greenbrae, California: Paradigm Press, 1986.

Anderson, Carol, Lee Campbell and Mary Ann Cohen. *Eternal Punishment of Women: Adoption Abuse.* Des Moines, Iowa: Concerned United Birthparents, Inc., 1981.

Anderson, Robert S., M.D. "Why Adoptees Search: Motives and More." *Child Welfare,* Vol. 67, No. 1, January/February, 1988, pp. 15–19.

Arms, Suzanne. *To Love and Let Go.* New York: Alfred A Knopf, 1983.

Baasel, Patricia. "Genetics and Your Child." *Ours. The Magazine of Adoptive Families.* July/August, 1988. Minneapolis, Minnesota.

Baran, Annette and Reuben Pannor. "Open Adoption as Standard Practice." Child Welfare, Vol. 68, No. 3, May/June, 1984, pp. 245–50.

Baran, Annette, Reuben Pannor and Arthur D. Sorosky, M.D. "Open Adoption." *Social Work,* March 1976.

Bok, Sissela. *Secrets: On the Ethics of Concealment and Revelation.* New York: Pantheon Books, 1982.

Burgess, Linda Cannon. *The Art of Adoption.* New York and London: W.W. Norton and Company, 1981.

Demick, Jack, Ph.D. and Seymour Wapner, Ph.D. "Open and Closed Adoption: A Developmental Conceptualization." Family Process, Inc., 1988.

Depp, Carole H. "After Reunion: Perceptions of Adult Adoptees, Adoptive Parents and Birth Parents." *Child Welfare.* February, 1982.

Deykin, Eva Y., Ph.D.; Jon Ryan, B.S.; Patricia Patti, B.S.N. "Fathers of Adopted Children: A Study of the Impact of Child Surrender of Birthfathers." *American Journal of Orthopsychiatry,* 58 (2), April, 1988.

Deykin, Eva Y., Ph.D.; Lee Campbell, M. Ed.; Patricia Patti, B.S.N. "The Postadoption Experience of Surrendering Parents." *American Journal of Orthopsychiatry.* April, 1984.

Dusky, Lorraine. *Birthmark.* New York: M. Evans and Co., Inc., 1979.

Fisher, Florence. *The Search for Anna Fisher.* New York: Fawcett Crest Books, 1973.

Freud, Sigmund. *Family Romances.* In J. Strachey (Ed. and Trans.) The Standard Edition of the Complete Psychological Works of Sigmund Freud, Vol. 9. London: Hogarth Press, 1959, pp. 235–241.

Ganson, Harriet C., Ph.D. and Judith A. Cook, Ph.D. "The Open Records Controversy in Adoption: A Woman's Issue?" Paper presented at the 81st Annual Meeting of the American Sociological Association. New York, 1986.

Genevie, Louis, Ph.D. and Eva Margolies. *The Motherhood Report: How Women Feel about Being Mothers.* New York: Macmillan Publishing Co., 1987, pp. 288–9.

Gilligan, Carol. "In A Different Voice." *Psychological Theory and Women's Development.* Cambridge: Harvard University Press, 1982.

Gilman, Lois. *The Adoption Resource Book.* New York: Harper and Row, 1984.

Glenn, Jules, M.D. "The Adoption Theme in Edward Albee's 'Tiny Alice' and 'The American Dream.' *Psychoanalytic Study of the Child.* vol. 29. New York: International Universities Press, 1974, pp. 413–429.

Gustavson, Carol. "Exploring the Myths in the Adoption Experience: An Educational Outreach." New Jersey: Adoptive Parents For Open Records, (unpublished paper).

Holden, Constance. "The Genetics of Personality." *Psychiatric Times,* January, 1988.

Hocksbergen, R.A.C., ed. *Adoption in Worldwide Perspective.* Berwyn, Pennsylvania: Swets North American, Inc., 1986.

Hyatt, Carole and Linda Gottlieb. *When Smart People Fail.* New York: Penguin Books, 1987.

Ingalls, Kate. *Living Mistakes: Mothers Who Consented to Adoption.* Winchester, Massachusetts: Allen & Unwin, 1984.

Jung, C.G. and C. Kerenyi. *Essays on a Science of Mythology,* Princeton, New Jersey: Princeton University Press, 1963

Kirk, H. David (Rev.) *Shared Fate: A Theory and Method of Adoptive Relationships.* Port Angeles, Washington: Ben-Simon Publications, 1984.

Klaus, Marshall H. and John H. Kennell. *Parent-Infant Bonding.* St. Louis, Missouri: The C.V. Mosby Company, 1982.

Krementz, Jill. *How It Feels To Be Adopted.* New York: Alfred A. Knopf, 1983.

Lenz, Elinor. *Once My Child, Now My Friend.* New York: Warner Books, 1981.

Lifton, Betty Jean. *Lost and Found.* New York: Harper and Row, 1988.

Maxtone-Graham, Katrina. *An Adopted Woman.* New York: Remi Books, Inc., 1983.

McKaugham, Molly. *The Biological Clock.* New York: Doubleday, 1987.

Melina, Carl M., M.D. and Lois Melina, M.A. *The Physician's Responsibility in Adoption, Part 1: Caring for the Birthmother.* Journal of the American Board of Family Practice, Vol. 1, No. 1.

Millen, Leverett, Ph.D. and Samuel Roll, Ph.D. "Solomon's Mothers: A Special Case of Pathological Bereavement." *American Journal of Orthopsychiatry,* 55.3, July, 1985, pp. 411–18.

Miller, Jean. *Toward a New Psychology of Women.* Boston: Beacon Press, 1976.

Monthly Vital Statistics Report. Vol. 36, No. 4. National Center for Health Statistics. July, 1987.

Pannor, Reuben; Annette Baran and Arthur D. Sorosky, M.D. *"Birth Parents Who Relinquished Babies for Adoption Revisited."* Family Process. Vol. 17, No. 3. September, 1978, pp. 329–37.

Pannor, Reuben; Fred Massarik and Byron Evans. *The Unmarried Father.* New York: Springer Publishing Company, 1971.

Paton, Jean M. *The Adopted Break Silence.* Philadelphia, Pennsylvania: Life History Study Center, 1954.

Pogrebin, Letty Cottin. *Among Friends: Who We Like, Why We Like Them, and What We Do With Them.* New York: McGraw Hill, 1987.

Riben, Marsha. *Shedding Light on the Dark Side of Adoption.* Detroit, Michigan: Harlo Press, 1988.

Rillera, Mary Jo. *Adoption Encounter.* Westminster, California: Triadoption Publications, 1987.

Rubin, Suzanne. *Adoption: Beyond the Veil.* Los Angeles, California: Concerned United Birthparents (unpublished paper) August, 1986.

Rynearson, Edward K., M.D. "Relinquishment and Its Maternal Complications: A Preliminary Study." *American Journal of Psychiatry* 139:3, March, 1982. pp. 338–40.

Sanders, Patricia and Nancy Sitterly. *Search Aftermath and Adjustments.* Costa Mesa, California: ISC Publications, 1981.

Sants, H.J. *"Genealogical Bewilderment in Children with Substitute Parents."* London: British Journal of Medical Psychology, 1964, Vol. 37, pp. 133–141.

Silber, Kathleen and Phyllis Speedlin. *Dear Birthmother.* San Antonio, Texas: Corona, 1983.

Silverman, Phyllis, Ph.D. "The Grief of the Birthmother." *Helping Women Cope With Grief.* Beverly Hills, California: Sage Publications, 1981.

Simpson, Eileen. *Orphans: Real and Imaginary.* New York: Weidenfeld & Nicolson, 1987.

Sobol, Michael F. and Jeanette Cardiff. *Family Relations,* October, 1983, pp.477–83.

Sorosky, Arthur D., M.D.; Annette Baran, MSW; and Reuben Pannor, MSW. *The Adoption Triangle: The Effects of the Sealed Record on Adoptees, Birth Parents, and Adoptive Parents.* New York: Anchor Press/Doubleday, 1979.

Viorst, Judith. *Necessary Losses.* New York: Simon and Schuster, 1986.

Watson, Kenneth W. "Birth Families: Living with the Adoption Decision. *Public Welfare.* Spring, 1986.

Winkler, Robin C. and Margaret van Keppel. *Relinquishing Mothers in Adoption.* Melbourne, Australia: Institute of Family Studies, 1984.

Winkler, Robin C.; Dirck W. Brown; Margaret van Keppel; and Amy Blanchard. *Clinical Practice in Adoption.* New York: Pergamon Press, 1988. p. 82.

Winnicott, D.W. *Primary Maternal Preoccupation. In Collected Papers: Through Paediatrics to Psychoanalysis.* New York: Basic Books, 1958.

Wishard, Laurie and William Wishard. *Adoption: The Grafted Tree.* San Francisco, California: Cragmont Publications, 1979.

Adoption, Reunion and Post-Reunion Resources

The organizations listed below all have a national perspective. They will be happy to direct you to local resources.

Adoptees Liberty Movement Association (ALMA)
Headquarters:
Box 154 Washington Bridge
New York, NY 10033

Adoptive Parents for Open Records (APFOR)
9 Marjorie Drive
Hackettstown, NJ 07840

American Adoption Congress (AAC)
Cherokee Station
P.O. Box 20137
New York, NY 10028

American Adoption Congress Hotline
(for information on support groups in your area, call: 505-296-2198)

Concerned United Birthparents (CUB)
2000 Walker Street
Des Moines, IA 50317

International Soundex Reunion Registry (ISSR)
P.O. Box 2312
Carson City, NV 89702

National Organization for Birthfathers and Adoption Reform
(NOBAR)
P.O. Box 1993
Baltimore, MD 21203

Orphan Voyage
2141 Road 2300
Cedaredge, CO 81413

People Searching News (Periodical)
P.O. Box 22611
Fort Lauderdale, FL 33335

Post Adoption Center for Education and Research (PACER)
2255 Ygnacio Valley Road Suite L
Walnut Creek, CA 94598

Triadoption Library
P.O. Box 638
Westminster, CA 92684